MW00605912

# Windows® 2000 Kernel Debugging

ISBN 0-13-040637-6
90000
9 780130 406378

# PRENTICE HALL PTR MICROSOFT® TECHNOLOGIES SERIES

## NETWORKING

- Microsoft Technology: Networking, Concepts, Tools
  **Woodard, Gattuccio, Brain**
- NT Network Programming Toolkit
  **Murphy**
- Building COM Applications with Internet Explorer
  **Loveman**
- Understanding DCOM
  **Rubin, Brain**
- Web Database Development for Windows Platforms
  **Gutierrez**

## PROGRAMMING

- Windows 2000 Kernel Debugging
  **McDowell**
- Windows Script Host
  **Aitken**
- The Windows 2000 Device Driver Book, Second Edition
  **Baker, Lozano**
- Win32 System Services: The Heart of Windows 2000 and Windows 98, Third Edition
  **Brain, Reeves**
- Programming the WIN32 API and UNIX System Services
  **Merusi**
- Windows CE 3.0: Application Programming
  **Grattan, Brain**
- The Visual Basic Style Guide
  **Patrick**
- Windows Shell Programming
  **Seely**
- Windows Installer Complete
  **Easter**
- Windows 2000 Web Applications Developer's Guide
  **Yager**
- Developing Windows Solutions with Office 2000 Components and VBA
  **Aitken**
- Multithreaded Programming with Win32
  **Pham, Garg**
- Developing Professional Applications for Windows 98 and NT Using MFC, Third Edition
  **Brain, Lovette**
- Introduction to Windows 98 Programming
  **Murray, Pappas**
- The COM and COM+ Programming Primer
  **Gordon**
- Understanding and Programming COM+: A Practical Guide to Windows 2000 DNA
  **Oberg**
- Distributed COM Application Development Using Visual C++ 6.0
  **Maloney**
- Distributed COM Application Development Using Visual Basic 6.0
  **Maloney**
- The Essence of COM, Third Edition
  **Platt**
- COM-CORBA Interoperability
  **Geraghty, Joyce, Moriarty, Noone**
- MFC Programming in C++ with the Standard Template Libraries
  **Murray, Pappas**
- Introduction to MFC Programming with Visual C++
  **Jones**
- Visual C++ Templates
  **Murray, Pappas**
- Visual Basic Object and Component Handbook
  **Vogel**
- Visual Basic 6: Error Coding and Layering
  **Gill**
- ADO Programming in Visual Basic 6
  **Holzner**
- Visual Basic 6: Design, Specification, and Objects
  **Hollis**
- ASP/MTS/ADSI Web Security
  **Harrison**

## BACKOFFICE

- Microsoft SQL Server 2000 Optimization Guide
  **Fields**
- BizTalk: Implementing Business-To-Business E-Commerce
  **Kobielus**
- Designing Enterprise Solutions with Microsoft Technologies
  **Kemp, Kemp, Goncalves**
- Microsoft Site Server 3.0 Commerce Edition
  **Libertone, Scoppa**
- Building Microsoft SQL Server 7 Web Sites
  **Byrne**
- Optimizing SQL Server 7
  **Schneider, Goncalves**

## ADMINISTRATION

- Windows 2000 Cluster Server Guidebook
  **Libertone**
- Windows 2000 Hardware and Disk Management
  **Simmons**
- Windows 2000 Server: Management and Control, Third Edition
  **Spencer, Goncalves**
- Creating Active Directory Infrastructures
  **Simmons**
- Windows 2000 Registry
  **Sanna**
- Configuring Windows 2000 Server
  **Simmons**
- Supporting Windows NT and 2000 Workstation and Server
  **Mohr**
- Zero Administration Kit for Windows
  **McInerney**
- Tuning and Sizing NT Server
  **Aubley**
- Windows NT 4.0 Server Security Guide
  **Goncalves**
- Windows NT Security
  **McInerney**

## CERTIFICATION

- Core MCSE: Windows 2000 Edition
  **Dell**
- Core MCSE: Designing a Windows 2000 Directory Services Infrastructure
  **Simmons**
- MCSE: Implementing and Supporting Windows 98
  **Dell**
- Core MCSE
  **Dell**
- Core MCSE: Networking Essentials
  **Keogh**
- MCSE: Administering Microsoft SQL Server 7
  **Byrne**
- MCSE: Implementing and Supporting Microsoft Exchange Server 5.5
  **Goncalves**
- MCSE: Internetworking with Microsoft TCP/IP
  **Ryvkin, Houde, Hoffman**
- MCSE: Implementing and Supporting Microsoft Proxy Server 2.0
  **Ryvkin, Hoffman**
- MCSE: Implementing and Supporting Microsoft SNA Server 4.0
  **Mariscal**
- MCSE: Implementing and Supporting Microsoft Internet Information Server 4
  **Dell**
- MCSE: Implementing and Supporting Web Sites Using Microsoft Site Server 3
  **Goncalves**
- MCSE: Microsoft System Management Server 2
  **Jewett**
- MCSE: Implementing and Supporting Internet Explorer 5
  **Dell**
- Core MCSD: Designing and Implementing Desktop Applications with Microsoft Visual Basic 6
  **Holzner**
- MCSD: Planning and Implementing SQL Server 7
  **Vacca**
- MCSD: Designing and Implementing Web Sites with Microsoft FrontPage 98
  **Karlins**

PRENTICE HALL PTR MICROSOFT® TECHNOLOGIES SERIES

# Windows® 2000 Kernel Debugging

Steven McDowell

Prentice Hall PTR, Upper Saddle River, NJ 07458
www.phptr.com

Library of Congress Cataloging-in-Publication Data

McDowell, Steven.
Windows 2000 kernel debugging / Steven McDowell.
p. cm. – (Prentice Hall PTR Microsoft technologies series)
ISBN 0-13-040637-6
1. Microsoft Windows (Computer file) 2. Operating systems (Computers) 3. Debugging in computer science. I. Title. II. Series.

QA76.76.O63 M396 2001
005.4'4769–dc21 00-050190

Editorial/Production Supervision: *Jane Bonnell*
Acquisitions Editor: *Mary Franz*
Marketing Manager: *Dan DePasquale*
Manufacturing Buyer: *Maura Zaldivar*
Copyeditor: *Marti Jones*
Composition: *Sean Donahue*
Cover Design: *Design Source*
Cover Design Direction: *Jerry Votta*
Interior Series Design: *Gail Cocker-Bogusz*

© 2001 by Prentice Hall PTR
Prentice-Hall, Inc.
Upper Saddle River, NJ 07458

Prentice Hall books are widely used by corporations and government agencies for training, marketing, and resale.

The publisher offers discounts on this book when ordered in bulk quantities. For more information, contact Corporate Sales Department, phone: 800-382-3419; fax: 201-236-7141; email: corpsales@prenhall.com
Or write Corporate Sales Department, Prentice Hall PTR, One Lake Street, Upper Saddle River, NJ 07458.

Product and company names mentioned herein are the trademarks or registered trademarks of their respective owners.

All rights reserved. No part of this book may be reproduced, in any form or by any means, without permission in writing from the publisher.

Printed in the United States of America

10 9 8 7 6 5 4 3 2 1

ISBN 0-13-040637-6

Prentice-Hall International (UK) Limited, *London*
Prentice-Hall of Australia Pty. Limited, *Sydney*
Prentice-Hall Canada Inc., *Toronto*
Prentice-Hall Hispanoamericana, S.A., *Mexico*
Prentice-Hall of India Private Limited, *New Delhi*
Prentice-Hall of Japan, Inc., *Tokyo*
Pearson Education Asia Pte. Ltd.
Editora Prentice-Hall do Brasil, Ltda., *Rio de Janeiro*

# CONTENTS

# PREFACE

## Audience

There are two primary audiences for this material: support persons and device driver developers. Familiarity with the basic architecture of Windows 2000 is assumed. Those sections that discuss device driver debugging also assume knowledge of device drivers and the C programming language. The book is fundamentally about using the Microsoft tools to debug device drivers and perform post-mortem crash dump analysis of kernel-mode failures.

## Book Organization

The approach taken here will lead you on a journey from understanding basic Windows 2000 debugging concepts, through the interpretation of the stop screen, to an overview of the tools. Chapter 2 contains all of the information required to set up the debugging environment. Chapter 3 switches gears and examines the Windows 2000 stop screen. Chapter 4 wraps up the introductory material with a tour of the debuggers.

After presenting this information, we'll spend three chapters actually using these tools to do debugging and to examine hardware-specific state. Chapters 5 focuses on using the debugging tools to perform debugging tasks, and Chapter 6 follows a path that examines a target's hardware with the debugger. Chapter 7 will have us momentarily switch gears and talk about extending the debugger with our own custom extensions.

Chapter 8 discusses the interesting and little-understood topic of remote-kernel debugging—that's debugging across a modem line or a network. Chapter 9 builds on the knowledge gleaned from the first eight chapters and talks about applying the techniques to examining memory dump files (as well as everything else you could want to know about dump files and the utilities to examine them). This is followed in Chapter 10 with a discussion of other tools provided by Microsoft to aid those debugging Windows 2000 device drivers. The book is concluded with a chapter devoted to debugging resources.

The appendixes attempt to bring into one place useful information that is normally scattered between header files, knowledge base articles, and the newsgroup archives. Appendix A is a complete reference of the options and commands available in the Microsoft Kernel Debuggers. Appendix B provides a listing of the bug check codes generated by Windows 2000, along with their often-undocumented parameters, and common causes. Appendix C enumerates the NT status codes, simply because they are not referenced in any other available hard-copy documentation, and they're invaluable when reading a stop screen.

## A Word about Versions

Microsoft is revising the tools described in this book at an amazing clip, with each revision generally improving on the last. At the same time, prerelease builds of Windows Whistler and related versions of debugging tools are arriving almost weekly at times. Amid this flurry of activity, it is impossible to write a book on a specific version of any one tool. The approach taken here is to capture what is common and most current when discussing the tools and their various features. Except where noted, what is stated about the tools is true across versions. What are ignored are the idiosyncrasies of the specific versions of each of these tools. Once the debugging tools stabilize, as Microsoft heads from Windows 2000 into Windows Whistler and Windows NT 4.0 becomes a memory, it is hoped that this book will be revised to reflect the specifics of the shipping version of the tools and the operating system.

## This Book Isn't Endorsed...

Although parties within Microsoft were aware that this book was being written over the past year, it is not endorsed by Microsoft, nor was Microsoft's cooperation solicited or offered during its writing. Likewise, as I wrote the majority of this text, I was a member of the Windows NT Engineering Team at NCR Corporation and the System Software Team at Network Engines. Both NCR and Network Engines kindly encouraged and supported the effort, but no one at either company officially reviewed or endorsed this work. The contents of this book are the responsibility of the author alone. No materials that would be considered confidential or proprietary by any of these companies were used in the preparation of this work.

## Book's Web Site

This book has a web site at *http://www.aint-it-good.com/kerneldebug.htm* that includes a multitude of good, related information. Look there for updated pointers to information about kernel debugging and crash dump analysis for both Windows 2000 and Windows Whistler. I encourage everyone to check in there to see what's available.

## Acknowledgements

There are many people who have contributed to this book in one way or another. It was written over a very interesting year in my career. I kept my editors continually frustrated as my focus drifted through the various tides. The first thanks must go to Mary Franz at Prentice Hall for keeping the faith. She has Strommer, Kimball, McBath, Joy, and the amazing Durham sisters to blame for my continually late drafts (thanks, guys, for the wonderful distractions!). Marti Jones is an amazing copyeditor. Thanks for the help, Marti.

Special thanks to Robert Denn—this one's better because of your touch. Raynor made me feel the need to write this book. If it weren't for Marty Seyer, one of a long line of wonderful mentors, I wouldn't write at all. The bulk of this book was written under three very generous and effective managers: Thanks to Rita Anderson, Bob Williamson, and Bob Wambach for allowing me the time to work on this when I should have been fighting fires in the lab. The NT Engineering Team at NCR was an amazing collection of OS engineers—it was a shame to see it disbanded. They inspired me every day. They were replaced in my world by an even more amazing bunch at Network Engines, who are out there inventing the future. Thanks, guys.

Lee Fisher at Microsoft provided excellent input that caused me to clarify many assumptions that I held about the debugging tools. I also had the opportunity to teach this material at the 1999 USENIX NT Symposium; the class provided invaluable feedback that forced me both to clean up some of the material and to reevaluate the target audience (thanks to Dan Klein at USENIX for allowing me to teach!). The book is immeasurably better because of these people.

Finally, my son, Christopher Riley, is the ultimate motivation for my doing anything—that, and competition with Parsons. Oh, and thanks, Mom!

O N E

# Introduction

**CHAPTER OBJECTIVES**

- Why Debug?
- Setting Goals for Debugging

*It sometimes seems that system crashes and Windows 2000 go hand in hand. Giving Microsoft its due, crashes appear to occur less frequently with each passing version and service pack; those that do occur are almost always caused by a misbehaving device driver. Still, if you work with NT in even the most nontrivial way, you have probably experienced at some point the dreaded "blue screen of death"—the NT stop screen. How do you read that confusing jumble of information? What does it all mean? This book will explain the stop screen before taking you to the next level.*

*This book will focus on explaining how the Microsoft debugging tools can help you not only to diagnose problems on running systems, but also to examine memory dumps (or "crash dumps") to provide post-mortem analysis of the failure. It will explore using the debugger when debugging your own kernel mode code. The focus is on the current versions of Windows 2000. No coverage is provided for Windows NT 3.51 or earlier systems.*

# Why Debug?

Before connecting a debugger for the first time or using tools to examine a crash dump, you should understand why it is that you're connecting that debugger to the target machine. Is it necessary? If you are debugging code, it probably is. If you experienced a stop screen and want to gather enough information to escalate to a higher level of support, it might not be necessary. If it is necessary, how far do you really need to probe? Some basic triage on the situation is needed to understand why it is you're doing what you are. This section presents discussion that leads to an understanding of when to—and when not to—debug.

## When Not to Debug

Although there are certainly times when connecting a debugger to a running (or recently stopped!) machine is the right thing to do, there are just as many times when it isn't the most appropriate course of action. There is a good number of problems that can be resolved through more traditional troubleshooting procedures.

Many times, a problem will be the result of misconfiguration of hardware and software components—for instance, changing the SCSI ID of a disk containing a boot partition will unfailingly generate a stop code of INACCESSIBLE_BOOT_PARTITION. It is very important that, before you decide to take a machine out of a production environment and connect a kernel debugger to it, you attempt every "easier" solution to the problem.

Failures manifest themselves in a variety of ways. The most catastrophic in a Windows 2000 environment is the dreaded stop screen. This recognizable blue screen occurs whenever the operating system kernel detects an inconsistency or encounters an error from which it cannot recover. Stop screens are discussed extensively in Chapter 3, but understand for now that, for many problems, the stop screen can provide enough information to understand whether a known issue caused the stop.

When dealing with any problem, it is imperative that you understand and always be aware that downtime in a live customer environment means money lost for someone. The most important goal for any troubleshooting session should be to get the user back up while attempting to understand exactly what went awry. If the problem is not catastrophic enough to keep a machine down, it might not be the best decision to bring it down to connect a debugger. If you have the luxury of developing code or troubleshooting the problem at hand in a lab (or other nonproduction environment), these limitations go away.

Often, a Windows 2000 stop screen will occur just one time in a given environment, due to some hardware anomaly (such as a power surge that causes memory to scramble or a noise on the system bus). It might also be that there is enough information available on the blue screen, coupled with an understanding of any changes made to the system just prior to the blue screen, to resolve the problem through other channels. In cases such as these, it may be the most prudent course to record the information from the stop screen and system event logs to attempt to duplicate the problem in a controlled lab environment.

The most important thing to attempt to do when diagnosing a Windows 2000 stop screen is to determine as soon as possible whether the failure is caused by a known problem or has occurred elsewhere. There are resources at Microsoft to accomplish this. Most hardware vendors that provide device drivers also provide some sort of on-line facilities to search for known problems. If you are in an IS or product development environment, I strongly suggest that you keep a good database of failure conditions that you encounter when servicing your customers—such databases prove invaluable over the long run.

**Tip** There is a number of resources available in tracking down known problems. The best source of information is Microsoft itself. Microsoft maintains a free web site (*support.microsoft.com*) that allows you to perform keyword searches of its entire database of known issues. This is called the *Microsoft Knowledge Base* and is very easy to use. Bookmark this page if you perform troubleshooting on any sort of regular basis. The knowledge base articles are also available as a part of the Microsoft Developer Network subscription (MSDN is also an indispensable tool), but I still find it more useful to go to the web site than to always swap CDs.

When examining the failed system, validate that all of the hardware components are on the Microsoft Hardware Compatibility List (HCL). If you contact Microsoft with a problem that occurs when you have unsupported hardware on your system, you will run into justifiable resistance. Placing a piece of hardware on the HCL is not a trivial matter. Hardware devices on the HCL go through rigorous testing and structured certifications. It is always a bad idea to use unsupported hardware. Eliminate these items first.

You should also examine the hardware to ensure that there are no conflicting hardware resources—I/O port assignments, DMA channels, interrupts, etc. Conflicts in these areas often lead to unexpected failures. You can easily examine resource assignments with the Windows 2000 utility `winmsd`. The advent and popularity of system buses, such as PCI and USB, are bringing plug-n-play into the server world, and Windows 2000 will be less susceptible to such conflicts. Until the ISA bus dies, though, these types of problems will persist.

The bottom line of this discussion is that, before you perform invasive and expensive procedures with a kernel debugger, you should exhaust all of the possibilities with more traditional troubleshooting techniques. Very often, someone else has found the problems encountered long before you found them. If you're working in a development environment, throw all of this advice out the window and just use the tools that you find most useful.

## When to Debug

Just as there are times when you want avoid debugging, there are just as many times when connecting the debugger is the correct thing to do. Connecting a debugger, or examining a crash dump, may be the correct course of action if you were not able to diagnose the failure using the more traditional techniques suggested earlier.

Connecting a debugger is the right thing to do if you are having a recurring stop screen and the stop screen isn't being caused by a known problem. If you don't have time to wait for Microsoft or a third-party hardware vendor to diagnose the problem for you, connecting a debugger can give you information that they will undoubtedly find useful. This might be the case in a critical production environment.

Once you decide that debugging is what you want to do, you must decide whether you want to debug a "live" system or look at a crash dump. Examining a working system is time-consuming and keeps the machine off-line for the duration. Often, it is better to find a quick work-around just to keep a computer running and to debug the failure from the crash dump. If a problem is not easily reproducible, a crash dump might also be the way to go.

Crash dumps are discussed in Chapter 6, but I'll point out a few facts here just to start you thinking. There is a global system option (accessible through the *system* applet in the control panel; look at the *advanced* tab) that causes the system to provide a memory dump whenever a system encounters a stop screen. This should always be enabled on production servers so that off-line analysis of failures can be achieved.

**Note** Beginning with Windows NT 4.0 Service Pack 4, Microsoft has provided the ability to force a memory dump with the use of a *dump switch*. A dump switch is essentially a board that plugs into one of the expansion slots on your computer and has a button protruding from the back of your machine. Depressing this button causes the system to experience a catastrophic failure on the bus, and the system will bug-check into a stop screen. These are harder to examine than the ordinary stop screen, because the obvious signs all point to a bus error, but you will be able to examine key data structures and other information pertaining to your system. The dump switch card is described on Microsoft's hardware development web site at *http://www.microsoft.com/hwdev/dumpswitch.htm*.

How far you should go with a debugger is a decision you have to make, given your circumstances. If you load NT symbols onto your machine, you can provide a very precise stack trace back to the developers responsible for the failing driver. If you are a developer, you will want to go as deep as you need to actually to resolve the problem.

A fortunate few outside of Microsoft have access to the source code for Windows 2000 (these include some development partners, premier support organizations, and more than a handful of university programs). These institutions can actually trace problems to their origin, using full source debugging of the kernel. Because source-level debugging of the kernel utilizes pretty much the same techniques as source-level debugging of ordinary device drivers and because the majority of the people reading this book are without such access, using the actual NT source code will not be mentioned again.

## Goals for the Debugging Session

Debugging in a live environment will force you to set parameters. Let your customer know how long the system will be down. If you exceed that, force a crash dump and take the analysis off-line. A key point to consider is that the longer customers' machines are down, the more they will expect their problems to be resolved.

A lab environment, on the other hand, is the ideal place to debug. Push yourself to your limits and you will understand the code and your tools better when you walk away. Kernel mode debugging is often frustrating and often infuriating, but that is what makes it interesting and worthwhile.

The goals you set depend entirely on the situation you are faced with in your debugging session. If the goal is maintaining customer satisfaction by resolving the problem, you should strive to find the fastest work-around and take the analysis of the failure off-line as quickly as possible. You should focus on the key questions, Is this a known problem? Is this problem reproducible? Do I have enough information recorded to escalate the problem to Microsoft or to the development staff at the hardware vendor?

On the other hand, if you are a device driver developer in a lab environment, you will want to exploit the tools to debug your code in the most useful ways that you can find. You will want to poke and prod with the sole goal of getting your software working. The goals you set depend on your environment, your organization, and your policies.

## Summary

What you should take away from this chapter is that, sometimes, it might not be the best decision to connect a debugger to a machine and debug. Sometimes, enough information is available from the stop screen or from a saved dump to troubleshoot the problem effectively. When the correct decision is to connect a debugger, you should have a clear understanding of the goals you are trying to achieve.

Exploratory debugging is certainly a good thing to do, and it's encouraged. Just make sure that you do it in the lab and not on a customer's machine. The bottom line is that we, as engineers, should strive toward a happy and running customer.

The rest of the book will focus on how to move forward with the Microsoft kernel debugging and crash dump analysis tools. The next chapter will take you through debugging concepts to prepare you better for what's to follow.

T W O

# Preparing for Kernel Debugging

**CHAPTER OBJECTIVES**

- Debugging Overview
- Different Architectures
- Concepts and Terminology
- Preparing the Machines

*This chapter presents an overview and introduction to Windows 2000 kernel debugging, along with the related concepts and terminology. Following this is a brief discussion of the different architectures that Windows 2000 supports and why there are different procedures for each of these architectures. Details on preparing the host and target systems for debugging and crash dump analysis tasks follow this. It wraps up with a discussion on preparing the host to run the debugger. Details of actually operating and configuring the debugger are saved until Chapter 4—I just provide the preparatory steps here.*

*Even if you have worked with kernel mode code on other platforms (such as Unix or VMS), you will still want to review the concepts as they are presented here. There are differences between the terminology and concepts, as they exist on other systems and on Windows 2000.*

# Debugging Overview

Kernel debugging is one of those efforts that seem to be a whole lot more complex than they really need to be. By taking the issues step by step and with the appropriate concepts laid out in order, the task of understanding how to debug a Windows 2000 system at the kernel mode level will become clear. To start this process of understanding, this section will answer the following questions that must be present to get started:

- What are the basic failure modes that might affect my Windows 2000 system?
- Which methods are available to analyze these failures?
- What tools are available to help me accomplish these tasks in a Windows 2000 environment?

## Failure Modes

What kinds of failures will cause a Windows 2000 system to misbehave? There are two general classes of problems: user mode and kernel mode. Obviously, you are most interested in kernel mode failures or you would not have picked up this book. It is important to understand that there are different types of debugging that can be performed on these failures. In the Windows 2000 architecture, badly written kernel-mode code will cause catastrophic failures. User-mode code can cause serious failures, as well. You need to be aware of these different operating modes that can cause failures and the types of debugging that are most effective in isolating those failures.

### KERNEL-MODE FAILURES

A failure in kernel mode is the most catastrophic event that can occur on an operating system like Windows NT. If there is a breach in the integrity of protected address spaces, if operating system data structures become inconsistent or corrupt, or if code executing in kernel mode misbehaves, important data can be lost or corrupted. Time, resources, and vital information are lost.

It is because failures in kernel mode are so catastrophic that the designers of Windows 2000 have built in self-check mechanisms to "stop" the system when it detects this sort of corruption. When this stop occurs, the familiar blue stop screen (known as the "blue screen of death") will be displayed on the main console. The target machine can be configured, through the System Control Panel applet, to behave in one of a number of different ways when the kernel fails. These options are:

- A snapshot of the memory contents at the time of the failure will be taken and written into a crash dump file.

- You can use a debugger to determine the state of the system as it currently exists.
- The stop screen will display momentarily, information will be put into the event log, and the machine will be restarted automatically.
- The stop screen will display, and nothing further will occur. This is the default behavior of Windows NT.

The default behavior of displaying a blue screen will at least allow you to isolate the components that were executing at the time of the failure. The configuration of these different types of behaviors, as well as detail on interpreting and using the information on the stop screen, will be discussed extensively in the next chapter.

### USER-MODE FAILURES

User-mode code can induce kernel-mode failures. This typically occurs with a defective DLL that accesses kernel-mode drivers or with misbehaving services. Most user-mode-driven catastrophic failures tend to be isolated in one of the environment subsystems (such as Win32); these have close relationships with kernel-mode code and call native NT services directly. It is out of the scope of this book to discuss user-mode failures, except to point out that, when they do occur, the techniques and tools presented here will help to isolate the failing DLL or service. From there, traditional user-mode debugging techniques can be applied to diagnose the failing user-mode component further. This is a case of using kernel debugging to pave the way for user-mode debugging (a much more pleasant task!).

## Types of Debugging

The focus of this book is on kernel debugging and crash dump analysis. When people use the term *kernel debugging*, they are talking about the examination of any code that executes as a part of the operating system. These components include not just the operating system, but also device drivers that have been loaded by the user or system administrator. You can freeze a running system to perform this examination (which this book will call *on-line debugging*) or you can perform a post-mortem examination on a copy of the memory image of a failed system (which is called *crash dump analysis*). To perform debugging tasks effectively, you must understand what these debugging modes are and when to use each.

### ON-LINE DEBUGGING

To perform live, real-time, debugging (either local or remote), you must connect a computer loaded with debugging and diagnostic software to the failing machine. This computer is called the *host* computer, so called because it hosts the debugger and the symbols necessary to translate addresses into meaningful symbolic names. The machine under examination is called the *target* computer. There are a couple of debuggers to choose from when using the Microsoft tools and one third-party tool. The Microsoft debuggers include *KD*, which is a simple command line interface to the debugging protocols, and *WinDbg*, which is a Windows GUI-oriented kernel debugging environment. There are tradeoffs and benefits to each, and the tool chosen should be appropriate to the specific task at hand. The third-party kernel debugger is called *SoftICE™* from NuMega™. A brief description of each of these debuggers is presented in the next section, "Debugging Tools."

A basic question is, When is on-line debugging most useful? There are some cases where post-mortem debugging is adequate, but on-line debugging seems to offer more. You will want to connect a debugger for on-line debugging in the following cases:

- To examine a system that has stopped responding but has not blue-screened.
- When watching or tracing through a device driver or other kernel-mode component prior to a failure.
- To extract information about a running Windows 2000 system that isn't otherwise available (more detail on this type of debugging is presented in Chapter 5).
- When it is impractical to take a memory dump (this might occur if you have 2 Gbytes of memory but not 2 Gbytes available to store a corresponding memory image).

Later in this chapter, I will show you how to enable kernel debugging on a target machine. In Chapter 4, you will begin to learn how to use the debugger.

## POST-MORTEM DEBUGGING

Post-mortem debugging (or crash dump analysis) offers you the ability to analyze a snapshot of a failed system. You can use the same debugging tools that you would use to perform on-line debugging to examine a dump file. Microsoft also offers a number of static analysis tools as a standard part of the Windows 2000 development environment to help you probe for the underlying failure (these tools are discussed in Chapter 10). Crash dump debugging is most useful in the following scenarios:

- The failing computer was not configured to use the kernel debugger.
- The failure occurred on a production server, and it was not feasible to take the machine off-line for on-line analysis.
- An error occurred in a remote location, and it was impractical to connect a debugger.
- You want a permanent record of the failure.

There are also tradeoffs in using the crash-dump facility to perform your debugging analysis. It is impossible, for instance, to use a crash dump to perform these types of actions:

- Examine the hardware (e.g., the PCI bus, the various controller chipsets, etc.).
- Watch the code execute or examine the data prior to a failure.
- Reproduce the failure from within the debugger.

Crash dump debugging can be a powerful and useful tool. It has both benefits and limitations. Chapter 7 will completely explore the topic of working with crash dumps and will discuss the additional tools provided for analyzing these memory images.

## Debugging Tools

The next logical question that must be answered is, What tools are available to perform debugging tasks? There is a number of tools available to accomplish your goals effectively. Microsoft supplies a simple command line debugger, KD, with every shipment of Windows NT. For a friendlier debugging environment, Microsoft includes a graphically oriented debugger, WinDbg, with each delivery of its development environment. There are also numerous tools, in addition to KD and WinDbg, that are useful for analyzing crash dumps; these will be covered in Chapter 9.

### THE KD DEBUGGER

Freely available on each Windows 2000 product CD is a debugger called, generically, KD. The KD debugger is strictly for performing kernel-mode debugging and crash dump analysis tasks. Versions of KD are available on Windows 2000 machines. Although this debugger does ship with the operating system, it isn't installed by default. The KD debugger has the following features and limitations:

- It's completely command-line-based.
- There is limited support for C source-level debugging.
- Remote debugging with KD is possible with the `remote` utility.
- Crash dump examination is supported.
- It isn't very friendly—it's not Windows based, and it relies on environment variables and command line options for configuration.

Whenever you read about KD, there is always the comment that it is the "tool of choice" for hard-core kernel-mode developers. I think a more apt statement would be that it is usable by only hard-core kernel mode developers. The biggest advantages that it has over WinDbg is that it is command-line-based, and it doesn't seem to hang up as much as WinDbg does. It is also completely free and readily available. We detail KD extensively in Chapter 4.

## WinDbg

The more popular alternative to KD is WinDbg. *WinDbg* is short for *Windows Debugger*, although it's more often affectionately referred to throughout the development community as "Wind Bag." The WinDbg debugger can be used to debug both user-mode and kernel-mode code, although not simultaneously. Most people who debug user-mode software do not usually use WinDbg for the task any longer, relying more on the integrated debugging tools with the Microsoft Development Environment. For those who need to perform kernel-mode debugging, WinDbg is by far the leading utility. The WinDbg debugger offers a range of features:

- WinDbg is a full-windowed debugger, allowing for multiple windows, each holding different information.
- It allows full-windowed source-level debugging of kernel-mode code.
- You can mix source- and assembly-level debugging.
- It's easy to find what you're looking for—everything is only a toolbar click away.
- It has menu-driven configuration (as opposed to KD's environment-variable-driven configuration).
- You can store multiple debugger configurations.
- WinDbg is freely available on the Microsoft web site.

The limitations? There are a few. WinDbg, for example, is notorious for hanging for no apparent reason. It does this a lot. This is the number one complaint voiced in the newsgroups and mailing lists. After years of shipping the same WinDbg, Microsoft has lately been releasing new versions of the debugging tools at a rapid clip. Each seems to be a little better than the last, but it still garners complaints from its users. Although it has its problems and is notoriously buggy, Microsoft makes strides forward with every release. This book will cover both KD and WinDbg, because WinDbg is clearly an evolution of KD, and they share a common general architecture and command set. I will get into the heart of WinDbg (and KD) in Chapter 4.

## NuMega SoftICE

No discussion of kernel debugging in the Windows 2000 environment would be complete without mentioning the one non-Microsoft kernel debugging tool. This tool is called *SoftICE* and is from a company called *NuMega*. There are numerous developers working with SoftICE to develop their device drivers, and those who use it tend to rave about its capabilities. It has some significant features:

- It provides the ability to perform kernel debugging on the same machine, using a different monitor, effectively eliminating the Microsoft approach of a host/target configuration.
- SoftICE supports Windows 98.

- It allows you to debug both user-mode and kernel-mode modules simultaneously.
- NuMega has a dedicated support staff there to serve you.

As with any product, there are some limitations:

- SoftICE isn't free.
- It can't be used to debug crash dumps.
- It can't be used to debug a blue screen that is polling for a debugger.
- It has reduced usability when used in a host/target configuration.

There is no question that SoftICE is a useful tool. You should explore whether it's the right tool for your support or development needs. For full information from the manufacturer, I encourage you to visit its web site at *www.numega.com* or to call (800) 4NU-MEGA ([800] 468-6342). NuMega has an excellent reputation in the development communities.

This book will not discuss SoftICE any further. It is sufficiently different in operation from the Microsoft tools—and equally complex to them—that each chapter would essentially have to be done twice—once for KD/WinDbg and once for the NuMega tool. SoftICE is also very well documented and supported by its manufacturer; something that isn't necessarily true for the Microsoft tools. The remainder of this book will focus on presenting kernel debugging and crash dump analysis through the eyes of the more popular, although more maligned, Microsoft tools.

## Concepts and Terminology

Before exploring actual debugging practices, you should understand and agree on some basic Windows 2000 kernel debugging concepts and terminology. This section isn't meant to be an exhaustive glossary of debugging terms, but rather a presentation of common debugging terms and concepts to minimize confusion. The goal is to ensure that, when you encounter these words and terms throughout the rest of this book or when you communicate with other developers, everyone is on the same page.

### Stop Screen

The most common diagnostic aid that you will have at your disposal when dealing with Windows 2000 kernel-mode failures is the Windows 2000 stop screen. It isn't a tool in any interactive sense, but it provides the initial debugging information and, in many cases, an adequate diagnosis can be made from the stop screen alone.

You've already read a little about the Windows 2000 stop screen. If you have started developing device drivers, you have probably caused more than a few. If not, you have talked to someone who has experienced one. If these stop screens did not exist, there wouldn't be a need for this book. Windows 2000 stop screens are known by a couple of different names, used interchangeably, such as the *blue screen of death, BSOD, bug check,* just *blue screen*, or, generically, the *stop screen.*

Stop screens are, quite simply, the operating system's way of throwing up its hands and crying foul; an internal check somewhere in kernel-mode has failed, and the component that caught the inconsistency has called a routine called `KeBugCheck()` (or `KeBugCheckEx()`) to freeze the system. This is directly analogous to the "panic" in the Unix world.

The blue screen contains enough useful information to describe the configuration of the machine at the time it failed to identify the exception that caused the bug check and to provide a simple stack trace to show the flow of system code when the exception occurred. There is enough information within the blue screen to at least determine whether you have seen the problem before. If it is a known problem, your debugging session can end there; if not, you can apply some debugging techniques to drill down a little further and find the offending component or piece of code.

When the blue screen occurs, the system will take one of several courses of action. Each of these is dependent on the user's having configured the options to trigger the action—Windows 2000 out of the box will do nothing but display the stop screen when a kernel-mode exception occurs. These actions can be one of the following:

- Simply display the stop screen (this is the default).
- Display the stop screen briefly, then restart the system (useful for unattended installations or time-critical systems).
- Display the stop screen while copying the contents of memory to a dump file (more useful for post-mortem analysis).
- Display the stop screen and poll for a debugger to be connected.

Later in this chapter is a section on configuring the target machine to enable these different behaviors. If you want to skip ahead or explore on your own, the actions are configured in the Recovery dialog box of the system applet in the control panel.

As for the actual contents and meanings of the stop screen, you need to keep reading. The next chapter is devoted entirely to understanding the Windows 2000 stop screen. That chapter will talk about how to understand what you see and how that might lead you to understand better why the machine failed.

## Symbols and Builds

Without symbolic information to guide us and provide reference, debugging something as complex as a kernel-mode component in a modern operating system would be tedious to the point of impossibility. Just imagine something as already tedious as the stop screen further obscured with a stack trace that provided only virtual addresses instead of module names. Fortunately, Microsoft had enough good graces to provide symbolic information for all of its shipping versions of Windows NT. Microsoft even went beyond what many operating system vendors have done and provided mechanisms for extracting symbolic information from code compiled with optimizations enabled. For those of us reared in the old Unix world, where you could have either symbols or optimized code but never both, this is rare luxury. But what are symbols? And where do they live?

When talking about symbols, people are really talking about *symbol tables*, although nobody ever really says "symbol tables" anymore. A symbol table is a cross-reference between an address in the code and some information that describes that address. These addresses correspond to function names and global variables. If you build a special version, called a *checked build*, information about local variables within functions and about where in the actual source code the functions live is included. Armed with this information, the debugger can allow you to single-step through kernel-mode components at the source-code level, not just at the assembly language level. This is pretty useful. A free build, contrarily, includes only very basic information about symbol locations. No source code information is available in a free build.

### CHECKED BUILD

As was just mentioned, there are two different ways to build a device driver: either *free* or *checked*. A checked build of the device driver is what you would build when doing initial debugging and device driver development. It's also very useful when there is a problem in the field or in a production environment, where *extra* checks or symbolic information is needed. The checked build is built with a complete complement of symbolic information available: it will resolve function names and local variables within functions, match source code line numbers with specific assembly language blocks within the code, and resolve global variables. This is all necessary to do full-blown source-level debugging on the driver or kernel module. Checked builds of kernel-mode components offer the additional benefits:

- The `assert()` family of macros is enabled, allowing in-line validation and sanity checking of data in your driver.
- Memory pool tagging is enabled.
- Checked versions of kernel modules provide an extra layer of sanity checking and detailed debugger output.

Microsoft even makes available (with a subscription to its invaluable *Microsoft Developer Network* [MSDN]) a complete checked build of Windows 2000 Workstation. The downside of running a checked build is that it can be significantly slower than a free build and that it's fatter and has a larger memory and disk footprint. A checked build of your driver can expose the internal operation of the code to prying eyes. Exposing the inner workings can be less than desirable if you are competing in the commercial marketplace and are protecting valuable intellectual property.

### FREE BUILD

Outside of the development environment, you are more likely to find free builds of both the operating system and device drivers. When drivers are built free, a limited amount of symbolic information is still included within the generated file. This information will allow you to look at a stack trace with a debugger and to determine the code flow through the driver. If you are a commercial device driver developer, you might be wary of releasing even this amount of symbolic information outside of your development group. You might also be wary of the increased footprint (both memory and disk) of your driver with this information embedded within it. Microsoft comes to the rescue here and allows you to extract the symbolic information from the executable driver into a special file called a *DBG file*. You use options on the *rebase* command to generate this DBG file.

Once this is generated, symbols are available to the support persons who need them but aren't necessarily passed on with the device driver. Also, as you might expect, the extra sanity checking that occurs with the checked build doesn't happen with the free build. The upside is that the code will run faster.

Microsoft makes available DBG files for each of its released operating systems on the product CD and on subsequent service pack CDs. These live on the product CD in the directory *support\debug\<platform>\symbols*, where *<platform>* is either *alpha* or *i386*, depending on whether the operating system installed was on an Intel architecture (IA) platform or a Compaq/DEC Alpha-based platform (note that Alpha platforms are described for Windows NT 4.0, support for Alpha being discontinued in Windows 2000). Each of the DBG files for the operating system components is separated into subdirectories corresponding to the module type, i.e., *<symbol_path>\sys* for device drivers that end with a*.sys*, and *<symbol_path>\DLL* for dynamic link libraries. The symbols can be used directly from the CDs on full releases of the operating system, but many service packs and checked builds will require you to extract them from a compressed archive onto your development machine. More discussion about using these symbols will occur a little later, when a demonstration of how to configure the debugger to use them is presented.

## Creating Your Own DBG Files

Creating and distributing DBG files isn't just for Microsoft. You can do it with your own device drivers or kernel modules. To do it, you use the *rebase* command found in the platform SDK (again, available as part of the MSDN subscription or available for download from the Microsoft support web site).

Prior to actually generating a symbol file from the executable, you need to know what the *base address* is for your executable. By default, the linker will build your driver to load at 10000, but before running the *rebase* command, you should verify that. To verify the default address, you use the *dumpbin* command as follows. In this example, a DBG file for the driver called *extmirr.sys* is created.

The *dumpbin* command produces a lot of output. To use the `rebase` command, you are actually interested in only the base address of the executable driver. This is in the second section in the output. For clarity, some of the output is stripped.

```
F:\drivers\i386\free> dumpbin /headers extmirr.sys
File Type : EXECUTABLE IMAGE
FILE HEADER VALUES
        <file header values omitted for readability>
OPTIONAL HEADER VALUES
        108 magic #
        5.10 linker version
        B300 size of code
        5820 size of initialized data
             0 size of uninitialized data
        302C address of entry points
             280 base of code
        ADE0 base of data
        10000 base of image ← This is what you're looking for!
            <remainder of this section and remaining sections omitted>
```

You can see from the output that this driver has an image base of 10000. This will be used in the *rebase* command when the debug information is extracted.

```
F:\drivers\i386\free> rebase -b 10000 -x . extmirr.sys
```

The debug file is now created. Note that the output is sent to the directory specified in the `-x` (for "extract debug information") option. Copy it to your symbol tree, then you're ready to debug.

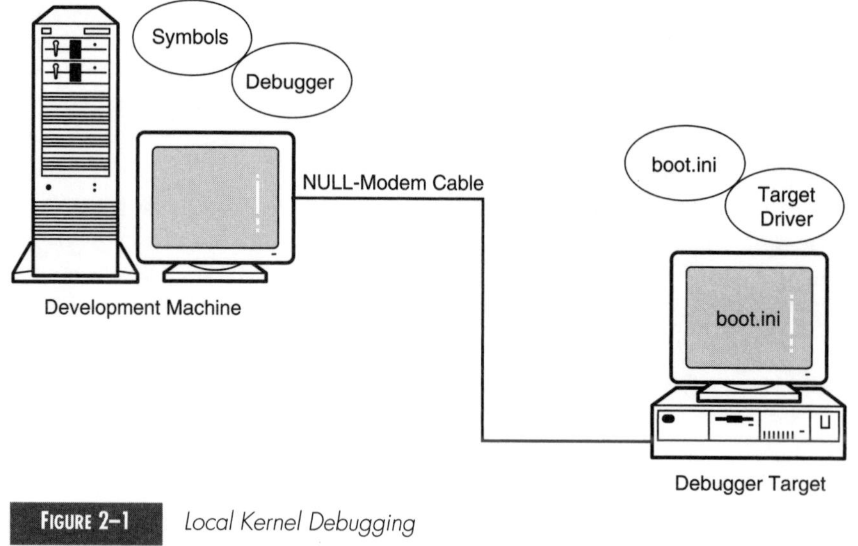


FIGURE 2–1 *Local Kernel Debugging*

# Debug Machines

There are two basic scenarios for on-line, live debugging. There is local debugging, where a development host machine is connected directly to a target machine (this is illustrated in Figure 2-1). There is also remote debugging, where a bridge, or proxy, machine lives between the host computer and the target computer, as is illustrated in Figure 2-2. In this section, the role of each of these computers is discussed. A detailed discussion of how to configure the actual debugger is in Chapter 4, whereas the configuration of the target computer and the initial preparation of the host computer are discussed later in this chapter.

### TARGET COMPUTER

To debug code effectively, you first need a computer to run the code being debugged. This can be a dedicated machine in your development environment that is loaded with the checked builds of the operating system and device drivers, or it can be a production machine that is experiencing stop screens. In either case, this machine is known as the *target computer*. The target computer is configured to load and execute the debugger client software as part of the kernel. It then responds to commands from the chosen debugger on the host development machine. Whenever the target computer is being debugged, it maintains a serial connection to either the host computer directly or through a proxy computer.

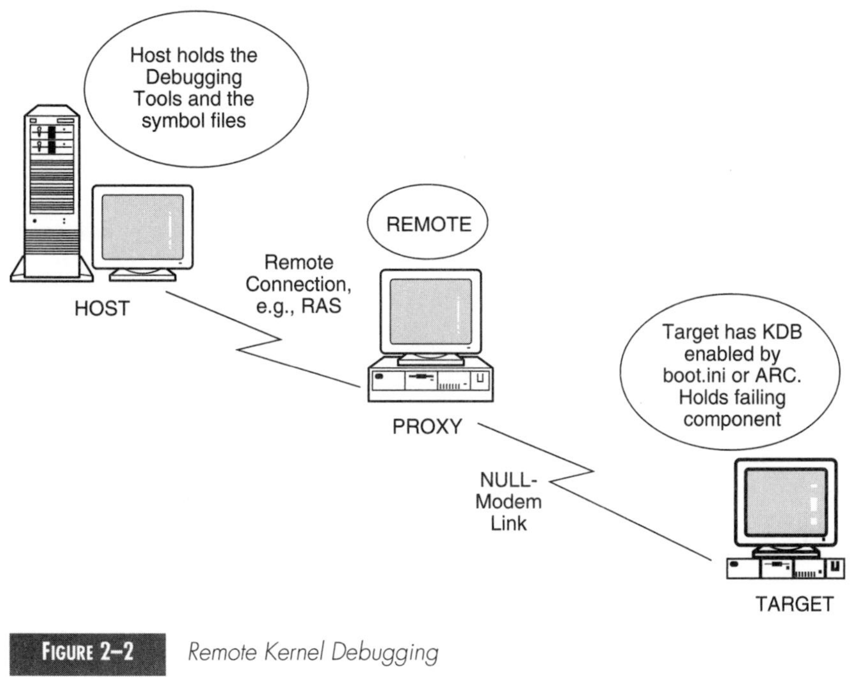


**FIGURE 2–2** *Remote Kernel Debugging*

## HOST COMPUTER

When talking about the *host computer*, I refer to the computer that the debugging tools are running on, the symbol files, and whatever source code is available to use for debugging. This is where you operate when diagnosing problems on the target machine. The configuration of the host machine doesn't require any boot-time modifications to be made, as the target does. All that is required is that the debugger of your choice is there, along with the symbols that match your target machine.

The debugger on the host communicates with the target through the use of a Microsoft proprietary debugging protocol. Details of the protocol can be gleaned from examining the various header files shipped with the Platform Software Development Kit (SDK) and the Device Driver Kit (DDK), but such details are not really relevant to the process of using the debugger to solve real-world problems. You should just take note that no symbolic information is transferred between the host and target computers and that it's a "lean and mean" protocol. If post-mortem dump analysis is all you are interested in, there will be no physical target computer, but there will still be a host computer. The host computer will be the computer hosting the debugging tools and, in this case, a copy of the crash dump file (the memory image of the target computer).

#### PROXY COMPUTER

The debugging information is transferred across the serial cable between the host and target computers in a local debugging environment. In a remote debugging environment, the debugging protocol is exchanged between the host and target computers through a *proxy computer* (see Figure 2-2). There are no real requirements on the proxy computer, except that it be equipped with the program called *remote* and that it have a serial connection with the target computer. Remote debugging is talked about in detail in Chapter 8.

## Preparing the Machines

There is a number of steps that you need to take before you should ever even start up the debugger and probe the innards of a target machine. You must perform the following basic steps before starting up the debugger for the first time:

1. Establish a physical connection between the host and target machines (or proxy and target).
2. Prepare the target machine.
3. Set up a symbol tree on the host.
4. Install the debugging tools.

The following sections will describe in detail the steps you need to take to configure the systems for a debugging session. What won't be touched on in this chapter is the actual configuration of the debugger—that is saved for Chapter 4.

### The Physical Connection

Interactive debugging between a host and target will not work without a physical connection between the two machines. If you are remote debugging, you must have a physical connection between the proxy machine and the target computer. For dump analysis, no physical connection is required—just a means of getting the saved dump file onto the host machine. You also have the option of remote debugging by directly placing a modem onto the serial port of the target machine, but that will be discussed in Chapter 8, when the entire subject of remote debugging is explored.

All communication between the host and target occurs across a NULL-modem cable. A NULL-modem cable is a cable that directly connects the transmit wire on one computer to the receive wire on the other and does the same crossover with the receive signal. The implementation of this is illustrated in Figure 2-3. The best way to obtain a NULL-modem cable is to buy one. It is relatively inexpensive and easy to come by. If you want to make your own, follow the diagram in Figure 2-3.

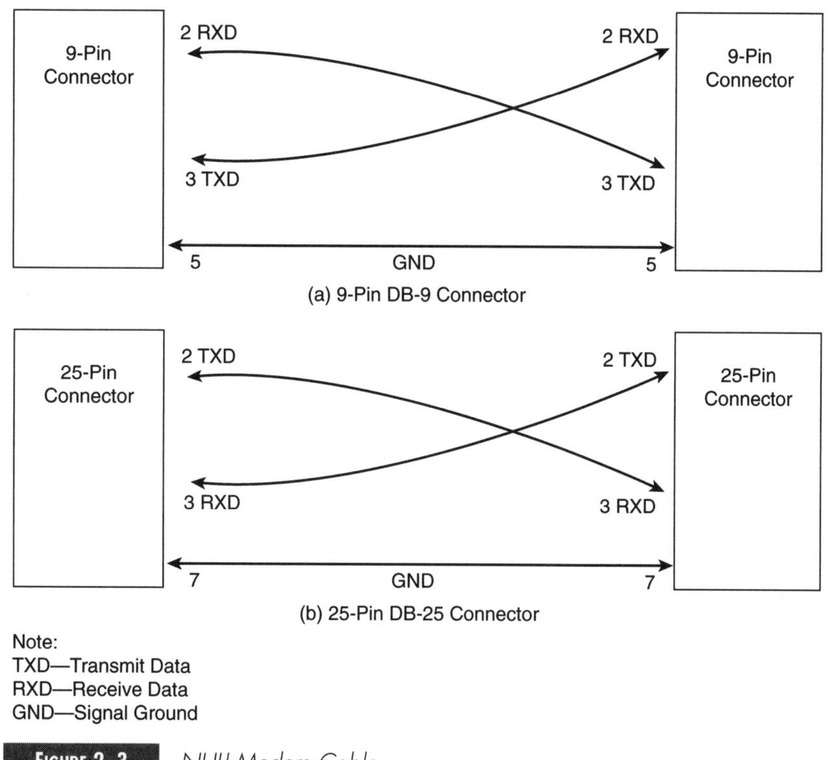


**FIGURE 2–3** *NULL-Modem Cable*

Once you have obtained a NULL-modem cable, you simply need to connect it between the host and target machines. You can use any available serial port (or COM port) and are not limited to the same port on each machine, e.g., you can connect the cable to COM1 on the host and COM2 on the target. When we actually configure the respective host and target computers, the data transmission parameters will be set.

## Target Configuration

Before you can debug, the target computer must be adequately prepared. First, the operating system kernel on the target machine must know to enable the debugger code. The target must also know whether this code is always active, where a debugger can break into the system at any time and effectively pause the system, or whether the debugger is active only after an exception that causes a stop screen. The following sections detail how to configure this behavior on the target computer.

More important than knowing when to activate the debugger on the target machine is knowing how to use the physical connection to the host

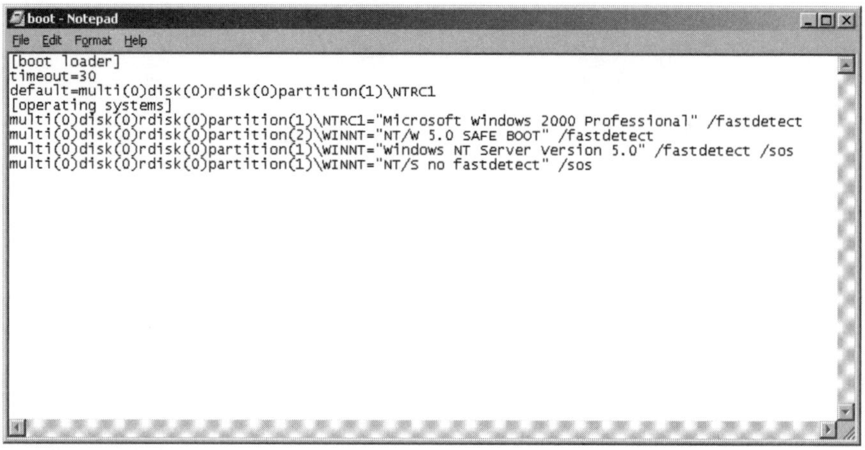

boot - Notepad

File Edit Format Help

```
[boot loader]
timeout=30
default=multi(0)disk(0)rdisk(0)partition(1)\NTRC1
[operating systems]
multi(0)disk(0)rdisk(0)partition(1)\NTRC1="Microsoft Windows 2000 Professional" /fastdetect
multi(0)disk(0)rdisk(0)partition(2)\WINNT="NT/W 5.0 SAFE BOOT" /fastdetect
multi(0)disk(0)rdisk(0)partition(1)\WINNT="Windows NT Server Version 5.0" /fastdetect /sos
multi(0)disk(0)rdisk(0)partition(1)\WINNT="NT/S no fastdetect" /sos
```

**FIGURE 2–4** *Sample boot.ini File*

computer. The target needs to be told which serial port the cable is connected to and which parameters should be used when communicating over that port.

Windows 2000 determines boot-time parameters based on the contents of a file that lives on the active boot partition. This file is a hidden file called *boot.ini*. The *boot.ini* file specifies not only which version of Windows 2000 to run, but also which options should be used when booting each instantiation of Windows NT on the system. The *boot.ini* lives in the root directory of the active partition of the boot drive. A sample *boot.ini* file is presented in Figure 2-4. Because it is a read-only hidden system file, you must change the attributes prior to editing the file. To change the attributes to edit the file, you execute the following command:

```
C:\> attrib -r -s -h boot.ini
```

Prior to modifying this file to enable debugging options, it might be instructive to examine exactly what each of the entries in each section means. The first section in the *boot.ini* file specifies the default instance of Windows 2000 that should be used to boot the machine. This doesn't have to be the instance that has the debugger enabled. If there are multiple versions or versions with multiple options of Windows 2000 on the machine when you boot, the loader will ask you to choose the one that you want to boot. There is a default timeout, so if you do not choose, the system will choose the default specified in this section for you. In the example, the first section is as follows:

```
[boot loader]
timeout=10
default=multi(0)rdisk(0)partition(1)\WINNT
```

In this example, the section name is `boot loader`. This defines the behavior of the boot loader at the system start time. The timeout value tells the loader how long to wait for the user to select an alternate operating system before going ahead and booting the default operating system. The default operating system is defined in the `default` parameter. The format of the entry is called *ARC format*, and it's both beyond the scope of the book and not really relevant to what happening here. Basically, it tells the boot loader which disk controller, disk, partition, and directory the instance of Windows 2000 lives in. It matches one of the entries from the next section. The next section lists the available operating systems, as follows:

```
[operating systems]
multi(0)disk(0)rdisk(0)partition(1)\WINNT="WinNT/S 4.0" /sos
multi(0)disk(0)rdisk(0)partition(1)\WINNT="WinNT/S 4.0 [VGA]" /basevideo
multi(0)disk(0)rdisk(0)partition(3)\WINNT="Win2000" /debugport=com1 /baudrate=115200
multi(0)disk(0)rdisk(0)partition(3)\WINNT="Win2000 [VGA mode]" /basevideo
```

You can see that, in this example, there are two versions of the operating system available for the user to boot. There are a Windows 2000 Server installation in the *WINNT* directory of the first partition of the boot disk and a Windows 2000 installation on the third partition of that same disk. You will note that, within quotes after the boot directory is specified, there is a text description of the operating system that is being booted. This is the text that is displayed in the boot menu. To enable the kernel debugger, you have two choices. You can modify the entry that corresponds to the instance of Windows 2000 that you are interested in debugging or you can create a new line for a debug-enabled version of the operating system. In either case, you enable the kernel debugger and specify the serial port to communicate on by appending options to the end of the entry. In the example, you can see that */sos* was already specified—it's the same place that you place the debugging flags.

There is a number of qualifiers that you can append to the end of a *boot.ini* entry to affect debugging. Note that each of these parameters must be preceded by a / character. For example, to enable the `BASEVIDEO` option, you would enter `/BASEVIDEO`. The supported boot parameters that are useful in a debugging environment are listed in Table 2-1.

**TABLE 2–1** *Boot Options*

| Options | Description |
|---|---|
| BASEVIDEO | **The standard VGA display driver will be loaded when booting Windows NT. This will get you out of a situation where the display adapter is configured for a higher resolution than is supported. Recent service packs for Windows 2000 make this a little-needed feature (e.g., the display control panel now forces you to verify new settings before applying them). This is still a useful feature for early service pack versions of Windows NT or for when a video adapter is changed without first making the appropriate changes in the video settings control panel.** |

**TABLE 2–1** *Boot Options (Continued)*

| Options | Description |
|---|---|
| BAUDRATE=<baudrate> | The speed at which the target communicates with the host is specified by this parameter. The valid values range from 9600 to 115200. The default without this argument specified is 9600 bps. If you experience debugger hangs at higher speeds, you should reduce the baudrate. Example: `/BAUDRATE=115200` sets the serial port baudrate to 115200 bps. |
| BOOTLOG | This option causes the Windows 2000 boot procedures to create a text file containing a log of the boot. This information is stored in %SystemRoot%\Ntbtlog.txt. |
| BREAK | This will force a breakpoint at HAL initialization time. This is useful for debugging at the start of the kernel intitialization.<br>You should note that this is a true breakpoint, and the system will stall indefinitely waiting to be serviced by the kernel debugger (contrasted with the target polling for a debugger at start-up time).<br>Also be aware that if the debugger is not enabled, and this flag is present, then the target machine will crash with a stop code of 0x78 (PHASE0_EXCEPTION). |
| BURNMEMORY=<#meg> | Specifies the amount of memory, in megabytes, that you want to restrict the computer from using. This is useful in testing low-memory behavior of the system without physically removing the memory. |
| CRASHDEBUG | This option instructs the operating system to activate the kernel debugger only when a stop screen occurs. The behavior of the system on an exception will be to display the stop screen, then continuously poll on the debugger's serial port, waiting for a debugger to respond. |
| DEBUG | This forces the debugger to be loaded into memory at all times, allowing the debugger to break into the running system at any time. |
| DEBUGPORT=<com#> | This tells the debugger to communicate over the serial port specific by the `com#` argument (you will replace the # with a 1 or a 2). If this option isn't specified, the system assumes COM2. Further, if this option is specified without either `/DEBUG` or `/CRASHDEBUG`, it will have the same effect as setting the `/DEBUG` option. Example: `/DEBUGPORT=COM1` configures the debugger to communicate over COM1. |
| INTAFFINITY | This flag causes interrupt affinity to the highest numbered processor when using the standard multiprocessor HAL (Halmps.dll). The normal behavior is to allow each processor to service interrupts. |
| KERNEL=<kernel><br>HAL=<hal> | You don't have to load a checked build of Windows 2000 just to use a checked build of the operating system. There is benefit to using a checked build, but you can just load the checked kernel with this option. If you do this, then *you must also load the corresponding hardware abstraction layer* (HAL; see the `/HAL` option), or your system will bug-check with a pretty blue screen. The procedure for doing this is as follows: |

**TABLE 2–1** *Boot Options (Continued)*

| Options | Description |
|---|---|
| `KERNEL=<kernel>`<br>`HAL=<hal>` *(cont.)* | 1. Copy the checked copy of *NTOSKRNL.EXE* from your checked build distribution media to the *<windows>\system32* directory; ensure that you call it something other than *NTOSKRNL.EXE*, or it will overwrite your existing kernel. For an example, I'll call it *NTOSCHECK.EXE*. Remember, if you are running on a multiprocessor system, you want the *NTOSKRNLMP.EXE* and not *NTOSKRNL.EXE*.<br>2. Select the appropriate HAL for your computer from your checked build distribution media and copy it to the *<windows>\system32* directory; also ensure that you rename it in the process. In our example, I'll call it *HALCHECK.DLL*. Refer to Table 2-2 to select the appropriate HAL.<br>3. Create a new *boot.ini* entry for this checked build by copying the line that currently boots your system onto a new entry line. Edit that one, adding the appropriate `/KERNEL` and `/HAL` options.<br>4. Reboot your system.<br>For example, add the following to the copied line of your *boot.ini*:<br>`/KERNEL=NTOSCHECK.EXE /HAL=HALCHECK.DLL` |
| `MAXMEM=<MB>` | This specifies the maximum amount of memory (in megabytes) that Windows 2000 will recognize when the operating system loads. This is useful in a debugging environment where you might want to test your driver under low-memory conditions without actually pulling memory from your computer. Example: `/MAXMEM=16` sets the amount of memory recognized by the machine to 16 MB. |
| `NODEBUG` | This option overrides any of the other debugger options and prevents the debugger from loading. This is useful to disable the debugger temporarily. |
| `NUMPROC=<#cpus>` | On a multiprocessor, this option will force the operating system to use only the number of processors specified. Example: On an eight-processor Windows 2000 Server, `/NUMPROC=4` forces only four processors to be used by the operating system. |
| `ONECPU` | Directs the operating system to use only one processor in a multiprocessing environment. This can be helpful in a debugging environment where you think a problem might be related to multiprocessor correctness and overall synchronization issues. Enabling this ensures single-CPU operation. |
| `PCILOCK` | This forces the kernel to use PCI resources that are assigned by the system BIOS. Normal behavior would be for the Windows 2000 plug-n-play component to configure each PCI card. |
| `SOS` | Windows 2000 will display diagnostic information as each device driver is loaded when this flag is set. |

After you have edited your *boot.ini* file to enable the debugger, ensure that the attributes protecting the file have been restored. The system will function without these attributes just fine, but they are there to protect you against accidental editing of this file:

```
C:\> attrib +h +r +s boot.ini
```

You must reboot the machine for the changes to take effect.

### Dealing with Blue Screens at Boot Time

It's very possible that you are experiencing a stop screen at boot time and cannot boot to modify the *boot.ini* file to enable the debugger. Or maybe the system isn't stable enough or staying alive long enough to do this. Or, more embarrassingly, you've corrupted the *boot.ini* file while making the changes talked about above, and now the machine just will not boot. Heroic measures are needed to rescue your *boot.ini* file. There are a couple of approaches to take, depending on how you configured your machine.

Before discussing how to fix a corrupted *boot.ini* file, I'll offer up a few suggestions on how to make your computer more maintainable. You should always make your boot partition a FAT partition. This makes it a very simple task to boot from a DOS diskette and fix whatever files are broken. Once Microsoft makes it easy to boot NTFS from a floppy, I will change that recommendation. Another recommendation that I always make is to install an alternate version of NT somewhere on your machine. That's easy in a big-money production environment but not always so easy where resources are scarce. If you have done either one of these, modifying a *boot.ini* file is not so hard. Just perform the following steps:

1. Boot from either the DOS boot floppy or from the alternate installation of NT.
2. Edit the *boot.ini* as you wish.
3. Reboot your machine.

If you didn't do either of the things I've described, it becomes a bit harder. You then have the following options:

1. Install another version of Windows 2000 on another partition, then perform the above procedure.
2. If you have a boot recovery disk, you can use this to edit the *boot.ini* and reboot.

Given one of these options, you should be able to configure your target system successfully to use the kernel debugger, or to recover from a corrupted *boot.ini* file.

## Preparing the Host

The previous section described how to establish a physical connection between a host and target machine for the debugger to communicate across. It also covered the configuration of the target computer to enable kernel debugging within that operating system. It is now time to talk about the preparation that must be taken prior to running the debugger on the host computer. The particulars of actually configuring the debugger are left to Chapter 4.

The steps that must be taken in preparing a host system to debug are as follows (in no particular order):

- Establish a physical connection between the host and target systems.
- Load the debugging tools onto the host computer.

- Create a symbol tree that matches the target machine.
- Configure the target computer to enable the kernel debugger.

You have already read about establishing the physical connection and configuring the target computer. The remainder of this section will focus on loading the debugging tools and creating a symbol tree that matches the target computer.

### SETTING UP THE SYMBOL TREE

Recall from the previous discussion in this chapter that symbol files are roadmaps into the binary files that make up the operating system. Symbol files translate addresses and offsets into symbolic names. They tell the debugger where data and functions live. They also provide the all-important line number information that allows the debugger to offer source-level debugging. They are vital to effective debugging.

The first step to setting up the symbol tree is determining which version of the operating system is executing on the target machine. The base version may be obvious, but service pack information and checked versus free build might not be so obvious. Although this information is kept in the registry (under *HKLM\Software\Microsoft\WindowsNT\CurrentVersion*), it is usually much quicker to run the *winmsd* utility from the command line. The version string lists the version, along with service pack information for your computer. This is illustrated in Figure 2-5.

Each Windows 2000 product CD, both free and checked, ships with a complete symbol tree intact on the media. These symbols live under the directory *support\debug\<platform>\symbols* on the product CD. If you are interested in debugging an Intel-based platform, the *<platform>* directory would be *i386*, whereas Alpha-based targets would be *alpha*. You can copy the entire symbols directory tree from the CD to your host machine using the Windows Explorer, or you can *xcopy* from the command line. If you are debugging a default configuration (single-CPU machine with a default HAL), you can even use the symbols directly from the CD, although it will be slow when loading the symbols into the debugger.

If you are running a service pack, things become more interesting. Microsoft has lately begun to ship symbols compressed on the service pack CD in the *support\debug\<platform>* directory. The details of how to decompress these vary by service pack, but will be covered in the release notes of the service pack. If you have hot fixes installed, you have to ask Microsoft for the symbol files relating to that hot fix. Install the service pack symbols on top of the base symbol tree—a service pack doesn't necessarily replace every file or driver. This will allow you to overwrite only those symbol files that have changed.

The symbol tree will have a number of subdirectories directly under the *symbols* directory. These correspond to the extension of the executable whose symbols are in them (e.g., *com*, *cpl*, *exe*, *dll*, *sys*, etc.).

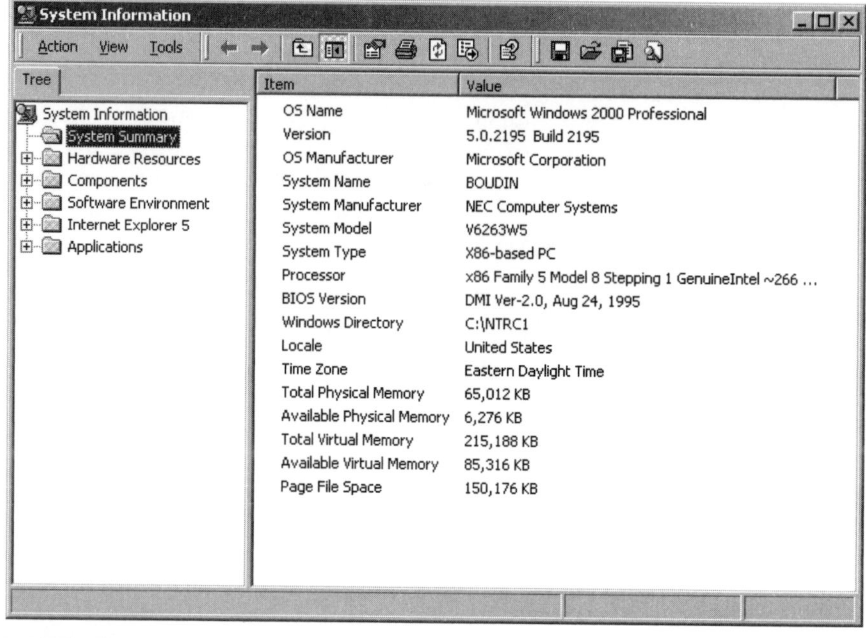


**FIGURE 2–5** *Using **winmsd** to Verify Version*

## CUSTOMIZING SYMBOLS

If your target is a multiprocessor computer or if it uses a special HAL, you must move some symbol files around before using them. Regardless of the actual name of the kernel and HAL that you booted your target from (recall that you can override the default kernel and HAL name with the `KERNEL` and `HAL` boot options—see Table 2-1), the debugger will always attempt to load symbol files *ntoskrnl.dbg* and *hal.dbg* for the kernel and HAL symbols.

If your computer is a simple multiprocessor, you need only replace *ntoskrnl.dbg* with *ntkrnlmp.dbg*. This is a simple rename operation, although you might want to save the original *ntoskrnl.dbg* file so that you can recover the change. This symbol file lives in the *EXE* subdirectory within the symbol tree (*ntoskrnl.dbg* is the symbol file for *ntoskrnl.exe*).

If your computer uses a special HAL (as many high-end servers do), there is a number of possibilities. There are many HAL files that ship with Windows NT. You computer manufacturer may also supply a custom HAL on its own media. Either way, you must rename the HAL that corresponds with your computer to *hal.dbg*. Again, you might want to take care to copy the original *hal.dbg* file. This symbol file lives in the *DLL* subdirectory of the symbol tree (because the HAL file is a DLL: *HAL.DLL*). The HALs shipped as a part of Windows 2000 are listed in Table 2-2.

**TABLE 2–2** *HAL Versions for Intel-Based Computers*

| HAL | Description |
|---|---|
| `HAL.DLL` | This is the standard HAL for the IA systems. |
| `HAL486C.DLL` | HAL for the 80486 Stepping C processor from Intel. |
| `HALAPIC.DLL` | Uniprocessor version of the *HALMPS.DLL*. |
| `HALAST.DLL` | HAL for AST SMP systems. |
| `HALCBUS.DLL` | HAL for Cbus-based computers. |
| `HALMCA.DLL` | HAL for MicroChannel architecture machines (PS/2 and others). |
| `HALMPS.DLL` | HAL for most multiprocessor machines. |
| `HALNCR.DLL` | HAL for NCR 35xx-series multiprocessor machines. |
| `HALOLI.DLL` | HAL for many older Olivetti SMP computers. |
| `HALSP.DLL` | HAL for the Compaq Systempro. |
| `HALWYSE7.DLL` | HAL for the Wys7 computer systems. |

### DEBUGGER FILES

The final step before actually running the debugger and performing kernel debugging tasks is to actually load the debugging tools on the host computer. As was pointed out earlier, there are two debuggers available to assist in kernel debugging: KD and WinDbg. The choice of which you want to use is personal, and I won't try to influence you here. Both will be installed in the example that follows.

The KD debugger is located on your operating system's distribution media in the *support\<platform>* directory.

To load KD, go to the appropriate support directory and copy the following files to a directory on your host machine:

- *<platform>kd.exe* (this is either *alphakd.exe* or *i386kd.exe*)
- *imagehlp.dll*
- *kdext<platform>.dll* (this is either *kdextalp.dll* or *kdextx86.dll*)

Once you've copied these files from the CD to your development machine, you can run them. Note that if the file *imagehlp.dll* is already loaded on your development machine, attempt to use that one first. Later versions of the platform SDK, the DDK, or the WinDbg tend to replace it. Copying over the later version might cause another tool to fail.

**Look in That Support Directory!**

You never know what useful utilities Microsoft will hide in the support directory. When Windows NT 4.0 Service Pack 4 shipped, Microsoft sneaked in an additional kernel debugger extension and a kernel memory space analyzer (both of which are described later in this book). The company never told anyone outside of its development partner community that these tools were there.

The moral of this story: You don't know what's out there until you look. So look!

Loading WinDbg is even easier. It installs as part of the platform SDK that ships as a part of the MSDN subscription. It is also available on the Microsoft support web site, currently at *http://msdn.microsoft.com/sdk/windbg.htm*. Run the setup program that ships as part of that distribution to install it.

# Summary

This chapter has covered a lot of ground. Basic kernel debugging topics were introduced, and basic terminology and concepts critical to kernel debugging were covered. The chapter then went on to explain how to set up the source and target machines for development. Supplementary to the text presented here, similar topics are covered in the Microsoft Workstation Resource Kit and in a number of articles on the Microsoft Knowledge Base (currently located on Microsoft's support web site at *suppport.microsoft.com*). If you have specific questions, I strongly encourage you to visit the knowledge base.

THREE

# The Stop Screen

#### CHAPTER OBJECTIVES

- Bug Checks
- Configuring Bug Check Behavior
- Anatomy of a Stop Screen
- Stop Screen Debugging Strategies

*The first indicator that debugging or crash dump analysis is necessary is the dreaded "blue screen of death" (BSOD) or, simply, the NT stop screen. It's confusing to look at. The information contained within it is important but may be a little hard to understand. If you are used to working with Unix, you'll both love the extra information it provides the support person and dread the lack of line number or file information you typically find in a Unix "panic." The stop screen is one of the most frequent tools that you will use to begin understanding a system failure on Windows 2000.*

*This chapter dissects the blue screen, beginning at its point of origin in the NT bug check. It provides pointers as to what to look for in the stop screen and what to do with that information. This chapter also discusses configuring the behavior of a Windows 2000 system at bug check time, and it shows you how to prepare for the next step: analyzing the state of the system either through "live" debugging or by analyzing the memory dump. It wraps up with a discussion of the most common stop codes that occur within a Windows 2000 system.*

# Bug Checks

A stop screen is an indication that one of the components of Windows 2000 has detected an instability in the system that would cause it to be unsafe or unwise to continue. Given the architecture of Windows 2000, the components that are able to cause catastrophic failures to the system all live in kernel mode. These include both the Microsoft-provided components that make the system work, as well as an array of device drivers from the various hardware vendors. The mechanism by which a stop screen occurs is called a *bug check.*

When the developers at Microsoft developed the Windows 2000 kernel, they embedded checks at various points within the software to ensure that the code was being fed information that was correct and stable. If the information or code flow is not as expected, the code calls the bug check function to cause the kernel to stop. Bug checks are also generated by the exception-handling routines in the kernel; these routines are called when basic exceptions occur, such as dereferencing null pointers or attempting operations at illegal interrupt levels. When the kernel stops, the blue screen will appear. Behavior beyond this is defined by the user and will be discussed further along in this section.

A good example of an explicitly called bug check can be found in the kernel module that implements and manages the virtual memory subsystem (the memory manager). As each process asks for memory to be allocated, the memory manager checks the list of free memory pages. If there are no more pages left to allocate and there are no pages that can be immediately freed up, the system will not remain useful. The memory manager will bug check. A much more common example is the case of referencing a pointer that is not valid, in which an exception will be thrown, and a bug check will occur. There are dozens of such cases.

The bug check is only the first step. It stops the system. It also provides the mechanism to alert the user to the actual problem that occurred. This is achieved by having a code defined that represents each possible failure. This code, called the *stop code,* is given to the bug check routine to display on the blue screen. A complete listing of the Windows 2000 stop codes can be found in Appendix B of this book.

Apart from the usual kernel-mode bug checks, there is the potential that an exception could occur in the hardware abstraction layer (HAL). This does not provide the usual stop screen or provide for a system dump. The HAL bug check is almost always caused by a nonmaskable interrupt (NMI) that is generated by the system hardware when a fatal error is detected. This error might be as simple as a memory error or as complex as a failing PCI card. When the HAL stop screen is encountered, basic hardware troubleshooting techniques should be employed. I'll talk about how to recognize this screen a little later in the section that dissects the stop screen components.

### How to Create a Bug Check Programmatically

There are two routines provided to kernel-mode developers to cause a bug check from device driver or other kernel-mode code. These routines are defined as follows:

```
VOID KeBugCheck(          IN ULONG NtStopCode )

VOID KeBugCheckEx(        IN ULONG NtStopCode,

                                          IN ULONG StopCodeParm1,
                                          IN ULONG StopCodeParm2,
                                          IN ULONG StopCodeParm3,
                                          IN ULONG StopCodeParm4 )
```

The only difference between the two calls is that one allows the caller to provide user-defined parameters that will be displayed in the blue screen and made available in the system dump. This is very useful for developers in understanding what went wrong in their code or with the system. The call to `KeBugCheck()` is actually written to call `KeBugCheckEx()`—so use `KeBugCheckEx()` and save yourself some cycles when stopping the machine.

Keep in mind that the system should be in either an unrecoverable or unknown (and potentially unstable) state before calling either of these functions. If it is at all possible to recover, that is the best bet.

There is a sequence of steps that the kernel follows as part of the processing of the bug check call. The first thing that occurs is that interrupts are disabled on all of the processors in the system. If interrupts were to occur, the state of the system that will be written to the dump (or made available to the debugger) would not be the same as when the bug check occurred.

The first line of the stop screen is then displayed. This is the line that contains the bug check code. No textual descriptions are provided at this point.

After the stop code is displayed, any device drivers that have registered bug check callbacks have their callback routines executed. A callback routine is a function defined by any interested device drivers that is called at bug check time. These functions typically do little except store state information in a structure that can be read and interpreted with a debugger executing on the saved crash dump file. Not all device drivers or kernel-mode components use bug check callbacks. They can be useful, and I will discuss them in Chapter 9.

Next, a check to see whether the debugger is enabled occurs. If the debugger is enabled, the remainder of the blue screen will not yet be displayed. Control is instead transferred from the bug check code to the debugger module in the kernel. The serial port configured for kernel debugging is continuously polled until the debugger responds. Once the kernel debugger is attached, the user determines any further action interactively. It is because everything comes to a sudden halt when the debugger is configured that you should configure only the target system to use the debugger when you actually have debugging to do. It can be an easy habit to leave the debugger enabled, so be careful!

If there is no debugger configured or if the debugger has allowed the system to proceed, the remainder of the stop screen information is determined and printed on the screen. This includes CPU and build number information, a listing of the loaded device drivers, and a module-level stack trace (with parameters).

Once the stop screen has been completely painted, either the system stops or the crash dump is written to the system page file. The behavior is user-selected. If the crash dump is written, it is saved to a permanent file when the system reboots. If there is not enough page file configured to hold the entire contents of memory, no crash dump will be written. Finally, the system either halts or is rebooted, behavior that is also configured by the user.

## Configuring Bug Check Behavior

There is a number of user-tunable parameters that control the behavior of the system when a bug check occurs. The things you must configure are whether a dump is taken, where that dump should go, whether the system will automatically reboot or simply hang, and what to do when the machine comes back up. These options are known as *recovery options* and are configured through the System Applet in the control panel.

To view or set the recovery options in Windows 2000, you must select the Startup and Recovery Button from the Advanced tab of the System Applet. This is illustrated in Figure 3-1.

Selecting the Startup and Recovery option will bring up the dialog box in which the actual recovery options can be set and modified. The top portion of the Startup and Recovery dialog is geared toward the various Windows 2000 startup options. This isn't really relevant to the current discussion on bug check behavior. It is the bottom section that is of interest. This dialog, as it appears in Windows 2000, is illustrated in Figure 3-2.

The first configurable item deals with logging an event to the system event log when the system stops. Because a catastrophic failure will force the system to halt operation immediately with interrupts turned off, there cannot really be any event log activity at the time the system stops. Instead, when this option is configured, an event is logged when the machine reboots. The message will indicate that a stop occurred, and it will preserve the stop code. This is illustrated in Figure 3-3.

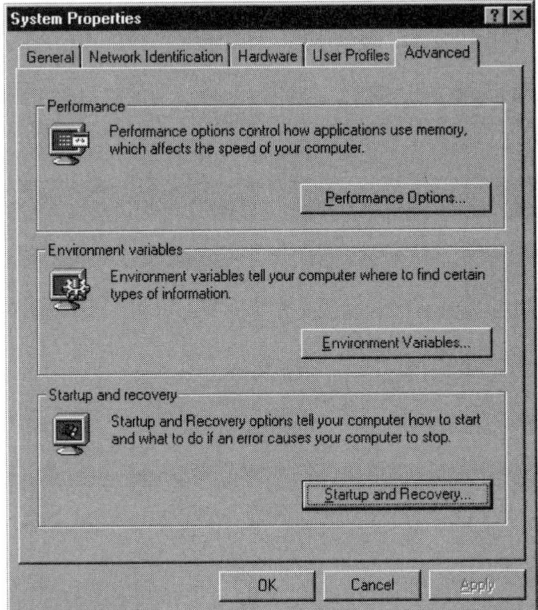


**FIGURE 3–1** *The System Applet on the Control Panel in Windows 2000*

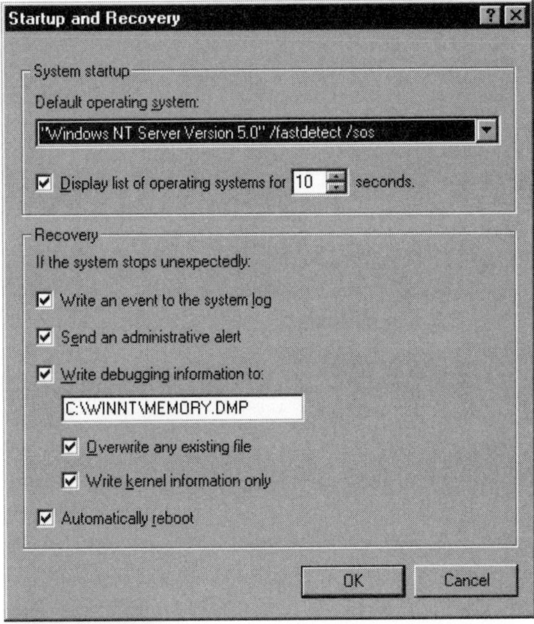


**FIGURE 3–2** *The Startup and Recovery Dialog in Windows 2000*

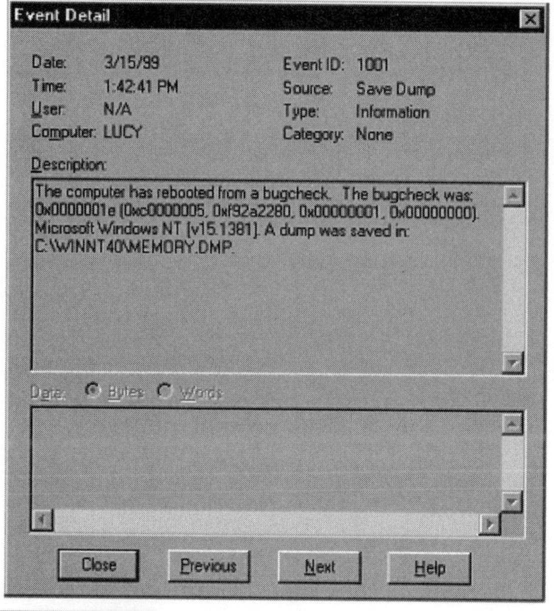


**FIGURE 3–3** *Recovery Event Log Message*

As with the event log message, an administrative alert can be sent when the machine is recovering from a bug check. When this option is enabled, an alert is sent to the domain administrator (or the local administrator on a stand-alone machine), informing of the bug check and subsequent reboot.

The third option allows the user to "write debugging information" to a specified file. This is the crash dump file. With this option selected, the system will save a copy of the system memory to the dump file specified. There are a couple of caveats that you must be aware of.

When the operating system attempts to create a crash dump, it does not immediately open the dump file and begin writing data. Remember that the system is in an unstable state, and opening files and writing to a file system can compromise the integrity of the data that you're attempting to save. If you're diagnosing a crash dump with a file system error, you want the file system data structures intact—not necessarily the state they'll be in if you start creating new files. Instead, the operating system will copy the contents of memory to the system paging file. For this to work, your paging file must be configured to match or exceed the size of main memory.

As the system is rebooting, it will detect that there is crash dump information stored in the paging file. This isn't a good thing from the perspective of the operating system because it needs the paging file to perform its virtual memory functions. The data must be moved out of the paging file as quickly as possible. This is accomplished by a background process called *dumpsave*. You don't need to do anything to make this happen. Dumpsave will run whenever a dump is detected in the paging file and transfer the contents of the dump into the dump file that you specified in the configuration screen.

Be aware that, as the system is coming up, you may receive a message that you are running low on virtual memory. This will correct itself as the available paging file is emptied of the dump information. To avoid this scenario, you can create either a very large paging file or an alternate paging file on a separate disk drive large enough to contain the dump information (Microsoft's preferred solution). This will keep enough page file space to manage normal operating system stress adequately during the boot cycle, while at the same time allowing dump files to be created.

Again, the size of the memory image can be quite large (up to 4 Gbytes on a 32-bit NT system). Ensure that, when you select the location of the system dump file, there is enough space on the selected volume. There are no restrictions on where you can locate the dump file in your system. Choose a location that will maintain enough free space.

The first suboption after setting the dump file location is a flag indicating whether to overwrite previous dump files. If this is set, a new dump will overwrite a previous file. If this is not selected, you must always take care to save the crash dump file to another location so that subsequent failures will have a place to write their information. The only real reason not to select this is if you are having a continuing failure and want to save the original dump file without the overhead of continuous dumps.

Windows 2000 gives you a second option relating to dump files that wasn't present in Windows NT 4.0. This is the option to save only kernel information. If you have a 4-Gbyte system and do not have that much space available for both a 4-Gbyte paging file and a 4-Gbyte dump file, this is the option to check. When this option is enabled, the dump file will contain only images of memory assigned to kernel address spaces. In many cases, this is enough to understand the failure when doing later analysis. There are also many cases when it will not be enough. My recommendation is that, unless you are short on disk space, you should keep this option disabled. A support engineer will want as much information as is available, and this option limits that.

The final option is a flag that determines whether the machine should reboot after encountering a system bug check. If enabled, the system will paint the blue screen, dump system memory, then reboot. The only reason for not selecting this option is if you are either experiencing continuous problems and don't want your machine to repeatedly cycle through stop screens or if you want to preserve the stop screen for some reason. Keep in mind that, if this option is selected, you will not receive a net alert informing of the failure until the machine has been manually rebooted.

The actual configuration information set by the Startup and Recovery dialog box is stored, like most things in Windows 2000, in the system registry.

TABLE 3–1 *Registry Key Entries Governing Recovery Options*

| Key | Description | Default Value |
|---|---|---|
| `AutoReboot` | Determines whether the machine will reboot after performing other bug check actions. | 1 |
| `CrashDumpEnabled` | Signifies whether a crash dump will be taken when the system bug checks. | 1 |
| `Dumpfile` | Specifies the location of the system dump file. | *%SystemRoot%\memory.dmp* |
| `Overwrite` | Is set to 1 if the dump file is to be overwritten. | 1 |
| `SendAlert` | Specifies whether a net alert will be sent after the machine has rebooted from a bug check. | 0 |
| `KernelDumpOnly` | Is set to 1 if only kernel-mode memory is to be included in the dump file. THIS IS VALID ONLY ON WINDOWS 2000. | 0 |

The recovery options are stored under the registry key `HKEY_LOCAL_MACHINE\CurrentControlSet\Control\CrashControl`. The subkeys used to govern recovery behavior are enumerated in Table 3-1.

# Anatomy of a Stop Screen

A bug check will always result in an NT stop screen. It might or might not create a system dump from the failing operating system image or perform any other of the configurable actions. The stop screen is different—it always exists. This screen appears cryptic at first but actually contains enough information to determine which device driver may be at fault in the failure. It also serves as a starting point to see whether the problem is a known one. The stop screen is illustrated in Figure 3-4.

Although there is only one stop screen format that you will see because of a bug check, there is actually another blue screen that may occur. This is the HAL blue screen. It does not fit the format or description of a bug check initiated blue screen. It occurs only when the HAL detects a catastrophic failure in the hardware that it cannot handle, usually in the

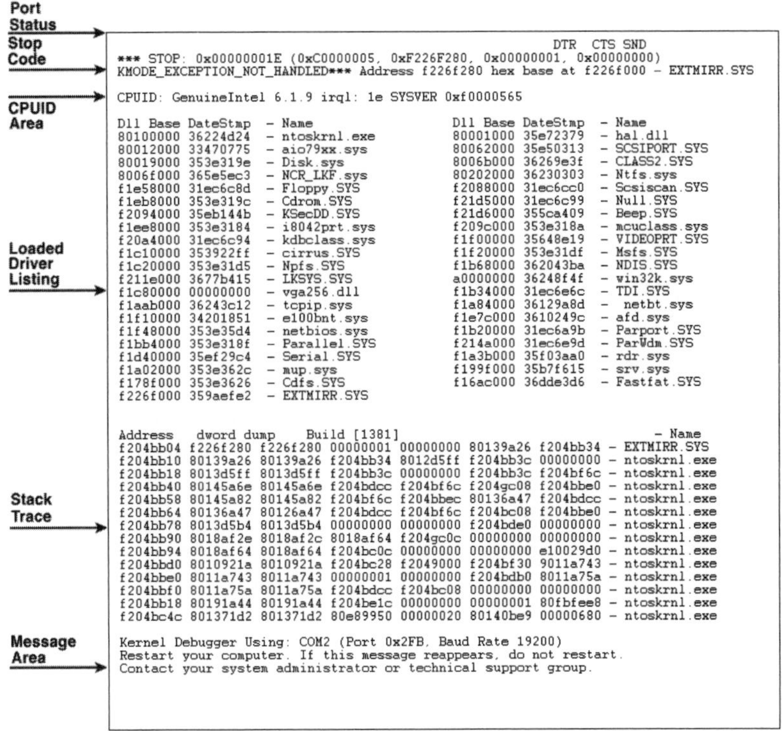


```
                                                              DTR  CTS SND
*** STOP: 0x0000001E (0xC0000005, 0xF226F280, 0x00000001, 0x00000000)
KMODE_EXCEPTION_NOT_HANDLED*** Address f226f280 hex base at f226f000 - EXTMIRR.SYS

CPUID: GenuineIntel 6.1.9 irql: 1e SYSVER 0xf0000565

Dll Base DateStmp  - Name                  Dll Base DateStmp  - Name
80100000 36224d24  - ntoskrnl.exe          80001000 35e72379  - hal.dll
80012000 33470775  - aio79xx.sys           80062000 35e50313  - SCSIPORT.SYS
80019000 353e319e  - Disk.sys              8006b000 36269e3f  - CLASS2.SYS
8006f000 365e5ec3  - NCR_LKF.sys           80202000 36230303  - Ntfs.sys
f1e58000 31ec6c8d  - Floppy.SYS            f2088000 31ec6cc0  - Scsiscan.SYS
f1eb8000 353e319c  - Cdrom.SYS             f21d5000 31ec6c99  - Null.SYS
f2094000 35eb144b  - KSecDD.SYS            f21d6000 355ca409  - Beep.SYS
f1ee8000 353e3184  - i8042prt.sys          f209c000 353e318a  - mcuclass.sys
f20a4000 31ec6c94  - kdbclass.sys          f1f00000 35648e19  - VIDEOPRT.SYS
f1c10000 353922ff  - cirrus.SYS            f1f20000 353e31df  - Msfs.SYS
f1c20000 353e31d5  - Npfs.SYS              f1b68000 362043ba  - NDIS.SYS
f211e000 3677b415  - LKSYS.SYS             a0000000 36248f4f  - win32k.sys
f1c80000 00000000  - vga256.dll            f1b34000 31ec6e6c  - TDI.SYS
f1aab000 36243c12  - tcpip.sys             f1a84000 36129a8d  -  netbt.sys
f1f10000 34201851  - e100bnt.sys           f1e7c000 3610249c  - afd.sys
f1f48000 353e35d4  - netbios.sys           f1b20000 31ec6a9b  - Parport.SYS
f1bb4000 353e318f  - Parallel.SYS          f214a000 31ec6e9d  - ParWdm.SYS
f1d40000 35ef29c4  - Serial.SYS            f1a3b000 35f03aa0  - rdr.sys
f1a02000 353e362c  - mup.sys               f199f000 35b7f615  - srv.sys
f178f000 353e3626  - Cdfs.SYS              f16ac000 36dde3d6  - Fastfat.SYS
f226f000 359aefe2  - EXTMIRR.SYS


Address   dword dump    Build [1381]                                 - Name
f204bb04 f226f280 f226f280 00000001 00000000 80139a26 f204bb34 - EXTMIRR.SYS
f204bb10 80139a26 80139a26 f204bb34 8012d5ff f204bb3c 00000000 - ntoskrnl.exe
f204bb18 8013d5ff 8013d5ff f204bb3c 00000000 f204bb3c f204bf6c - ntoskrnl.exe
f204bb40 80145a6e 80145a6e f204bdcc f204bf6c f204gc08 f204bbe0 - ntoskrnl.exe
f204bb58 80145a82 80145a82 f204bf6c f204bbec 80136a47 f204bdcc - ntoskrnl.exe
f204bb64 80136a47 80126a47 f204bdcc f204bf6c f204bc08 f204bbe0 - ntoskrnl.exe
f204bb78 8013d5b4 8013d5b4 00000000 00000000 f204bde0 00000000 - ntoskrnl.exe
f204bb90 8018af2e 8018af2c 8018af64 f204gc0c 00000000 00000000 - ntoskrnl.exe
f204bb94 8018af64 8018af64 f204bc0c 00000000 00000000 e10029d0 - ntoskrnl.exe
f204bbd0 8010921a 8010921a f204bc28 f2049000 f204bf30 9011a743 - ntoskrnl.exe
f204bbe0 8011a743 8011a743 00000001 00000000 f204bdb0 8011a75a - ntoskrnl.exe
f204bbf0 8011a75a 8011a75a f204bdcc f204bc08 00000000 00000000 - ntoskrnl.exe
f204bb18 80191a44 80191a44 f204be1c 00000000 00000001 80fbfee8 - ntoskrnl.exe
f204bc4c 801371d2 801371d2 80e89950 00000020 80140be9 00000680 - ntoskrnl.exe

Kernel Debugger Using: COM2 (Port 0x2FB, Baud Rate 19200)
Restart your computer. If this message reappears, do not restart.
Contact your system administrator or technical support group.
```

**FIGURE 3–4** *Example Stop Screen*

form of an NMI. An example of this might be a failure from the PCI bus controller. The HAL stop screen does not cause a dump or force a reboot. The configuration options for system recovery do not apply. There is nothing to do except perform basic hardware troubleshooting in an attempt to isolate the failing component. A typical HAL stop screen will print out a message in the form:

```
*** HARDWARE MALFUNCTION <code>
This system has halted. Call your hardware vendor for support
```

You should note that many newer HALs and some third-party support tools (such as NCR's State Saver) will generate a special bug check code when an NMI is encountered and generate a dump. There is hardware known as *dump switch cards* that does little more than generate an NMI when the user presses a button on the card. This is useful when a system is seemingly hung or unresponsive. Examination of the system dump file after a dump switch

### What Causes NMIs?

A nonmaskable interrupt, as its name implies, is an interrupt generated by the system hardware that cannot be ignored by the operating system. This is used almost exclusively to indicate a catastrophic failure of the underlying hardware.

The most common cause of an NMI is a memory error. This may be a simple parity error in non-error-correcting memory (ECC), or it may be a double-bit parity error in ECC memory. Either case should yield information that a parity error occurred in the HAL stop screen. If you get this error, then removing memory modules until the problem cannot be recreated is the correct approach to take.

An error on the either the PCI or MicroChannel bus will also cause a fatal NMI. These errors are caused when an adapter card on the bus generates some error or if the bus itself is broken (for example, there may be an electrical short in one of the adapter connectors causing an error). These bus errors are usually indicated by notation on the HAL stop screen that an IOCHK (I/O check condition), PERR (PCI parity error), or SERR (PCI system error) has occurred. The correct troubleshooting method is to remove adapter cards one at a time and attempt to duplicate the problem until the correct card is determined. Often, simply reseating the cards in the adapters in their slots after cleaning the connectors will solve this type of problem.

card has generated an NMI will usually yield the reason for the hang. This is discussed in detail in Chapter 7, when I talk about working with system dump files. Although there isn't much more to say about HAL stop screens, there is plenty to say about the more frequent bug check-driven stop screens. An examination of Figure 3-4 shows that there are six basic regions on a Windows 2000 stop screen. These are defined as follows:

1. Debug port status indicators (present only when kernel debugging is enabled)
2. Bug check information
3. CPU and version information
4. Loaded driver listing
5. Module-level call stack (or stack trace)
6. Message area

Each of these regions will be discussed separately in the following sections.

## Port Status Indicators

If you do not have kernel debugging enabled on the machine that has encountered the stop screen, you will not see the port status indicators on your blue screen. These indicators describe the state of the connection with the host debugger. If there is no debugger attached to the failing machine, it

**TABLE 3–2** *Port Status Indicators*

| Indicator | Meaning |
|---|---|
| MDM | The debugger is using modem control on the serial port. |
| CD | Carrier detected. |
| RI | RS-232 signal Ring Indicator. If a modem is attached to the debugger serial port, this indicates that it is ringing (as if a support person were dialing in to debug over a modem). |
| DSR | RS-232 signal Data Set Ready. This indicates that a debugger is attached and ready to communicate (at least from a serial-port point of view). |
| CTS | RS-232 signal Clear To Send. This indicator appears when the attached debugger can receive more information. |
| SND | This indicator appears whenever the failed machine is actually sending data across the serial port. |
| RCV | This indicator appears whenever the failed machine is receiving information across the serial port (i.e., the debugger is talking). |
| FRM | There was an RS-232 framing error on the transmitted data. This should correct itself. |
| OVL | There was an RS-232 buffer overflow. This should correct itself. |
| PRT | A parity error was detected on data traversing the serial port. The system should recover from this. |

will continuously poll for one, and you will see the SND message flash. The meanings of the acronyms that are displayed are straightforward and informational. They are described in Table 3-2.

Most of the port status indicators refer directly to signals on the RS-232 serial port. To understand better how RS-232 works and for a complete description of the protocol, I urge you to consult the excellent *RS-232 Made Easy* by Martin Seyer, published by Prentice Hall.

## Stop Code Data

The next section of the stop screen is the most critical to understanding the system failure. It is the actual stop code and parameters, as passed to `KeBugCheckEx()`. It tells what went wrong, although not necessarily why it went wrong. From the illustration in Figure 3-4, we can examine the sample stop code as follows:

```
*** STOP: 0x0000001E (0xC0000005, 0xF226F280, 0x00000001, 0x00000000)
KMODE_EXCEPTION_NOT_HANDLED
*** Address f226f280 hex base at f226f000  EXTMIRR.SYS
```

The first line indicates that a bug check occurred, what that bug check was, and the parameters passed into the bug check call. These parameters will be different for each possible stop code (see a complete listing in Appendix B). In this example, the stop code was 0x1E. The bug check handling routine that populates this screen attempts a lookup to give a name to the actual stop code. This is printed on the second line in this section. In this example, it is KMODE_EXCEPTION_NOT_HANDLED. This is a generic stop code indicating that a basic error, such as an errant pointer, has occurred.

After the stop code has been displayed, Windows 2000 attempts to resolve any addresses in the bug check parameter list back to their respective base device driver or kernel modules. For example, the second parameter in the bug check just described points to the device driver *EXTMIRR.SYS*. You can manually see this by comparing the address in the second parameter with the list of loaded device drivers—an exercise we will take when we discuss the loaded device driver list. The bug check routine attempts to resolve any addresses it finds in the bug check parameters; this example had just one valid address.

What do the rest of the parameters mean? It's different for each possible stop code, but for the purposes of illustration, I'll define these here. The stop code listing in Appendix B explains that the parameters for stop code 0x1E are as follows:

- The actual exception code that wasn't handled
- The virtual address of the code that excepted
- Parameter 0 of the exception, if any
- Parameter 1 of the exception, if any

The exception code in this example is 0xC0000005. Appendix C explains that the exception code indicates "access violation." The blue screen has already told us that the offending driver pointed to by parameter 2 is the driver *EXTMIRR.SYS*. The meanings of parameters 3 and 4 aren't clear, so we'll just go on what we have.

Given this simple example, we know that the *EXTMIRR.SYS* driver attempted to access memory that it wasn't supposed to. In fact, the *EXTMIRR.SYS* driver was modified to generate this example by referencing a null pointer. The remainder of the blue screen simply provides more clues (keep in mind that not all stops are so self-evident).

## System Information

Following the stop code data is information that attempts to describe the underlying kernel. It doesn't do a fantastic job of imparting useful information, but it will give you some information. Again, from Figure 3-4, we get the following identification string:

```
CPUID: GenuineIntel 6.1.9 irql: 1e SYSVER 0xf0000565
```

The CPUID parameter is generated by querying the underlying processor for its CPUID string and version information. In this case, it's a genuine Intel processor. The version information explains that it's some revision of a Pentium Pro (the Pentium Pro identifies itself as a P6). This information does not indicate how many processors are in the system or even whether it is a multiprocessor system. This parameter does differentiate between the various brands and models of CPU (e.g., AMD, etc.).

The second parameter indicates the interrupt request level (IRQL) of the machine at the time the blue screen was generated. If you recall from the discussion of the how bug checks are handled, all interrupts are disabled when the blue screen is generated. Because of this, every blue screen will indicate `1e` as the IRQL. Note that this is not the IRQL at the time of the failure.

The final parameter is the system version information. It describes exactly two things: the major build number and whether that build was a free build or a checked build (refer to Chapter 2 for detail on the differences between the two types). The high byte in the version string is either an `f` or a `c`, indicating "free" and "checked," respectively. The lower half of the version string is a hexadecimal representation of the major build number. In this example and on all Windows 2000 systems, this number is 565, which translates to build 1381. Don't rush to do the conversion yourself—later in the stop screen, the number is decoded for you as part of the stack trace.

What's missing is the service pack information. No place on the stop screen informs the user of the service pack level of the underlying operating system. You can often derive this information by comparing the date stamps of the loaded device drivers, but that is an awkward method. Given all of this information, all that has really been determined is that this is a free version of the operating system running on an Intel Pentium Pro platform.

## Loaded Driver List

The next section in the stop screen lists each device driver that is currently loaded into the operating system. It also enumerates the base address of each driver and the date stamp from the driver (in hexadecimal). The list is formatted into two columns, each containing the three pieces of information just described. The following items are from the sample shown in Figure 3-4:

```
Dll Base DateStmp - Name
80100000 36224d24 - ntoskrnl.exe
80012000 33470775 - aio79xx.sys
```

The column entitled `Dll Base` lists the address of each device driver that was loaded into system memory. If you are a driver developer, you might notice that it's not the address you expected. This is because the address reflects the actual location where the driver was loaded, and this may or may not be the address at which the driver was built to live. When a device driver is built, it is linked to a "preferred load address" that is configured with the build environment utilities *bind* and *rebase*. If the device driver developer did not specify a preferred address, the linker invents one. For a complete discussion of this topic, please refer to the documentation accompanying the Device Driver Kit (DDK) provided by Microsoft.

The second parameter is the timestamp, indicating the date that the component was built. This isn't a date as you might expect it—it is displayed as the hexadecimal representation of the number of seconds since January 1, 1980. This is not a friendly format that you can simply glance at and quickly understand the date. It is useful only if you compare the timestamp displayed against the actual executable. You will want to do this to compare a given device driver against known binary files to determine service pack levels or to verify that the correct third-party driver is loaded.

How do you compare timestamps on two executables when all you have on the stop screens is a long, seemingly meaningless number? Fortunately, Microsoft gives us a method to look up the timestamp on an executable. This is accomplished using the *dumpbin* command. The following example demonstrates how to look up the timestamp on the *videoprt.sys* driver:

```
C:\winnt\system32\drivers> dumpbin /headers videoprt.sys
Dump of file videoprt.sys

PE signature found

File Type: EXECUTABLE IMAGE

FILE HEADER VALUES
             14C machine (i386)
               9 number of sections
        35C76F41 time date stamp Tue Aug 04 16:29:53 1998
               0 file pointer to symbol table
               0 number of symbols
              E0 size of optional header
             30E characteristics
                   Executable
                   Line numbers stripped
                   Symbols stripped
                   32 bit word machine
                   Debug information stripped
```

As you can see, the timestamp on this file is 35C76F41, which translates in English to "Tue Aug 04 16:29:53 1998". Is this the same driver that is displayed on the sample stop screen in Figure 3-4? The *videoprt.sys* driver (the information is found midway down the second column, in the loaded driver section) has a date stamp of 353e318a. I don't know what that date is, but it's older than the one that we just obtained by executing the *dumpbin* utility. The answer is that they don't match.

## Call Stack

The call stack traces the flow of execution prior to the bug check. It presents a flow at the module level (as opposed to the debugger view of actual function's call execution). It also provides a list of arguments passed to each successive call. An excerpt of the call stack from the sample stop screen in Figure 3-4 is as follows:

```
Address     dword dump  Build [1381]
f204bb04 f226f280 f226f280 00000001 00000000 80139a26 f204bb34  - EXTMIRR.SYS
f204bb10 80139a26 80139a26 f204bb34 8012d5ff f204bb3c 00000000  - ntoskrnl.exe
f204bb18 8013d5ff 8013d5ff f204bb3c 00000000 f204bb3c f204bf6c  - ntoskrnl.exe
```

The first thing that you might notice is that the build number is included as a part of the header on the stack. Unlike the build number presented earlier in the system information section of the stop screen, this build number is in decimal.

Following the header is the actual stack trace. This is read from the bottom up, with the topmost entry being the last driver that executed. Each module is listed in the far right-hand column. In the example, the last driver to execute would be the *EXTMIRR.SYS* driver. In attempting to diagnose the bug check, this may be the offending driver that caused the failure or it may be another in the stack. There is no real way to tell. What it does provide, however, is a listing of the drivers involved in the failure.

The seven columns of numbers to the left of the driver name have limited use in a stop screen. The first column indicates the stack frame address for the call. Without a debugger connected, there is no use for this information, except maybe to examine quickly for stack frame corruption. The second and third columns are the return address for the function call that generated the stack trace entry. Why that number appears twice is a mystery. The final four columns represent the arguments passed to each function. Without knowing what the function is that's being called (remember, these are module names), the parameters are not very useful. You can visibly scan them to see whether any of the addresses that may be passed between functions match any of the loaded device drivers. If so, add that driver to your list of suspects.

## Message Area

The final area of the stop screen is the message area. This provides the status information as to the state of the dump (should one be taken). If there is no dump, a message indicating that you should call your support person is displayed. It is relatively useless for any troubleshooting function. Windows 2000 also includes verbiage in the message area with customized messages for certain stop codes.

## Stop Screen Debugging Strategies

Given a stop screen, can you diagnose a problem? The answer varies. What you can usually do with a Windows 2000 stop screen is to figure out whether this is a known problem with Windows 2000. You can possibly determine which device driver is responsible for the failure or which is at least involved. You can verify that the correct device drivers are loaded. If you are a device driver developer, you can quickly scan to see whether your driver is in the stack. If you want more detail into the failure, you must either have a debugger connected or use one to examine the crash dump.

From a support standpoint, the primary function when examining a stop screen is determining whether the blue screen is a known problem and ascertaining an expedient work-around. The Microsoft Knowledge Base, also included with Microsoft Developer Network (MSDN) and TechEd subscriptions, is the primary source of information in determining whether a problem is known. Search for the key words *stop code* or *blue screen* and you will be inundated with known problems that generate certain stop screen characteristics. If your stop screen matches one described in the knowledge base, the knowledge base article will usually provide you status and point you to any hot fixes or service packs that address the problem.

If there isn't a knowledge base article that indicates a known problem from Microsoft's perspective, a third-party driver vendor might be the key. Before approaching a device driver vendor, you must first isolate suspect drivers. A driver is suspect if any of the addresses in the stop code indicate a memory location within that device driver. Windows 2000 will attempt to resolve any addresses for you and print the appropriate message below the actual stop code on the blue screen. A driver should also be suspect if it is in the stack trace and is not called *ntoskrnl.exe* (*ntoskrnl.exe* usually indicates that a system function was called, although they have also been known to fail). If you have isolated a suspect driver, you should contact the technical support organization that supports the device driver to see whether you have a known problem.

Some stop codes do not indicate a misbehaving device driver but rather point to a system corruption or configuration problem. The stop code should be looked up in Appendix B and its parameters checked to see whether there is an obvious solution. Failing any of these methods, the next step will be to connect a debugger and probe more deeply. If you are a device driver developer, this might be the first approach you want to take.

# Summary

This chapter demonstrated that there is an abundance of information to be found in the Windows 2000 stop screen. It may be the dreaded "blue screen of death," but it provides the first clues to unraveling the mystery of a catastrophic failure. The blue screen is just the first point in debugging a failure—a crash dump will need to be examined to truly understand what went wrong with the operating system. Whether you, as a support person, look at the dump or the dump is forwarded on to someone who will analyze it, you should always keep the option enabled. The remainder of this book will talk about exploring the operating system and crash dump files with the available Microsoft tools.

FOUR

# Overview of WinDbg and KD

**CHAPTER OBJECTIVES**

- WinDbg vs. KD
- Tool Configuration
- Command Windows
- Debugger Extensions

*You either have a blue screen that you want to understand, or there's a crash dump that needs examining, or maybe you just want to do some basic debugging of your device driver. This chapter provides the first look at the two related tools to do all of that—KD and WinDbg, the Microsoft kernel debuggers.*

*Chapter 2 discussed enabling kernel debugging on the target computer and in establishing the physical connection. This chapter will pick up that discussion and will walk through the kernel debugger. Most of the relevant screens and configuration options will be discussed. You will get a feel for what these tools are and will understand some of the limitations. You will also understand what you need to do to navigate the tools to get the information you are looking for.*

This chapter touches on the use of many of the Windows and configuration commands, but it is by no means exhaustive. For an exhaustive reference for many of these options, consult the WinDbg help file in Appendix A of this book and the documentation available in the Windows 2000 Device Driver Developer's Kit (DDK).

## WinDbg vs. KD

There are two tools provided by Microsoft that are capable of examining both a running kernel and a kernel image contained within a crash dump. These are WinDbg, the graphical kernel debugger, and KD, the command-line-based debugger. There are similarities between WinDbg when operated from the WinDbg command window and KD when run from the command line. I'll talk more about the various windows later in this chapter.

Which debugger should you use? WinDbg is the more user-friendly of the two. It is easy to navigate and use for anyone familiar with operating Windows-based programs. It provides multiple views of the running system. KD, on the other hand, is a command-line-operated program that brings with it all of the limitations of console-based applications.

Microsoft is continuing the development of WinDbg as it progresses down its Windows roadmap toward Windows Whistler and beyond. The future of KD remains less clear. Windows NT 4.0 shipped only with KD in the support directories. Windows 2000, on the other hand, ships with WinDbg. Microsoft has been very active in improving what was once an interminable tool into something that is respectable to work with. What was once shipped only with a subscription to the Microsoft Developer Network (MSDN) now ships with every copy of the operating system.

This chapter will address KD explicitly only where differences exist—you should assume that anything stated as true for the WinDbg command window will be correspondingly true for the KD command line. The major difference traditionally between the command line of WinDbg and KD is that KD supports only a subset of the built-in commands that you will find in WinDbg. This is changing as Microsoft merges the KD and WinDbg code bases (they have these builds in beta test as this book goes to print). KD also has some unique startup restrictions and requirements, so those will be covered in more depth.

Microsoft has pointed out to me during the development of this book that WinDbg is a multithreaded application and is prone to periodic lockups, due to synchronization issues. KD is a single-threaded application that does not suffer from these issues and, thus, does not encounter the lockups that WinDbg does. Again, WinDbg is under active development, so what is true as I write this may not be true of versions that appear after. Always rely on your own experience with regard to stability issues. When in doubt, check with Microsoft.

Also, you should note that both KD and WinDbg were enabled with the capability to provide rough debugging of user-mode code. This is a book about kernel debugging and, as a consequence, will cover only the information relevant to kernel-mode debugging with the tools. If there are options that make sense only when doing user-mode debugging (such as attaching to a running process), they will not be discussed.

# Configuring WinDbg

You cannot simply run WinDbg and expect it to work. It is a complex piece of software that was designed for multiple purposes and, as such, must be configured for what you are trying to accomplish. To use WinDbg for kernel-mode debugging, the following steps must occur:

- The debugger must be told that it is debugging kernel-mode code and not user-mode code.
- The communications port and speed information needs to be provided.
- A path to the proper symbol tables must be provided.

These settings can be saved either as a *workspace* (which will be discussed later in this section) or can be set on the command line when the debugger is initially started up. A list of the relevant command line startup options is presented in Table 4-1.

Beyond these core parameters that must be configured, WinDbg allows you to configure (and remember) window layouts, colors, fonts, and all of the other things that you are used to tweaking in a normal Windows application. Saving these layouts is achieved through WinDbg *workspaces*, which will be discussed later in this section.

**TABLE 4–1** *WinDbg Command Startup Options*

| Option | Meaning |
|---|---|
| `?` | Open the WinDbg help file. |
| `Ad` | Automatically display the Open Crash Dump dialog box at startup. |
| `G` | Immediately execute the *go* command when the debugger begins—this will cause the debugger to begin immediately polling for the target computer. |
| `I` | Ignore the default workspace. This is as if running without any defined configuration. |

**TABLE 4–1** *WinDbg Command Startup Options (Continued)*

| Option | Meaning |
|---|---|
| `K[platform port speed]` | This starts the debugger in kernel debugging mode. The options specify the platform (i.e., x86 or alpha), the communication port (COM1 through COMn), and the port speed (e.g., 9600, 115200). |
| `L[text]` | Sets the title of the debugger window to *text*. |
| `M` | Begin the debugger in minimized mode. |
| `R filename` | Start the debugger and execute the commands contained in the command file specified. The commands are placed one per line. Once the debugger has executed the commands listed, it will present the normal command prompt. |
| `R command` | Execute the specified debugger command before presenting the debugger command prompt. A caveat with this method of passing in a command is that you cannot use spaces in the command. Instead, substitute an underscore. For example, `/R.opt_dllt1_tlloc.dll.` |
| `W name` | Load the named workspace instead of the configured default workspace when loading the debugger. |
| `Y "path"` | Start the debugger, using the specified symbol path. |
| `Z crashfile` | Start the debugger with the specified crash dump file loaded. |

**Save the Workspace!**

The WinDbg debugger provides the ability to save the layout and configuration of a debugging session in a named workspace. Once you have configured a debugger the way that you want it for a given session, that configuration should be saved so that you don't have to configure it again. This is accomplished by selecting the appropriate workspace item from the FILE menu.

Workspaces are useful if you maintain settings for different debugging scenarios (e.g., connected to a live machine but also to debug crash dumps). They are also useful for saving the window layouts for an active debugging session that you want to leave and come back to at a later time. Workspaces in WinDbg can be an invaluable aid to your productivity.

## The .opt Command

Most of the configurations that can be entered and saved from the configuration menus and startup options can also be set from the command line. This is useful if you need to change something quickly. It can also be useful if you are configuring items from within a command file.

To set the option you want, you must enter the *.opt* command on the WinDbg command line in the command window. This is followed by the option that you want to set. For example, the following command sequence sets the symbol path to a new directory:

```
>.opt DllPath "c:\beta3symbols\"
```

Complete lists of the items that can be modified with the *.opt* command are summarized in Table 4-2. The list for a particular version of WinDbg can be found by issuing the command `help .opt` from the command line.

**TABLE 4–2** *Options That Can Be Set with .opt for Kernel Debugging*

| Option | Meaning |
|---|---|
| `AsmRaw [on \| off]` | If this setting is on, it displays raw data when disassembling. |
| `AsmSymbols [on \| off]` | If this setting is on, symbols will be shown when disassembling a block of memory. |
| `AutoReloadSrcFiles [on \| off]` | If this setting is on, source files that have changed will be automatically reloaded by the debugger. |
| `BackgroundSym [on \| off]` | If this setting is on, load the symbols in the background. |
| `BrowseOnSymError [on \| off]` | If this setting is on and IgnoreAll is off, the debugger prompts the user for assistance when any errors are encountered in loading symbols. |
| `CaseSensitive [on \| off]` | Case sensitivity is enabled when this setting is on; otherwise, any commands and symbols are interpreted without regard to character case. |
| `CommandRepeat [on \| off]` | When this setting is on, ENTER repeats the last command. |
| `DllPath ["path"]` | This command specifies the path that is searched for symbols. |
| `IgnoreAll [on \| off]` | When this option is set to on, all symbol files are loaded. This includes any symbol files that contain errors.<br>Conversely, if this setting is off and the `BrowseOnSymError` is set to off also, do not load symbol files that contain errors. Do not prompt the user.<br>If this setting is off and the `BrowseOnSymError` is set to on, any error loading symbols will cause a dialog box to be displayed, allowing the user to specify a |

**TABLE 4-2** *Options That Can Be Set with .opt for Kernel Debugging (Continued)*

| Option | Meaning |
|---|---|
| `IgnoreAll [on \| off]` *(cont.)* | different symbol file or to cancel the symbol load operation for the corrupt symbol file. |
| `KdBaudRate [`*`baud`*`]` | When kernel debugging is enabled, this specifies the kernel debugger baudrate (9600, 14400, 19200, 38400, 56000, 57600, etc.). |
| `KdCacheSize [`*`size`*`]` | With kernel debugging enabled, this option specifies the kernel debugger cache size, in MB. If you do not specify size, the cache status is displayed. If size is 0, the cache is disabled. |
| `KdEnable [on \| off]` | When set to on, then kernel debugging is enabled. |
| `KdGoExit [on \| off]` | If this option is set to on, exiting from a kernel debugging session will cause a *go* command to be automatically sent to the target. |
| `KdInitialBp [on \| off]` | When set to on, the kernel debugger will stop at the initial breakpoint. |
| `KdPlatform [x86 \| alpha]` | Specifies the kernel debugger target system, either X86 or Alpha. |
| `KdPort [`*`port`*`]` | Specifies the kernel debugger communication port (COM1, COM2, etc.). |
| `KdUseModem [on \| off]` | If this setting is on, the kernel debugger serial connection uses modem controls. This is not settable through the Options menu. |
| `MasmEval [on \| off]` | If this setting is on, it turns on the MASM-style (Macro Assembler) expression evaluation. |
| `UnicodeIsDefault [on \| off]` | If this setting is on, it evaluates all UINT pointers as Unicode strings. |
| `Verbose [on \| off]` | If this setting is on, it turns on verbose output mode for information about what the debugger is doing in certain circumstances. |

## Configuring for Kernel Debugging

To perform kernel-mode debugging, the debugger must first be told that it is debugging in kernel mode. This is accomplished with one of three methods. First, the `-k` command line option can be specified when starting the debugger (see Table 4-1). This is the more cumbersome method, but it works.

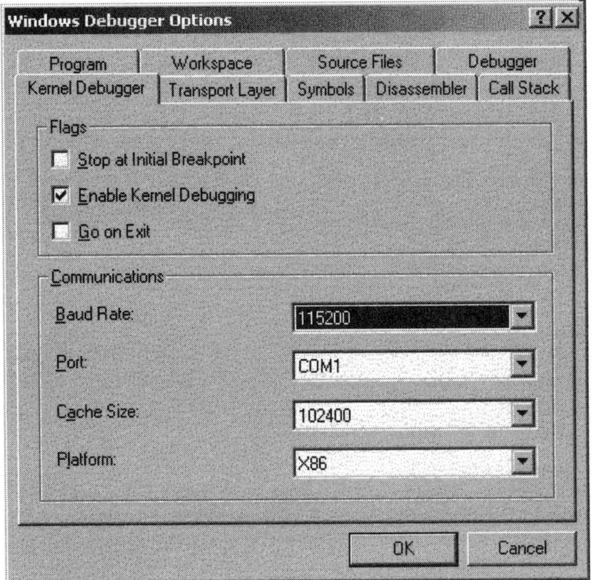


FIGURE 4–1 *Configuring for Kernel Debugging*

Not much better is manually setting the options with the *.opt* command in the command window. The relevant options in this command are the *KdInitialBp, KdEnable, KdGoExit, KdBaudRate*, and *KdPort* commands. Refer to Table 4-2 for their arguments. This method is most useful when configuring WinDbg from a command file.

The best and easiest method of configuring WinDbg for kernel debugging is to start WinDbg and use the setup screens. To configure the parameters for kernel debugging, select the ***Options*** choice on the ***View*** menu list in WinDbg. Select the ***Kernel Debugger*** tab. This is illustrated in Figure 4-1.

Looking at the options under the kernel debugging tab, some of these might seem obvious. To enable kernel debugging, you must check the kernel debugging box. Be sure to set the communication port for the port that you connected the debugging cable to, and set the speed for the connection to match the speed that you configured the target to use. Also set the platform type to match the architecture of the target machine. These four options provide the absolute minimum configuration that you need to perform to enable kernel debugging with WinDbg.

The other options might not be so obvious. The *"go on exit"* choice causes WinDbg to send a *go* command to the target whenever the debugger is normally terminated (e.g., the *go* command will not be sent when the debugger hangs and is terminated from the NT Task Manager). This is useful to prevent the target system from remaining in a suspended state, thinking that it is still being debugged when, in fact, the debug session is terminated. It is good to leave this option enabled.

The "*stop at initial breakpoint*" option causes the target to be stopped at a breakpoint early in the boot process. This is relevant when you are debugging problems that occur during the initialization phase or want to set breakpoints before the system gets too far into the boot process. This has its usefulness, but if you are doing many reboots without restarting the debugger, it can rapidly become annoying to have enabled.

Rather than read information from the target computer every time you need it, WinDbg will cache the information. This can be a big performance gain. The cache size option defines the size of this cache. Be aware that normal debugging operations, such as single stepping or setting the *go* command, will invalidate the information within this cache. The default cache size is 100 Kbytes. This is usually sufficient, but you might want to tweak the value to see whether you can increase performance when debugging over very slow serial links.

Once the kernel debugging parameters have been satisfactorily configured, you should test out the configuration from the WinDbg command window by connecting to a target (enter the *g* command, immediately followed by a *.break* command). You should see output indicating a successful connection, as follows:

```
>g
Thread Create: Process=0, Thread=0
Kernel debugger waiting to connect on com2 @ 115200 baud
Kernel Debugger connection established on com2 @ 115200 baud
Kernel Version 2000 Free loaded @ 0x80400000
Module Load: NT (symbol loading deferred)
>
```

Save the kernel debugging configuration by saving the workspace. The next time the debugger is started with this workspace active, the settings you have chosen will be active. If you debug multiple machines with different settings, you can save different workspaces containing the kernel debugging configuration for each.

## Setting the Symbol Path

Debugging is difficult without the symbol files that match the components on the target machine available to the debugger. At a minimum, you should have a directory set up that contains the symbol files for the kernel (*ntoskrnl.exe*) and the device driver you are debugging. If you are diagnosing system problems or crashes, you should have a complete set of symbol files loaded.

For the debugger to use these symbol files effectively, it must be told where they live. The files can be split among multiple directory trees (a driver in development might have its symbol files in the build tree, not the standard symbol path) or can all be in the same directory tree. The choice is yours.

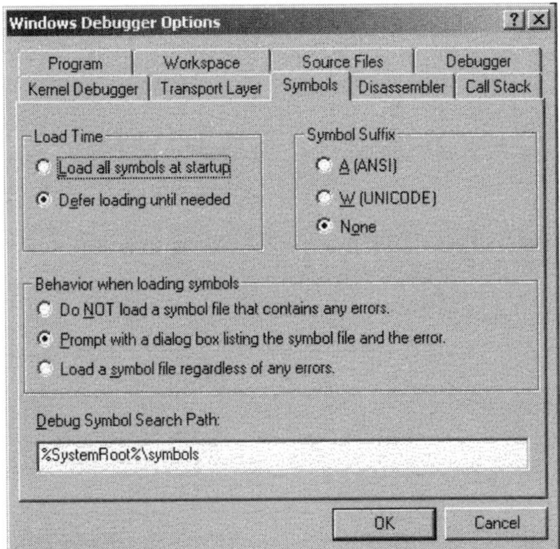


**FIGURE 4–2** *Symbol Path Configuration Window*

There are three mechanisms for telling WinDbg where the symbol files live: a command-line argument, an *.opt* command, or the graphical user interface. Once configured to use a given symbol tree, the configuration should be saved into the workspace. If you do not do this, you will be reentering the information the next time that you use the kernel debugger.

To configure the symbol path using the user interface, you must select the ***Options*** item from the ***View*** menu. Select the Symbols tab. You will see a data entry screen that looks like the one shown in Figure 4-2. There are numerous options on this screen.

At the bottom of this entry dialog is a box that is labeled ***Debug Symbol Search Path***. It is here that you will enter a list of paths in which to search for the appropriate symbol files. If there is more than one path, separate them with semicolons.

# Configuring KD

Unlike WinDbg, KD must be configured before being executed. This is done with either command line arguments or through environment variables. Because of this limitation, it is best to start KD from within a batch file. This minimizes the errors that can occur when starting a program with many startup options.

The KD debugger is not really named *KD*. It is instead named for the platform on which it is being executed. For example, on an Intel architecture platform, the debugger's name is *i386kd*. On an Alpha architecture platform, it is called *alphakd* (note that the Alpha platform is discontinued on Windows 2000).

## Startup Environment Variables

Unlike WinDbg, where the configuration can be set after the debugger has been started, KD relies on the use of environment variables and command-line arguments to control its configuration. These environment variables are summarized in Table 4-3. Some of the environment variables can be overridden with command-line options. The KD command-line options are summarized in Appendix A of this book.

An example of a batch file that can be used to start KD enabled for kernel debugging is illustrated below:

```
@echo off
Set _NT_DEBUG_PORT=COM2
Set _NT_DEBUG_BAUD_RATE=115200
Set _NT_SYMBOL_PATH=C:\Beta3Syms\
Set KDQUIET=1
I386kd
```

In this batch file, you can see that `i386kd` is being started using COM2 as the link to the target machine. That link is running with a baudrate of 115200 bps. The symbol tree lives in *C:\Beta3Syms*, and the debugger will start with `KDQUIET` set so that the annoying messages about Ctrl-C being set are not triggered. It really is that easy.

## Navigation Keys

Once in the KD kernel debugger, you may be left with no prompt. This will be the case if you connect to a running system. KD is controlled with Ctrl keys. Ctrl keys are activated by depressing the Ctrl key on your keyboard simultaneously with the appropriate key to match the function that you wish to activate. For example, to activate the Ctrl-R function, you would depress the R key on the keyboard while holding down the Ctrl key. This might seem basic, but with the proliferation of Windows applications, it is surprising how few people actually use control sequences anymore.

TABLE 4–3 *KD Environment Variables*

| Variable | Meaning |
|---|---|
| `_NT_DEBUG_PORT=<COMX>` | Sets the communication port used by the KD debugger to that specified, e.g., `_NT_DEBUG_PORT=COM2`. The default is COM1. |
| `_NT_BAUD_RATE=`*<baudrate>* | Forces the baudrate of the connection to the target machine to be the rate specified. The default is 9600 bps. |
| `_NT_SYMBOL_PATH=`*<drive:path>* | Tells the debugger to use the symbols found in the specified path. |
| `_NT_ALT_SYMBOL_PATH=`*<drive:path>* | Provides an alternate path for looking for symbols. This is useful if you keep your device driver symbol files in a location apart from the system symbol files. |
| `_NT_DEBUG_EXTENSIONS=`*<dll list>* | Provides a list of kernel debugging extension dynamic linked libraries (DLLs) to load when starting the debugger. The default is *kdextx86.dll* (or *kdextalpha.dll* on Alpha platforms). Multiple DLLs are specified by separating each item in the list with semicolons. |
| `_NT_DEBUG_LOG_FILE_OPEN=`*<file>* | Causes the specified file to be created, with all debugging information logged to that file. |
| `_NT_DEBUG_LOG_FILE_APPEND=`*<file>* | Appends log information to an already existing log file. If the file doesn't exist, it is opened. |
| `_NT_DEBUG_CACHE_SIZE=`<br>*<size_in_bytes>* | Sets the size of the cache used to hold information from the target machine, minimizing the number of times the target must be asked for that information. |
| `KDQUIET` | When interrupting KD with a Ctrl-C sequence, a message box is displayed that an error did not occur but that the user requested a break. This option, if set, disables this message box. It is recommended that you disable this message box. |

Entering a Ctrl-C while running KD will cause the debugger to be activated on the target computer. This will freeze the target computer and give control of that system to the KD session. This is what you would need to do to initially break into a running system. A summary of the remaining control sequences is provided in Table 4-4.

**TABLE 4–4** *KD Ctrl Keys*

| Control Sequence | Meaning |
|---|---|
| Ctrl-C | Tells the debugger to break into the target machine. |
| Ctrl-B Enter | Exits the debugger. |
| Ctrl-R Enter | Forces a resynchronization of communication between the host and target machines. |
| Ctrl-K Enter | Toggles the use of the initial breakpoint. |
| Ctrl-V Enter | Forces the debugger into verbose mode, where additional information about the operation of the debugger is displayed. This is not very useful information for an ordinary debugging session. |
| Ctrl-D Enter | Provides additional debugging information regarding the operation of the debugger. This is not very useful, except to those debugging the debugger. |

# A Tour of the WinDbg Windows

The current version of WinDbg is, above all else, a graphical debugger designed for the Windows environment. It has the look and feel, and shares the basic operation, of most Windows programs. Hot keys operate as you would expect in any other Windows program. You can drag-and-drop, cut-and-paste, or perform any other operation that you would in the Windows world. This might seem as though the obvious is being stated, but previous releases of WinDbg broke many of the rules of well-behaving Windows programs—it was a very nonstandard piece of software.

Figure 4-3 illustrates a typical layout of an active debugging session with WinDbg. You will notice that most of the information that is available can be opened in its own window. There is a toolbar along the top that will open these windows or provide debugging functions, such as stepping through code. Holding the mouse above each of the toolbar items will cause the function of that button to be displayed.

This section will provide a brief tour of the functionality provided by each of the various windows. It will not delve deeply into the underlying functionality, but rather will provide you a basis for finding your way around the tool when you are ready to apply the techniques spelled out in the rest of this book.

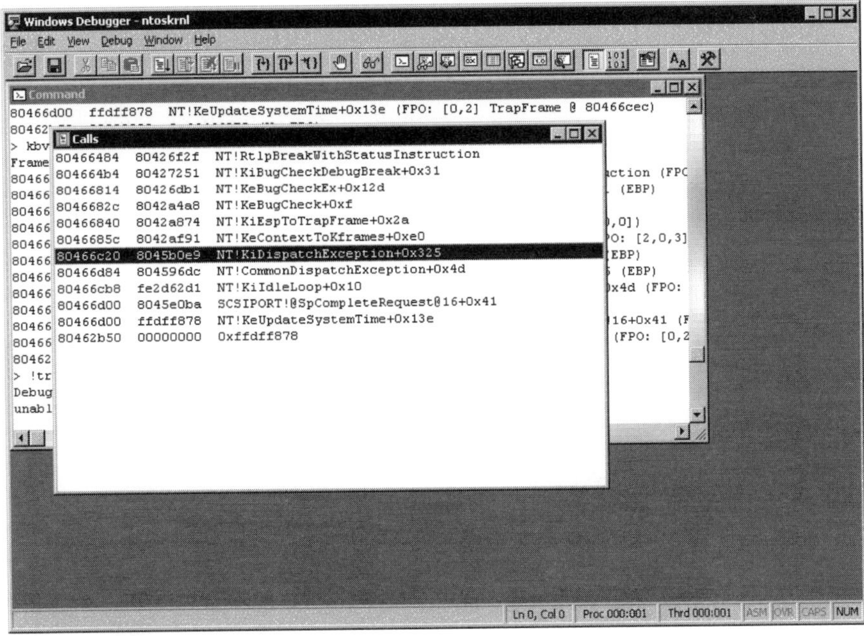

FIGURE 4–3 *Typical WinDbg Workspace*

## Understanding the Windows

Each of the windows within WinDbg can be triggered either from the toolbar or from the debugger's ***View*** menu item. This is also the menu item that will allow you to configure the font and colors used by the various windows. Finally, the ***Debugger Options*** window is available from this menu; the option window is discussed throughout the book where configuration is discussed and will not be covered in this section.

When saving a workspace, the window positioning, font, and color scheme currently being employed will be saved. The next time that the workspace is opened, this configuration information will be in effect.

### COMMAND WINDOW

The command window is always present when you first start WinDbg (unless you've configured a workspace without it!). It provides the textual interface to the debugger. If messages are printed from a driver or kernel component on the target machine, the output of that message will arrive on the command window. All of the commands that will be discussed throughout this book will be entered in the command window. It is analogous to the prompt on the KD tool.

### WATCH WINDOW

When watching a variable, you are displaying its value at every program interruption. For example, if you are watching a variable named `index` and you are single-stepping through the execution of some piece of code, then after every single-step, the value of the variable `index` will be displayed.

The most convenient way to do this is to enter the variable name or address in the left pane of the watch window. The data value associated with the variable will be displayed in the right pane after the next execution stop. The target must be stopped before the requested watch can take effect.

### MEMORY WINDOW

The memory window is used to display some range of data values on the target system. These values are not updated after every stoppage of the target system in the way that watch variables are. When opening this window, you will be prompted for an address expression. This expression can be the name of any valid symbol, or you can type in an address. You will also be prompted for the display type. Display modifiers, such as those used in the watch window and the command line, are unnecessary with the memory window.

### CALL STACK WINDOW

The call stack window will display the call stack at the time of the last system stoppage. It will be updated when a breakpoint is hit, a single-step occurs, or a bug check is encountered. If the target system is stopped, the call stack window will be updated.

Double-clicking on a line in the call stack window will bring up a disassembly window. This disassembly window will contain the disassembled code for the location specified by the stack entry. If source code is available for the module, a source window will also open. This source window will highlight the line of code that is represented in the stack. Used in this manner, the call stack window can be a very powerful tool.

You can configure the behavior of the call stack window by selecting the Options item on the View menu. The Call Stack tab has a number of options about the amount and type of information that you can see when using this window.

### LOCALS WINDOW

The locals window shows the variables that are local in scope to the function that is currently being stepped through or the function that was current at the time of the failure. This window is updated whenever a variable's value is changed and control is returned to the debugger. Obviously, the content of the locals window will change if the debugger is stopped in the context of a different function—in that case, the window will display the variables local to the new current function.

The display type for each of the variables can be overridden by adding the appropriate format modifier to the value.

You should also note that structures are, by default, not expanded (you will see only the structure name, not its values). If you want to examine the individual elements within a structure, you must click on the plus symbol in the far left column. It will change to a minus symbol, and the elements of the structure will be spelled out.

### REGISTER WINDOW

The register window will display the contents of the system registers for the current processor context. By highlighting a value in the right pane, you can modify the contents of the register. This is updated each time the target machine is stopped, and control is transferred back to the debugger.

To change the current processor context on a multiprocessor computer, you can use the ~ command from within the command window. This command sets the debugger's processor context to that specified by the user. This is talked about later in this chapter, when context is discussed.

### FLOATING-POINT WINDOW

The floating-point window will display the contents of the floating-point registers for the current processor context. By highlighting a value in the right pane, you can modify the contents of the register. This is updated each time the target machine is stopped, and control transferred back to the debugger.

### DISASSEMBLY WINDOW

The disassembly window shows a range of memory addresses, disassembled and turned into assembly language code. If symbols are available, any addresses that can be resolved into symbols are resolved. This window is started in the following three manners:

- The user requests that it open up, using the View menu. In this case, the code at the program counter address is disassembled and displayed.
- A stack location is clicked on, causing the window to open to the location specified in the stack entry.
- The target stops and transfers control back to the debugger (such as in the case of hitting a breakpoint). The disassembly window is generated and code at the current program counter address is displayed. This behavior can be disabled by the user.

There are options governing the behavior of the disassembly window that can be found on the ***Disassembler*** tab of the ***Options*** dialog box (found on the ***View*** menu). These can be used to configure the amount and type of information that can be shown when the code is disassembled.

#### SOURCE WINDOW

The source window is a little different from the rest of the windows that have been talked about previously, in that it isn't brought up from the options under the View menu. To open a source file for editing, reference, or setting breakpoints, you select the File→Open combination. Opening a source file in this manner will cause the source window to open.

The source window will also open as a result of a breakpoint or a double-click on a stack location in the stack window. If the target system is stopped at a location that the debugger knows how to resolve back to a source file, the source window will open with the currently executing line highlighted. The same will occur if you double-click on a stack frame entry in the call stack window.

There are a couple of options that control the behavior of the source window. Like most options, these are configured through the View→Options menu sequence. These options control the paths that are searched for source files and some general formatting options for viewing source code in the source window.

## Using the WinDbg Command Window and KD Prompt

Commands are entered and status is displayed in the WinDbg command window. This is also true of the KD command prompt. In KD, this is the only option for executing commands and displaying status. WinDbg, as has been pointed out, has numerous windows for displaying data. Even so, most of the action in WinDbg occurs in the command window.

### Command Types

There are three broad groupings of commands in WinDbg:

- Built-in commands that control the basic operation of the debugger with regard to the target.
- Dot commands (so named because they are preceded with a period) that control the configuration and local operation of the debugger.
- Debugger Extension commands that execute functions present in external, dynamically loaded libraries (extension DLLs). There is also a number of extension commands that are internal to the debugger and control the operation and configuration of the loaded DLLs.

There are many commands shared by WinDbg and KD. For instance, the same debugger extension DLLs are used in both. Where differences exist, these will be pointed out.

## Built-In Commands

This section lists a logical view of the built-in commands for controlling the debugger from the WinDbg and KD command lines. Details on using these can be found in Appendix A of this book.

### CONTROLLING TARGET STATE

| Command | Meaning |
|---|---|
| *G* | This is the first command you will enter once in the debugger. It tells the target system to "go." |
| *Bx* | This is the series of commands that control breakpoints. This is easier from the window interface than from the command line, but it is certainly doable. |
| *FP* | This displays or modifies floating point registers on the target machine (WinDbg only). |
| *P* | This causes a stopped target system to execute a single program step. |
| *R* | This modifies or displays the contents of the registers on the target system. |
| *Q* | This causes the debugger to quit execution. |

### DETERMINING CURRENT TARGET STATE

| Command | Meaning |
|---|---|
| *F* | This locates a symbol in memory. |
| *Kx* | This is the series of commands that display the target's stack frame. |
| *LN* | This finds symbols near a given address. It is useful for finding a module or function that is related to a suspect address. |

#### MANIPULATING TARGET MEMORY

| Command | Meaning |
|---|---|
| *A* | This will assemble directly into memory (KD only). |
| *Cx* | This is the series of commands that compare two ranges of memory locations. |
| *Dx* | These are commands that cause target memory to be displayed on the debugger. |
| *Ex* | This enters data into a contiguous memory range. |
| *F* | This fills a range of memory on the target machine with a known value. |
| *Nx* | This moves memory between one range of memory and another on the target machine. |
| *Sx* | This searches the target's memory for a given pattern. |
| *Ux* | This disassembles a range of memory. |

## Dot Commands

The Dot commands are so named because they are prefixed with a period. These commands, by and large, control the debugger's configuration and local operation. These are useful when scripting a debugger operation with debugger command files. These are also useful when performing quick configuration from the command line (the *.opt* command has already been extensively discussed).

It is important to note that the Dot commands are not valid in KD. These are implemented only as part of the WinDbg debugger. Detail of the operation of each of these commands is found in Appendix A of this book and in the Microsoft DDK help file.

#### LOG FILE COMMANDS

| Command | Meaning |
|---|---|
| *.logopen* | Start logging all commands and command-line output to a log file. |
| *.logappend* | Log all commands and output to a log file, appending to the end of an existing log file. |
| *.logclose* | Close the log file. |

### COMMAND FILE COMMANDS

| Command | Meaning |
|---|---|
| *.source* | Causes a text file containing a list of debugger commands to be opened and executed. |
| *.open* | The same as the *.source* command. |

### DEBUGGING COMMANDS

| Command | Meaning |
|---|---|
| *.reboot* | Causes the target machine to reboot. |
| *.break* | Forces the target machine to stop execution and transfer control to the KDB module. |
| *.resync* | Causes the communication between the source and target to be resynchronized. |
| *.reload* | Reloads the current symbol information. |

### CONFIGURATION COMMANDS

| Command | Meaning |
|---|---|
| *.opt* | Sets a multitude of options. Detailed elsewhere in this chapter. |
| *.title* | Causes the title on the WinDbg debugger window to be set to a title specified by the user. |

## Debugger Extensions

The kernel debuggers have the ability to be extended with external DLLs that are loaded as needed. These DLLs are known as *debugger extensions.* Users can write their own application-specific debugger extensions (an activity covered in Chapter 9). Microsoft provides a set of default kernel debugging extensions used to examine data within a target's kernel address space in a formatted and friendly matter.

### Kernel Debugging Extensions

Microsoft provides kernel-debugging extensions as a part of each operating system release. It does this because each debugger extension must match the build number and type (i.e., checked or free) of the target. If they don't match, the information returned by the various commands is suspect. The debugger attempts to match the version of the target operating system automatically with the available debugger extensions. The extension DLLs are named for the platform being debugged—*kdextx86.dll* for Intel-based platforms and *kdextalpha.dll* for Alpha-based platforms.

There is no way to determine from the name of the DLL which version it supports. The only way to do this is to load the DLL into the debugger and check the version. There are numerous built-in commands provided to work with debugger extensions. These are described in Chapter 9 of this book.

### Custom Debugger Extensions

The debugger provides the facilities to load custom debugging extensions. These are loadable libraries that you can develop to facilitate debugging your custom device driver. Chapter 9 of this book completely describes building your own debugger extensions to work with WinDbg and KD.

## Summary

This chapter provided an in-depth overview of the WinDbg and KD debugging tools and options. It provided the reader with an understanding of the differences between WinDbg and KD. It also provided extensive detail on the various options that can be used to configure the tools. You should walk away from this chapter with an understanding of how the debugging tools are used and configured.

FIVE

# Kernel Debugging

## CHAPTER OBJECTIVES

- Approaching Debugging
- Controlling the Target
- Working with Symbols
- Basic Kernel Debugging Procedures

*Up to this point, the book has focused on the tools and concepts required to debug in a Windows NT environment. Now it's time to actually be performing some debugging tasks.*

*The challenge in explaining how to debug is that there are a number of different scenarios that may require different approaches. The underlying technology and procedures may be similar, but the order and depth of the procedures will vary, based on what you are trying to achieve. For example, a device driver writer will be primarily focused on source-level debugging and understanding where code that he or she is familiar with has failed. A support technician, in contrast, will simply want to identify a failing component.*

*The approach taken in this chapter is to explain the most common debugging procedures. These procedures are then used as building blocks when explaining how to approach the more common debugging scenarios best. This is extended into the next chapter, where the concepts are expanded into understanding how to look inside the Windows NT kernel to understand some of the more complex relationships.*

*It's important to note that everything within this chapter is applicable to both live system debugging and crash dump analysis. The examples shown will be generated against a live system. Crash dump analysis is more thoroughly covered in Chapter 7.*

## Approaching Debugging

Anyone using debugging tools is doing so in order to understand the behavior of a system. The system may be failed outright, it may be hung, or the user may just be interested in understanding how the underlying system works. The most common use of a debugger is in diagnosing failures, and that will be the immediate focus.

There are a number of failure types on Windows NT that will cause you to use the debugger. The most common is to understand a system that has stopped with a bug check. This is also the type of debugging that is typically done when debugging a crash dump.

There are some common steps that must be followed whenever debugging a failure on Windows NT:

- Use the bug check information to understand the type of failure.
- Isolate the offending code by examining the stack and trap frame.
- Ensure that the proper drivers are loaded.
- Record as much state as might be relevant, e.g., the active IRP, current thread and process, etc.
- Repeat the information-gathering steps on each processor in a multiprocessor system.

Often, when probing with the debugger, there is other information that you will want to search out. You will want to dig deeper to truly understand the underlying behavior. This list provides some of the most essential steps when gathering information on a stopped system. If you find yourself debugging crashed systems on a regular basis, you may want to explore saving common debugging steps as debugger batch files (this was explained in the last chapter).

If you are using the debugger to assist in writing device driver code, you may well follow the steps above. After all, if your driver failed, you will want to know where the failure was. If the driver hasn't failed but you are performing basic debugging, there are other things that you will want to do:

- Examine Memory
- Watch Variable Changes
- Look at Register Values
- Step through Code

All of these things are described later in this chapter.

## Controlling the Target

When performing live debugging between a debugger and a target system, there are a number of commands that will need to be executed to control the debugging session. At various times, you will want to interrupt the execution of the running target to examine state. If that fails, you want to have the target stop itself, using a special key sequence. These are examples of some of the target control commands that are provided by the debugger.

The most basic commands issued in a debugging session are those that control the debugger's communication with the target machine. These, by their very nature, are procedures that are applicable only in live debugging scenarios; they are not needed for examining crash dumps.

### Telling the Debugger to GO

Before the debugger can begin talking to the target machine, it must be told that everything is set up and ready for debugging. This concept is called *go*. It isn't until the *go* command is issued to the debugger that debugging can begin. After a breakpoint has been hit, the *go* command must again be issued to release the target and allow debugging to continue.

There are four methods to tell WinDbg to go and begin debugging. The first is by typing "go" in the command window (you may also just type "g"). The second is to use the function key F5. There is a toolbar icon for *go* (see Chapter 4 for a description of the WinDbg toolbar). Finally, the first option under the DEBUG menu is GO. These are all equally effective.

If the target system is not correctly configured, you will see a message that says no debuggee is specified. This message means that the debugging information that was entered in the options menu is incorrect. Go back and verify that the debugger is configured for kernel debugging. If the debugger is correctly configured, a message will display that says the debugger is waiting for data on the configured serial port.

In contrast to WinDbg, KD does not require the initial *go* command. When active, KD is always searching for debugging packets. KD needs a command to go only after the target has been stopped, such as after hitting a breakpoint. The command to tell KD to go after the target is halted is simply *g*.

## Breaking into the Target

When running, the debugger is always listening for debugging traffic from the target machine. The target machine is configured for kernel debugging. The only item that remains before useful work can be done is to stop the target and turn control over to the debugger module in the target's kernel. If the target computer is not stopped, no debugging can occur. There are a number of ways to achieve this. These are detailed as follows.

### STOPPING FROM THE DEBUGGER

Much like telling the debugging to go, there are a number of mechanisms for halting the target machine in WinDbg. The first is by typing ".break" in the command window. There is also a toolbar icon for Break (see Chapter 4 for a discussion of the toolbar). Pressing the Ctrl and Break keys simultaneously will also stop the debugger. Finally, you can choose the Break option on the DEBUG menu.

The options are more limited in the KD environment. Using KD, you simply press the Ctrl and C keys simultaneously to break into the target machine. If you see the KD prompt, the target is stopped.

### THE ATTENTION KEY SEQUENCE

Suppose that the target is not responding to the debugger's request to stop (this occasionally happens), how do you force the target to break? The answer is the attention key sequence. By pressing the Ctrl and Break keys together on the target machine, you force the kernel on the target machine to pass control to its kernel-debugging module. This should get the attention of the debugger so that you can proceed with your debugging session.

### THE DUMP SWITCH

There are rare circumstances when the machine is completely locked up. The debugger cannot make it stop, nor can the attention key sequence. Or maybe the machine is hung at a remote location and you want to force a dump for later analysis. In these cases, you can utilize a dump switch card.

The dump switch card works by forcing a hardware fault, which, in turn, triggers a nonmaskable interrupt (NMI). The operating system cannot ignore an NMI, nor can it continue to operate. When the NMI is triggered, the NMI handling routine in Windows NT will, in turn, force a bug check to occur. If a debugger is attached, control will go there. If there is no debugger configured and system dumps are enabled, a dump will be taken. Failing that, the system will simply reboot.

More detailed information about dump switch cards, as well as a reference design for building one, can be found at Microsoft's hardware development web site. That site is at *http://www.microsoft.com/hwdev*.

## Verifying the Target's Version

Before the debugger can work correctly, the version of the kernel debugger extension used by the tool must exactly match the operating system version on the target machine. The reason for this is that many of the debugger commands key the information that they display by reading variables and by reading information at known locations from these variables. This kind of information can change from build to build. Microsoft always makes new debugger extensions available when the builds of the operating system change.

Most the commands in the debugger extension will complain if the versions do not match. You can also verify the version by executing the *!version* debugger extension. Don't confuse the debugger extension command for finding the version with the built-in version command, which lists the versions of the debugging tools but not which OS build it matches. Examples of each follow:

```
> !version
Free Extension dll for Build 2096 debugging Free kernel for Build 2096
```

## Handling WinDbg Hangs

The number one fact of using WinDbg to do kernel debugging is that WinDbg will eventually stop responding. It will eventually just lock up on you, and there is nothing that you can do to make it respond again. You will have to go into the task manager and kill the debugger. Some versions and builds of WinDbg are better than others, but every version up to this point will fail eventually.

There are things that you can do to increase the stability of the debugging environment. If you are experiencing continuous hang, the first thing that you should do is lower the baud rate of the debugging connection. There is also a command, *.resync*, which purports to resynchronize communication between the debugger and the target. This command rarely fixes any problems, but it's worth a try.

The other helpful hint is to save your workspace (a process described in Chapter 4) whenever you are in the middle of any sort of complicated debugging. If you do this, you will be able to restore your environment quickly after restarting WinDbg.

## Working with Symbols

The last chapter provided extensive discussion of matching symbols with what is being debugged on the target machine. Essentially, if the symbols don't match, the output from the debugging tools cannot be trusted.

### LOADING AND VERIFYING

The first step in a debugging session, once the target has been stopped, is to have the debugger query the target to decide which symbols it should load. If the debugger was configured correctly, the symbols will load, and debugging can occur with the right information.

The command to load the symbols is the kernel debugging extension command *!reload*. This command queries the target machine for the list of loaded modules. It then goes through each of the configured symbol search paths to see whether it can match the loaded module with a symbol file. When a match is found, that symbol file will be loaded.

There are times when a module will appear to match but won't exactly. In these cases, the debugger will display a message that a given symbol file has a mismatched timestamp or an incorrect checksum. When this occurs, you should manually verify that the symbol file matches what's loaded on the target machine. In some cases, it won't matter because the module isn't one that is in the failure path—in this case, the symbols for that module aren't being used to diagnose a problem or to control the output of the debugger.

The only time that you don't need to execute the *!reload* command is when the debugger is attached and has been told to go prior to the target booting. When the target boots, if it is attached to the debugger, it will automatically send module information as each module is loaded. In this manner, the debugger is automatically updated. The debugger is also automatically updated whenever a module is loaded while it is attached, as in the case of dynamically loaded device drivers.

#### What Happens If Different Modules Have the Same Basename?

If there is more than one loaded driver or kernel module with the same basename (for example, *extmirr.sys* and *extmirr.dll*), the debugger will not be able to locate the symbols for these modules.

Specifying the file with the extension present, such as in *x extmirr.sys!**, will not work. This is because the "." operator is already used by the debuggers in a different context and cannot be ambiguously overloaded.

When building modules with multiple components, you must take care not to use the same basename for the libraries and base executable.

For more information on this topic, please reference Microsoft Knowledge Base article Q170116, "PRB: Can't Find Symbols in Modules When exe's Have Same Basename."

### UNDERSTANDING SYMBOL FORMATS

It's impossible to perform system debugging without working with symbols. They'll show up in stack traces, and you will use them when setting breakpoints. It is important to understand what a symbol looks like and, if it isn't yours, where it came from.

All functions and global variables are separate and distinct symbols. When viewed in the kernel debugger, the symbols are usually prefixed by the name of the module and a separator. For example, the global variable *var1* in the module *testmodule* would be displayed as *testmodule!var1*.

### KERNEL FUNCTION PREFIXES

It is almost impossible to look at a stack trace that doesn't contain some number of entries from the Windows NT kernel. Understanding the control flow through the kernel (as described in the stack trace) can often lead to a better analysis of the underlying problem.

The Windows NT kernel is broken up into a number of separate and distinct components. Even though there are separate components, core kernel functions are always associated with the module *ntoskrnl*. The first two letters of each function name can determine the actual kernel component that the function lives in. For example, the object manager external routines are all prefixed with *Ob*; the function *ObReferenceObjectByHandle* is a function in the object manager. A complete listing of NT kernel prefixes is found in Table 5-1. Most exported functions in each module are described in the Device Driver Kit (DDK).

TABLE 5-1 *Common Kernel Function Prefixes*

| Prefix | Kernel Component |
|---|---|
| Ke, Ki | Core Kernel Functions |
| Mm, Mi | Memory Manager |
| Ob | Object Manager |
| Ps | Process Manager |
| Pnp | Plug-n-Play (PNP) Manager |
| Po | Power Management Functions |
| Se | Security Subsystem Functions |
| Ex | Executive Functions |
| Rtl | Kernel Mode Run Time Library |

# Basic Debugging Procedures

It is important to learn some basic debugging commands and concepts before attempting to diagnose and solve problems with the debugging tools. This section details some of the more common procedures used when debugging kernel mode drivers and failures.

## Verifying Device Drivers

One of the first steps in diagnosing an unknown failure is ensuring that the system is running the correct version of the questionable device drivers. Another tactic for determining where the system stopped is resolving a questionable pointer back to the range of addresses used by a particular device driver. Chapter 3 talked about how to derive this information from the blue screen. A better source of information on which drivers are loaded onto a target machine and which memory ranges that driver owns is found through the kernel debugger.

The kernel debugger command *!drivers* provides basic to detailed information about the drivers that are loaded onto the system. Like many commands in the kernel debugger, the argument passed to the command determines the amount of information that is actually displayed.

The *!drivers* command provides three views of device driver state. The first view, obtained with no arguments to the command, is the most common. It lists the loaded device drivers and their creation times, and it provides enough basic information to verify whether the correct driver is loaded.

An abbreviated example of the *!drivers* command is as follows:

```
> !drivers
Loaded System Driver Summary

Base       Code Size        Data Size       Driver Name        Creation Time
80400000 122600 (1161 kb)  3ffc0 ( 255 kb) ntoskrnl.exe   Fri Mar 12 17:53:05 1999
80001000  121a0 (  72 kb)   3e20 (  15 kb)      hal.dll   Thu Mar 04 23:05:40 1999
f9010000   1960 (   6 kb)   1040 (   4 kb)  BOOTVID.dll   Mon Mar 01 20:27:40 1999
f8c00000   b280 (  44 kb)   1e00 (   7 kb)      pci.sys   Fri Mar 12 17:16:39 1999
f8e80000   67a0 (  25 kb)   13e0 (   4 kb)   isapnp.sys   Mon Mar 01 19:36:43 1999
f91c8000    780 (   1 kb)    4a0 (   1 kb) intelide.sys   Thu Feb 25 01:31:18 1999
f8e88000   4480 (  17 kb)    9e0 (   2 kb)  PCIIDEX.SYS   Thu Feb 25 01:31:18 1999
f8e90000   5d20 (  23 kb)    800 (   2 kb) MountMgr.sys   Sat Feb 13 14:14:58 1999
fe2f7000  19700 ( 101 kb)   2300 (   8 kb)   ftdisk.sys   Tue Mar 02 23:59:57 1999
```

This view gives you a very quick indication of which drivers are loaded into the system and when those drivers were built. The drivers are listed in the order that they were loaded into the system. The code and data size fields indicate the sizes statically allocated when the drivers were linked. Following this is the actual name of the device driver and the date that the device driver code was compiled.

The second view that is available is generated by adding a flag, 2, to the *!drivers* command. This command describes the memory layout of each driver resident in memory. An abbreviated example of this output is:

```
> !drivers 2
Loaded System Driver Summary

Base      Code   Data  Locked  Resident  Standby  Loader Entry  Driver Name
80400000 122600  3ffc0     0      4b0       30    fe52b848      ntoskrnl.exe
80001000  121a0   3e20     0       44        0    fe529f68           hal.dll
f9010000   1960   1040     0        c        0    fe529ee8       BOOTVID.dll
f8c00000   b280   1e00     0       2c        8    fe529e68           pci.sys
f8e80000   67a0   13e0     0        c       10    fe529de8        isapnp.sys
f91c8000    780    4a0     0        4        0    fe529d68      intelide.sys
f8e88000   4480    9e0     0        c        8    fe52afa8       PCIIDEX.SYS
f8e90000   5d20    800     0       10        8    fe52af48      MountMgr.sys
fe2f7000  19700   2300     0       1c       48    fe52aea8        ftdisk.sys
f9100000   1280    520     0        8        0    fe52ae28      Diskperf.sys
```

This view can let you know whether a given device driver is using an excessive amount of memory pages. After displaying the same base address, code, and data sizes as the basic drivers command, it goes on to describe how the driver is using memory pages. The command provides a count of pages that are locked, resident, or marked as standby. Following this is the loader entry point for the file and the actual driver name.

The final view offered by the *!drivers* command breaks down the structure of the loaded driver file. It provides the same basic information as does the *dumpbin* command in the Windows NT. The information is useful primarily to device driver writers who want to ensure that the file loaded on the target system is the same file that is on their debugging machine. The output is abbreviated to provide a representative example of the command:

```
> !drivers 4
Loaded System Driver Summary

Base        Code Size         Data Size        Driver Name         Creation Time
80400000 122600 (1161 kb)  3ffc0 ( 255 kb) ntoskrnl.exe   Fri Mar 12 17:53:05 1999

SECTION HEADER #1
   .text name
   5F973 virtual size
     440 virtual address
   5F980 size of raw data
     440 file pointer to raw data
       0 file pointer to relocation table
       0 file pointer to line numbers
       0 number of relocations
       0 number of line numbers
68000020 flags
         Code
         Not Paged
         (no align specified)
         Execute Read

Debug Directories(1)
    Type        Size      Address  Pointer

    misc         110         7fe0     7fe0Image Name: exe\ntoskrnl.dbg
```

## Looking at the Bugcheck Information

You need to understand what the failure is—reference back into the driver list to see if there's a likely suspect.

## Examining the Stack

What was the system doing when it failed? What was it doing just before it failed? These are the important questions that must be answered when diagnosing a failure condition. The stack is the roadmap that provides this information.

### WHAT IS A STACK?

A stack is nothing more than a basic data structure that is agreed upon by the processor, the operating system, and the compiler. This data structure holds parameters that are passed between called functions. These parameters are stored in a consistent manner within Windows 2000.

The register set within the processor provides registers that assist in the management of the stack. The first of these is the stack pointer. The stack pointer keeps track of the current location on the top of the stack (a stack is said to "grow" in memory). The stack pointer is the ESP register on 32-bit Intel processors.

A stack is typically divided into sections known as *frames*. These frames contain the local variables, passed parameters, and other linking information. The EBP register on 32-bit Intel processors contains a stack-frame pointer. This identifies the specific point within the current stack from for the called procedure. To use the stack frame base pointer, the called function usually copies the contents of the stack pointer (the ESP register) into the frame pointer (again, the EBP register) before putting local variables on the stack. This allows easy access to data passed on the stack, the return instruction pointer, and any local variables used by the called function.

A stack trace is a listing of each function called by detailing the stack frames that live on the call stack. This procedure is known as *unwinding the stack*. This provides a history of where the process, or thread, has been.

Once the debugger knows the boundaries of a frame, using the operating system's calling conventions, it can retrieve the return address saved within that frame and map it to the name of the procedure containing that address.

Registers hold the frame pointer address and stack pointer address for the current frame. Each procedure call pushes the return address onto the stack, and the child procedure then pushes the parent's frame pointer address onto the stack before it alters the frame pointer and stack pointer to build its own frame.

When there is a problem, the problem code is almost always on the stack. If the stack becomes corrupt because of the failure, the path to the failure may still be there.

It's important to note that a stack is specific to a thread and process. When the debugger is invoked, it enters in the context of the process and thread that were running at the time the target stopped. It also enters on the CPU that took the command to stop the debugger. In the event of a stop screen, the failed CPU is the current CPU used to derive this information.

To examine the current stack from the command line, you use variations of the *k* command. The basic command provides output as follows:

```
> k
80466484  80426f2f  NT!RtlpBreakWithStatusInstruction+0x1
804664b4  80427251  NT!KiBugCheckDebugBreak+0x31
80466814  80426db1  NT!KeBugCheckEx+0x12d
8046682c  8042a4a8  NT!KeBugCheck+0xf
80466840  8042a874  NT!KiEspToTrapFrame+0x2a
8046685c  8042af91  NT!KeContextToKframes+0xe0
80466c20  8045b0e9  NT!KiDispatchException+0x325
80466d84  804596dc  NT!CommonDispatchException+0x4d
80466cb8  fe2d62d1  NT!KiIdleLoop+0x10
80466d00  8045e0ba  SCSIPORT!@SpCompleteRequest@16+0x41
80466d00  ffdff878  NT!KeUpdateSystemTime+0x13e
80462b50  00000000  0xffdff878
```

This call stack is in the reverse order that it generated; for example, the first procedure that was called in this chain was at the address `0xffdff878` (obviously, no symbol information was available for this module or, more likely, it lives in user-mode space). It then called `NT!KeUpdateSystemTime`, and so on, until it stopped in `NT!RtlpBreakWithStatusInstruction`.

The first column provides the address of the frame pointer for each entry on the call stack. The second column provides the return address for the call (the address that is jumped to on the RETURN instruction). The final column provides the module and function describing the location of the procedure call. Note that, if there is no symbol data available, an address is used.

An additional level is available by modifying the command with the *b* and *v* options, as follows:

```
> kbv
FramePtr  RetAddr   Param1   Param2   Param3   Function Name
80466484  80426f2f  00000003 804664cc 00000000
NT!RtlpBreakWithStatusInstruction+0x1  (FPO: [1,0,0])
804664b4  80427251  00000003 0006e978 80466c90 NT!KiBugCheckDebugBreak+0x31
(EBP)
80466814  80426db1  00000000 00000000 00000000 NT!KeBugCheckEx+0x12d (EBP)
8046682c  8042a4a8  00000030 00000202 80466894 NT!KeBugCheck+0xf (FPO: [1,0,0])
80466840  8042a874  80466c90 0006e978 80466c3c NT!KiEspToTrapFrame+0x2a (FPO:
[2,0,3])
8046685c  8042af91  80466c00 00000000 80466894 NT!KeContextToKframes+0xe0 (EBP)
80466c20  8045b0e9  80466c3c 00000000 80466c90 NT!KiDispatchException+0x325
(EBP)
```

```
80466d84  804596dc  0000000e 00000000 00000000 NT!CommonDispatchException+0x4d
(FPO: [0,80,0])
80466cb8  fe2d62d1  00000000 00000023 00000023 NT!KiIdleLoop+0x10 (No FPO)
80466d00  8045e0ba  00000001 00000002 000000d1
SCSIPORT!@SpCompleteRequest@16+0x41 (FPO: [2,0,2])
80466d00  ffdff878  00000001 00000002 000000d1 NT!KeUpdateSystemTime+0x13e (FPO:
[0,2] TrapFrame @ 80466cec)
80462b50  00000000  80462b58 80462b58 80462b60 0xffdff878 (No FPO)
```

The *b* modifier to the call tells the debugger to detail the arguments to the call. The arguments are printed in columns three through five. The *v* modifier provides additional information describing FPO and trap frame address information as part of the final column.

## Trap Frames

There is a special case of the stack frame structure. This occurs when a trap occurs and normal processing flow must be interrupted. It's called the *trap frame.*

When a trap occurs (a trap is a system-level exception or unexpected condition), and Windows 2000 is able to intercept it, the operating system creates a trap frame. This records the state of each processor's register set at the time of the failure.

The debugger provides the *!trap* command to examine the state of the trap frame. This is the command called with the address of the trap frame. This means that a little digging must be performed to find out the address of the trap frame.

Recall from the previous discussion, the following stack trace was generated:

```
> kb
<params deleted> NT!RtlpBreakWithStatusInstruction+0x1 (FPO: [1,0,0])
<params deleted> NT!KiBugCheckDebugBreak+0x31 (EBP)
<params deleted> NT!KeBugCheckEx+0x12d (EBP)
<params deleted> NT!KeBugCheck+0xf (FPO: [1,0,0])
<params deleted> NT!KiEspToTrapFrame+0x2a (FPO: [2,0,3])
<params deleted> NT!KeContextToKframes+0xe0 (EBP)
<params deleted> NT!KiDispatchException+0x325 (EBP)
<params deleted> NT!CommonDispatchException+0x4d (FPO: [0,80,0])
<params deleted> NT!KiIdleLoop+0x10 (No FPO)
<params deleted> SCSIPORT!@SpCompleteRequest@16+0x41 (FPO: [2,0,2])
<params deleted> NT!KeUpdateSystemTime+0x13e (FPO: [0,2] TrapFrame @ 80466cec)
```

Note that, in the bottommost entry in the stack, the trap frame is listed out as an argument on the far right side of the listing. This trap frame can now be examined with the *!trap* command:

```
> !trap 80466cec
eax=ffa9cd68 ebx=80466cec ecx=80466c90 edx=0006e978 esi=01509bc8 edi=00000000
eip=f8c1aa93 esp=804664f8 ebp=00000000 iopl=0         nv up di ng zr ac pe cy
vip=0    vif=0
cs=f858  ss=0010  ds=0003  es=7251  fs=93fc  gs=6814              efl=000000f9
ErrCode = 00000000
F8c1aa93  a024f0dfff          mov         al, [ffdff024]
```

The contents of the trap frame include the register set, the error code, and the instruction that was saved as a part of the trap frame. This gets you back from whence you came.

**Dealing with Corrupt Trap Frames**

If the trap frame is corrupt or cannot be found using the techniques described, there is a trick to derive it from other available information.

First, dump the first child's EBP register on the stack, using the *dd* command. Continue to dump until you see two 23s back to back. When you find this line in the dumped data, subtract 0x30 from the address at the beginning of that line and run a *!trap* against the results.

Reference the Microsoft Knowledge Base article Q159672, "How to Find the Trap Frame If It Is Corrupt," for more detailed information on this topic.

### Finding the Stack with Context and Exception Records

Encountering a stop code of KMODE_EXCEPTION_NOT_HANDLED may provide you with a corrupted stack history (or at least one that the *k* commands can't find). There is still a method to derive it through the context and exception records.

First, look at the first parameter to the `NT!PspUnhandledExceptionInSystemThread` call on the stack. Use the *kb* command, which displays the stack parameters, to find this value.

This parameter is a pointer to the structure that contains its own pointer to exception information. Using the *dd* command on that value will dump that information.

The first value in this dumped area is the address of the exception record. The exception record can then be displayed in a formatted way using the debugger command *!exr*. The second parameter in this data is the address of the context record for the exception. It can be displayed with the debugger command *!cxr*.

Note that, after running the *!cxr* command, any subsequent *!kb* command will dump the stack based on the information contained in the context record. This provides the call stack where the unhandled exception occurs. The debugger can continue.

## Examining Memory

There are a number of commands available to examine operating system memory structures. These include looking at virtual memory, the underlying physical memory, and the mapping structures that translate physical to virtual addresses.

## Virtual Memory Usage

The most basic command to understanding memory use in a Windows 2000 system is the *!vm* command. Sample output is provided below.

```
> !vm

*** Virtual Memory Usage ***
   Physical Memory:    16269   (   65076 Kb)
   Page File: \??\C:\pagefile.sys
      Current:     98304Kb Minimum:     98304Kb Maximum:    196608Kb
   Available Pages:     1660   (    6640 Kb)
   Modified Pages:       784   (    3136 Kb)
   NonPagedPool Usage:   797   (    3188 Kb)
   PagedPool 0 Usage:   2748   (   10992 Kb)
   PagedPool 1 Usage:    283   (    1132 Kb)
   PagedPool 2 Usage:    272   (    1088 Kb)
   PagedPool Usage:     3303   (   13212 Kb)
   Shared Commit:        272   (    1088 Kb)
   Special Pool:           0   (       0 Kb)
   Shared Process:      1452   (    5808 Kb)
   Total Private:       8135   (   32540 Kb)
            inetinfo.exe       1295 (     5180 Kb)
            services.exe        826 (     3304 Kb)
            lsass.exe           779 (     3116 Kb)
            winlogon.exe        714 (     2856 Kb)
            explorer.exe        689 (     2756 Kb)
            msdtc.exe           675 (     2700 Kb)
            snmp.exe            582 (     2328 Kb)
            svchost.exe         568 (     2272 Kb)
            SPOOLSV.EXE         550 (     2200 Kb)
            svchost.exe         530 (     2120 Kb)
            csrss.exe           252 (     1008 Kb)
            tlntsvr.exe         236 (      944 Kb)
            llssrv.exe          168 (      672 Kb)
            mstask.exe          135 (      540 Kb)
            dfssvc.exe           90 (      360 Kb)
            smss.exe             40 (      160 Kb)
            System                6 (       24 Kb)
PagedPool Commit:     3303    (   13212 Kb)
Driver Commit:         749    (    2996 Kb)
Committed pages:     14188    (   56752 Kb)
Commit limit:        37682    (  150728 Kb
```

In addition to general virtual memory statistics, such as committed pages, pool usage, etc., it contains driver usage by the various system services. This information can all be used to characterize system memory usage.

## Lookaside Lists

Lookaside lists are mechanisms that allow optimized memory allocations by preallocating a certain amount of memory. This allows the system to provide memory on demand without the overhead of invoking the memory management routines.

When a driver asks the system to use a lookaside list, it provides a tag that identifies the list. This tag facilitates tracking tools. The *!lookaside* command provides insight into the list usage. If you know the address of the list you want to look at (perhaps from the output of a *!process* command), you can provide that. Run with no arguments, detail is provided on all system lookaside lists. See the truncated example that follows:

```
> !lookaside

Lookaside "CcTwilightLookasideList" @ 8046a020  Type =  6f5a0 NonPagedPool
    Current Depth  =     62900   Max Depth   =    48738
    Size           =   7641456   Max Alloc   =    7690000
    AllocateMisses =   7641584   FreeMisses =         4
    TotalAllocates =        39   TotalFrees =         0
    Hit Rate       =       90%   Hit Rate    =       60%

Lookaside "IopSmallIrpLookasideList" @ 8046c8c0 Type =  6f5a9 NonPagedPool
    Current Depth  =      4096   Max Depth   =    48738
    Size           =    640426   Max Alloc   =   724224
    AllocateMisses =   7641584   FreeMisses =         0
    TotalAllocates =       240   TotalFrees =         0
    Hit Rate       =       98%   Hit Rate    =      100%
```

The output of this command includes the module that owns the list, the pool type it was allocated from (paged or nonpaged pool), and statistics about the sizing and usage of the command. This demonstrates the effectiveness of the allocation strategies.

## Processes and Threads

There are a couple of commands available for examining basic process and thread structures. The most basic of these is the *!process* command. When run without any arguments, the currently executing process on the current CPU at the time the debugger was invoked is displayed. The following is an example of the process command:

```
> !process
PROCESS 80462b50  Cid: 0000    Peb: 00000000  ParentCid: 0000
    DirBase: 00030000  ObjectTable: fe528f08  TableSize: 125.
    Image: Idle
    VadRoot 0 Clone 0 Private 0. Modified 0. Locked 0.
    DeviceMap 0
    Process Lock Owned by Thread 0
    Token                             e1000750
    ElapsedTime                       21:23:00.0593
    UserTime                          0:00:00.0000
    KernelTime                        0:13:21.0312
    QuotaPoolUsage[PagedPool]         0
    QuotaPoolUsage[NonPagedPool]      0
    Working Set Sizes (now,min,max)  (4, 50, 450) (16KB, 200KB, 1800KB)
    PeakWorkingSetSize                4
    VirtualSize                       0 Mb
    PeakVirtualSize                   0 Mb
```

```
    PageFaultCount                   1
    MemoryPriority                   BACKGROUND
    BasePriority                     0
    CommitCharge                     0

        THREAD 80462de0  Cid 0.0  Teb: 00000000  Win32Thread: 00000000 RUNNING
```

As you can see, it provides a number of process metrics for the running process. This includes pointers to a number of other structures (such as the process's object table, etc.) that may be useful in examining the underlying system. There is also summary information for the threads owned by the process.

An example of using this information is to look into the structure pointed to by the token field. Looking at the output, you can see that it points to address `0xe1000750` as the token owned by the process. The *!token* command is used to provide formatted output:

```
> !token e1000750
TOKEN e1000750  Flags: 9  Source *SYSTEM*  AuthentId (0, 3e7)
    Type:                    Primary (IN USE)
    Token ID:                3ea
    ParentToken ID:          0
    Modified ID:             (0, 3e9)
    TokenFlags:              0x9
    SidCount:                4
    Sids:                    e10008d0
    RestrictedSidCount:      0
    RestrictedSids:          0
    PrivilegeCount:          21
    Privileges:              e10007d4
```

To drill further down and actually examine the thread owned by the process, you would use the *!thread* command. You can see in the sample process output above that the address of the thread owned by the process is located at virtual address `0x80462de0`. Here's output of the *!thread* command on that address:

```
> !thread 80462de0
THREAD 80462de0  Cid 0.0  Teb: 00000000  Win32Thread: 00000000 RUNNING
IRP List:
unable to get IRP object
Not impersonating
Owning Process 80462b50
WaitTime (seconds)      0
Context Switch Count    20692
UserTime                  0:00:00.0000
KernelTime                0:13:21.0312
Start Address 0x00000000
Stack Init 80467030 Current 80466d80 Base 80467030 Limit 80464030 Call 0
Priority 16 BasePriority 0 PriorityDecrement 0 DecrementCount 0

ChildEBP RetAddr  Args to Child
0006ed08 00000000 00000000 00000000 00000000 +0xffffffff
```

This provides detailed information and statistics on the thread structure. This information includes any IRP information, stack address, and any events that the thread is waiting on.

## Summary

This chapter has covered a lot of ground. It has gone from describing basic failures into some sophisticated debugging extension commands. There is no set method for using the kernel debugger. There are basic methods for deriving the location of a failure, and there are methods for examining system data structures. Using these tools to solve real-world problems requires experience and a lot of trial and error. This chapter provided basic understanding of the more common functions used to examine a failed system. A full listing of commands is provided in Appendix A. I encourage you to experiment with these commands on a system that is okay to force failures on.

S I X

# Debugging the Hardware

**CHAPTER OBJECTIVES**

- Using WinDbg/KD
- I/O Ports
- Memory-Mapped Hardware
- PCI Bus
- HAL Bus Handlers
- MPS Table
- SCSI
- USB
- Interrupt Controllers

*Most, though certainly not all, device drivers actually control devices that live within the computer. This chapter will describe how to delve into and explore the hardware regions of the target computer through the debugger interface. It's possible to read and write hardware ports and to probe the BIOS, the SCSI bus, and the PCI bus. You may also want to take a look at the state of the processors or chipsets within the computer. All of this is possible.*

*This chapter will talk about, in the execution of the provided examples, some of the more common things to look for, such as how to read and interpret PCI status registers. This chapter will not get into device specifics but will focus more on the generalities that affect most driver developers and support persons. The assumption is that, if you are looking at the hardware devices, you should understand what you are looking at. It is beyond the scope of this book to offer instruction on computer engineering. Where applicable, the reader is pointed to the appropriate documentation.*

## Can I Do This with WinDbg/KD?

The kernel debuggers provide a remarkably good environment for accessing a machine's underlying hardware. The kernel debugging extensions provide the ability to read and write a variety of formats to a CPU's I/O ports. Memory-mapped registers are accessed, as are any other system virtual addresses.

The kernel extensions provide a window into some of the underlying device structures. This provides an easy-to-read representation of the underlying data. These extensions were designed with the hardware device driver writer in mind.

Keep in mind that most of what is detailed in this chapter is valid only while attached to a live system. Most of the hardware commands will not work correctly on a crash dump. There are exceptions; examining structures that mirror hardware state (such as `!bushnd`) will work. Anything that directly reads or modifies hardware will not work.

## Accessing I/O Ports

Basic hardware device driver development will mandate that you occasionally read and write from I/O port locations. These are locations that are not mapped into memory but live on the processor's I/O bus. Most chipset functionality, for example, lives in I/O space.

The kernel debuggers do not offer native support for reading and writing to I/O port locations. The functionality is, however, offered up through the kernel extension dynamic linked libraries (DLLs). The reason for this is that the implementation of the I/O functions varies among architectures, and all architecture-specific functionality is relegated to the extension DLLs.

The basic commands for reading and writing to I/O port locations are `!iX` and `!oX`, where *X* is replaced by one of the standard data type modifiers. Table 6-1 illustrates the valid input and output combinations.

**TABLE 6–1** *I/O Port Commands*

| Command | Description |
|---|---|
| `!ib <port>` | Input an 8-bit BYTE from the given I/O port location. |
| `!iw <port>` | Input a 16-bit WORD from the specified I/O port. |
| `!id <port>` | Input a 32-bit DWORD from the I/O port. |
| `!ob <port> <value>` | Write an 8-bit BYTE to the specified port location. |
| `!ow <port> <value>` | Write the specified 16-bit WORD value to the I/O port location. |
| `!od <port> <value>` | Write a 32-bit DWORD to the specified port location. |

Notice that there are no I/O commands for reading and writing to 64-bit registers. The word from Microsoft is that they are on their way as the 64-bit Windows initiative kicks into high gear. Validate this information against the latest builds of the extension DLLs that ship with your media—64-bit support could be there at any time.

## Reading/Writing Memory-Mapped Registers

Memory-mapped registers, such as those that live on devices attached to the PCI bus, do not require explicit support from the kernel debugger. The Windows 2000 operating system sees to it that these addresses are mapped into the normal system virtual address space. As such, you can use the normal mechanisms that you would use to read and write normal memory locations on memory-mapped hardware.

As you use the commands to read and write memory on mapped hardware addresses, be aware that some locations may be read-only at the hardware level—you can write to them, but the write will have no effect. Also, writing to read-only hardware will usually not cause an exception, as would writing to a read-only memory page. This is because the protection is implemented at the device level and not as a function of the NT memory management system.

Another issue to be aware of with memory-mapped hardware is that watch points on memory addresses may not function correctly. Watch points are implemented with the memory management hardware, whereas data on the device may change without going through the mechanisms provided by the operating system. If a device changes its own memory-mapped regions, the watch point will not trigger. It may, on the other hand, trigger if a driver or other process manipulates that memory.

# Working with the PCI Bus

The PCI bus is the current internal bus of choice for system developers. Microsoft and Intel will tell you that ISA and MicroChannel and all of the others are dead. All new cards being developed conform to the PCI specification. This is with good reason. PCI cards provide high-speed bus access with true plug-n-play functionality. They are easy to write software for, and the operating system can support all types of cards with a minimum of effort. The odds are that, if you are writing a hardware-based device driver, it probably has to interact with the PCI devices on the system.

There is a number of commands provided by the kernel debugging extensions to view the configuration of the PCI buses in the target system. There are also the facilities to drill down into the actual device state. This section will demonstrate how this is done.

## Mapping the Bus

Windows 2000 maintains a logical view of the PCI bus structure in the underlying computer. There may be multiple buses or simply one PCI bus. Regardless of the number, the `!pcitree` command will enumerate layout:

```
> !pcitreeBus 0 (FDO Ext fe50e2d8)  0600 71808086 (d=0,  f=0) devext fe50dd28
Bridge/HOST to PCI  0604 71818086 (d=1,  f=0) devext fe50db28 Bridge/PCI to
PCIBus 1 (FDO Ext fe50cb38)No devices have been enumerated on this bus.
  0100 80789004 (d=b, f=0) devext fe50d7c8 Mass Storage Controller/SCSI
  0200 12298086 (d=10, f=0) devext fe50d468 Network Controller/Ethernet
  0300 00b81013 (d=12, f=0) devext fe4f70e8 Display Controller/VGA
  0601 71108086 (d=14, f=0) devext fe4f7d88 Bridge/PCI to ISA
  0101 71118086 (d=14, f=1) devext fe4f7b88 Mass Storage Controller/IDE
  0c03 71128086 (d=14, f=2) devext fe4f7828 Serial Bus Controller/USB
Total PCI Root busses processed = 1
```

This output is full of information useful to both support technicians and device driver developers. Provided above is a complete summary map of what the PCI buses look like on the system being debugged, along with pointers to more detailed information.

Ignoring all of the hexadecimal numbers for a moment, a quick glance shows that there are two PCI buses on this system. Further, there are numerous devices attached to these buses. The devices are enumerated in plain language in the far right column of the output.

For those who want to drill down further, more information is available. The first column of output for each device lists the logical location within the PCI bus namespace that the device is assigned.

The second column provides an unformatted view of the first configuration register for the PCI device. This register contains a vendor code and device type. The vendor code is the low-order word. For example, the first line of device enumeration is:

```
0600 71808086 (d=0,  f=0) devext fe50dd28 Bridge/HOST to PCI
```

In this example, the configuration register contains the value 71808086. The 8086 refers to the vendor (in this case, Intel), and the 7180 denotes the type of device (in this case, a HOST to PCI Bridge Device). A complete listing of vendor identifiers and device types can be found at the PCI SIG web site, *www.pcisig.com*. You can also pick up a soft copy of the specification from this site.

The next column indicates the device and function code for the device. The `d=` describes the device to the PCI bus. The `f=` describes the function of the PCI device.

Following this is a pointer to the device extension. The device extension is maintained by the device driver for the PCI device and contains a wealth of information about the state of the device.

## Drilling into the Device Extension

The device extension is a structure with a standard format that is maintained by the device drivers for hardware devices. A pointer to the device extension for each active piece of PCI hardware can be found with the `!pcitree` command. Given this pointer, it is possible to drill down with the `!devext` command:

```
> !devext fe50d7c8 PCIPDO Extension, Bus 0, Device b, Function 0.
  DevObj = fe50d710, PCI Parent Bus FDO Ext = fe50e2d8.
  Driver State = PciStarted
  Vendor ID 9004 (ADAPTEC)  Device ID 8078
  Subsystem Vendor ID 9004 (ADAPTEC)  Subsystem ID 7880
  Class Base/Sub 01/00  (Mass Storage Controller/SCSI)
  Programming Interface: 00, Revision: 01, IntPin: 01, Line Raw/Adj 0b/2c
  Enables ((cmd & 7) = 7): BMI   Capabilities Pointer = dc
  Driver State = PciStarted
  CurrentState:          System Working,  Device D0
  WakeLevel:             System Unspecified,  Device Unspecified
  Requirements: Alignment  Length    Minimum          Maximum
            Io: 00000100   00000100  0000000000000000 00000000ffffffff
        Memory: 00001000   00001000  0000000000000000 00000000ffffffff
        Memory: 00010000   00010000  0000000000000000 00000000ffffffff
  Current: Start            Length
       Io: 000000000000f800 00000100
   Memory: 00000000fedff000 00001000
```

The first thing you should notice is the format of the `!devext` command itself. Note that the syntax calls for a device type. This is because different device types maintain different fields within their respective device extension structures. In this example, the device type was specified as PCI. The various device extension structures are documented in the Windows 2000 Device Driver Kit (DDK).

The first line indicates that the device extension belongs to Device B on Bus 0. The second line provides a pointer to the Device Driver Object for this device (useful only if you are the device driver developer) and a pointer to the device extension of the actual PCI bus on which this device resides. Following this information, the output describes the state and configuration of the device.

A nice feature of this command is that it resolves the PCI Vendor and Device ID to readable names for the most common vendors and devices, respectively. You can very quickly look at this entry and know that it is the device extension for an Adaptec 7880 SCSI controller. The fourth line of output indicates that the device has been started on the PCI bus.

There is a description of the power management features on the device (in this case, "unspecified"). Following this, the next section details the alignment restrictions in place for the device. The final lines indicate the resources reserved on the bus for this device. In this example, a range of I/O port locations and memory locations has been reserved.

## Examining the Devices

The final mechanism for examining the PCI bus is the `!pci` command. This command enumerates each device on each PCI bus, providing a summary detail of each device. The output from this command is illustrated as follows:

```
> !pciPCI Bus 000:0  8086:7180.03  Cmd[0106:.mb..s]  Sts[2290:c....]
Device  Host bridge
01:0  8086:7181.03  Cmd[0007:imb...]  Sts[02a0:.6...]  PciBridge 0->1-1
PCI-PCI bridge
0b:0  9004:8078.01  Cmd[0017:imb...]  Sts[0290:c....]  Device
SubID:9004:7880  SCSI controller
10:0  8086:1229.02  Cmd[0007:imb...]  Sts[0280:.....]  Device  Ethernet
11
12:0  1013:00b8.00  Cmd[0003:im....]  Sts[0200:.....]  Device  VGA
compatible controller
13
14:0  8086:7110.01  Cmd[000f:imb...]  Sts[0280:.....]  Device  ISA bridge
14:1  8086:7111.01  Cmd[0005:i.b...]  Sts[0280:.....]  Device  IDE
controller
14:2  8086:7112.01  Cmd[0004:..b...]  Sts[0280:.....]  Device  USB host
controller
14:3  8086:7113.01  Cmd[0001:i.....]  Sts[0280:.....]  Device  Class:6:80:0
```

The columns list data as read from the PCI bus for each device. The first column contains the PCI device number. The second column provides a formatted view of the configuration register. This lists the vendor ID, followed by the device ID (note that this is the reverse of how the `!pcitree` command displays things).

The next two columns provide a representation of the command and status registers, respectively. For detail on the bit definitions and their interpretation, the reader is referred to the PCI Specification. The PCI Specification can be found at *www.pciorg.com*. The final column provides the class of the PCI device.

# Looking at HAL Bus Handler Information

The hardware abstraction layer (HAL) maintains an internal bus handler for abstracting the underlying system buses to the operating system. Beginning with Windows 2000, the debugger extensions offer up a view into these data structures, as queried from the HAL.

The command to view bus handler information is `!bushnd`. This command is provided in two flavors. Alone, `!bushnd` will provide a summary of the installed bus handlers:

```
> !bushnd
FE5280D4  bus 0, type InternalFE503F94  bus 0, type InterfaceTypeUndefined
FE503EF4  bus 1, type InterfaceTypeUndefined
FE503E54  bus 0, type Eisa
FE503CF4  bus 0, type Isa
FE4FDB74  bus 0, type PCI
FE4FD9B4  bus 1, type PCI
```

This output shows that there are multiple bus handlers installed. The first column specifies the address of the bus handler. The last column describes the type.

Taking the address of the bus handler for a given bus as an argument to the `!bushnd` command will yield output specific to the instance of the installed bus. In the following example, output from two different bus types is shown:

```
> !bushnd fe5280d4
Dump of bus handler FE5280D4
  Version                 0
  Interface Type (0) = Internal
  Bus Number              0
  Parent Bus Handler      00000000
  GetBusData              80008C9E      (_HalpNoBusData@24)
  SetBusData              80008C9E      (_HalpNoBusData@24)
  AdjustResourceList      80008CA4      (_HalpNoAdjustResourceList@12)
  AssignSlotResources     80010A0C      (_HalpNoAssignSlotResources@32)
  GetInterruptVector      8000C49E      (_HalpGetSystemInterruptVector@24)
  TranslateBusAddress     80007D74      (_HalpTranslateSystemBusAddress@24)
  IO......: 0:00000000 - 0:0000ffff (tran 0:00000000 space 1 (r@FE503010))
  Memory..: 0:00000000 - 0:ffffffff (tran 0:00000000 space 0 (r@FE503038))
  DMA.....: 0:00000000 - 0:00000007 (tran 0:00000000 space 0 (r@FE503088))

> !bushnd fe4fd9b4
Dump of bus handler FE4FD9B4
  Version                 0
  Interface Type (5) = PCI
  Bus Number              1
  Parent Bus Handler      FE4FDB74
  BusData                 FE4FDA20
  GetBusData              800060E0      (_HalpGetPCIData@24)
  SetBusData              800061AE      (_HalpSetPCIData@24)
  AdjustResourceList      8000E8E0      (_HalpAdjustPCIResourceList@12)
  AssignSlotResources     8000E06E      (_HalpAssignPCISlotResources@32)
  GetInterruptVector      80010472      (_HalpGetPCIBridgedInterruptVector@24)
  TranslateBusAddress     80007D74      (_HalpTranslateSystemBusAddress@24)
```

You can see from the output that the interface type and bus number are provided. These bus structures are kept in a tree, and the parent of the device is pointed to by the field labeled `Parent Bus Handler`. There is no parent bus handler in the first example, whereas the second example has a parent bus handler at 0xFE4FDB74 (which, referring back to the summary listing, is the first PCI bus).

Following the bus information is detail of the mapping between the bus functions and the underlying HAL routines implementing them. Also provided is the address of each of these functions.

Finally, if there is resource information (as in the first of the two examples), that is printed out. Resource information is usually not available on PCI bus types, unless they are directly bridged to an ISA or other legacy bus type.

# The MPS Table

On a multiprocessing computer that's based on Intel processors, the operating system and BIOS must understand and agree on the logical layout of the hardware. The routing between the various interrupts and the CPUs must be defined. The addresses and resources consumed by the system buses must be understood. All of this information is defined in the MPS table.

MPS stands for *Multiprocessing Specification*. This is a specification put forth by Intel and Microsoft, among others, that defines the layout and content of this information. The latest revision of the MPS is version 1.4. It can be obtained from Intel's Developer web site (a treasure trove of hardware-related technical information) at *developer.intel.com*.

The MP configuration information is actually located in two structures: the MP Floating Pointer Structure, which indicates that the system conforms to the MPS specification, and the MP Configuration Table, which is an option table that details the underlying configuration.

The MP Floating Pointer Structure contains a physical address pointer to the MP Configuration Table and other MP feature information bytes.

The MP Configuration Table, on the other hand, is composed of a series of pointers to configuration sections. The table consists of a fixed header containing pointers to subsequent configuration records. These records contain explicit information about APICs, processors, buses, and interrupts. If the system corresponds to one of a set of default configurations listed within the MPS, this table need not exist.

## The !mps Command

If all of this sounds complicated, that's because it is. Microsoft has been kind enough to provide a kernel debugging extension to locate and format the information contained within the MPS table for easy viewing. This is accessed with the kernel extension command `!mps`, as follows:

```
> !mps  BIOS Revision MPS 1.4          HAL = UP MPS 1.4 - APIC platform  OEM
ID          :INTEL      OEM Product ID :RD440LX DP    processor. EN BP L.APIC
ID 00 Vers 11
              Family 6, Model 3, Stepping 4, CPUID Flags 80fbff
  bus.        id 00, type PCI
  bus.        id 01, type PCI
  bus.        id 02, type ISA
  io apic.    EN id 01 vers 11 @ fec00000
  io int.     extint po=1 el=1, srcbus 02 irq 00 dst apic 01 intin 00
  io int.     intr   po=1 el=1, srcbus 02 irq 01 dst apic 01 intin 01
  io int.     intr   po=1 el=1, srcbus 02 irq 00 dst apic 01 intin 02
  io int.     intr   po=1 el=1, srcbus 02 irq 03 dst apic 01 intin 03
  io int.     intr   po=1 el=1, srcbus 02 irq 04 dst apic 01 intin 04
  io int.     intr   po=1 el=1, srcbus 02 irq 05 dst apic 01 intin 05
  io int.     intr   po=1 el=1, srcbus 02 irq 06 dst apic 01 intin 06
  io int.     intr   po=1 el=1, srcbus 02 irq 07 dst apic 01 intin 07
  io int.     intr   po=1 el=1, srcbus 02 irq 08 dst apic 01 intin 08
  io int.     intr   po=1 el=1, srcbus 02 irq 0a dst apic 01 intin 0a
  io int.     intr   po=1 el=1, srcbus 02 irq 0c dst apic 01 intin 0c
  io int.     intr   po=1 el=1, srcbus 02 irq 0e dst apic 01 intin 0e
  io int.     intr   po=1 el=1, srcbus 02 irq 0f dst apic 01 intin 0f
  io int.     intr   po=3 el=3, srcbus 00 irq 2c dst apic 01 intin 12
  io int.     intr   po=3 el=3, srcbus 00 irq 40 dst apic 01 intin 13
  lcl int.    extint po=1 el=1, srcbus 02 irq 00 dst apic ff intin 00
  lcl int.    nmi    po=1 el=1, srcbus 01 irq 00 dst apic ff intin 01
  extended table entries
  address.    bus 00 io port                    0 len 10000
  address.    bus 00 memory               4000000 len f9000000
  address.    bus 00 prefetch mem        fd000000 len 1dff000
  address.    bus 00 memory              fedff000 len 1201000
  address.    bus 00 memory                 a0000 len 20000
  address.    bus 00 memory                 d0000 len 18000
  child bus.  bus 02 is child of bus 00 subtractive
  bus comp.   bus 00 include ISA ranges
  bus comp.   bus 00 include VGA ranges
```

## Version Information

The output provides some interesting information from a diagnostic and informational standpoint. First, the system corresponds to the MPS 1.4 specification. It is also running a uniprocessor version of the HAL. This seems correct, because this is a multiprocessor motherboard populated with only one CPU.

The underlying hardware is an Intel motherboard RD440LX DP. This is always interesting, because often computer vendors are not shipping their own motherboards, but rather incorporating motherboards from external vendors—in this case, Intel. I now know that, to find updates and information on this board, I can look to Intel's web site, as well as to that of the well-known computer manufacturer from whom I thought I was buying a computer.

## Processor Entry Fields

For each processor in the system, there is a corresponding processor entry field describing the CPU. This entry is as follows:

```
processor. EN BP L.APIC ID 00 Vers 11
             Family 6, Model 3, Stepping 4, CPUID Flags 80fbff
```

All entry fields begin with an identifying mnemonic. In this case, it's `processor`. The `EN` indicates that the processor is enabled. The system boot processor will follow the `EN` with a `BP`. There can be only one boot processor in a given system.

The local APIC assigned to the CPU is detailed next. In this case, `L.APIC ID 00` means that local APIC 00 is the one assigned to the CPU. This is followed by the version of the local APIC—Version 11.

The next line details the type and stepping information for the processor being described. Refer to Intel's web site for information relating this information back to a CPU type. What is important here is that all CPUs should have matching stepping numbers and CPUID flags. If they don't match, problems can occur when trying to run NT in multiprocessing mode.

## Bus Entry Fields

Following the system information section of the displayed data, the actual configuration sections begin. The first of these describes the system buses. In this example, the output is as follows:

```
bus.         id 00, type PCI
bus.         id 01, type PCI
bus.         id 02, type ISA
```

In this example, there are three buses. There are two PCI buses, numbered 00 and 01. Bus 02 is an ISA bus. These buses could be any of the valid PC system buses. The first column indicates the entry type (`bus.`), the second indicates the bus ID, and the third describes the bus type.

Each bus in a system must have a unique bus ID if any of the following criteria are true:

- The bus does not share its memory address space with another bus.
- The bus does not share its I/O address space with another bus.
- The bus does not share interrupt lines with another bus.
- Any aspect of the bus as an independent entity is software-visible (such as PCI configuration space).

Special consideration must be given when assigning a bus ID for local buses that are designed to work in conjunction with another bus. If the bus looks like a part of another bus because it uses a subset of that bus's interrupts and address space, rendering it totally invisible to software, it does not need its own bus entry in the table. The two buses in this case are considered a single logical bus.

## I/O APIC Entry Field

The next section details all of the I/O APICs in the system. In this case, there is only one:

```
io apic.   EN id 01 vers 11 @ fec00000
```

The first column indicates the entry type. For I/O APICs, the type is simply `io apic.`. The `EN` indicates that the APIC is enabled. At least one APIC in every system must be enabled.

Following this is the APIC ID. In this example, the APIC ID is 01. This APIC is version 11 (derived from bits 0–7 of the I/O APIC's version register). The base address of the APIC is 0xfec00000. This is the physical address of the I/O APIC.

## Interrupt Entry Fields

After the I/O APIC entry field comes a series of lines describing interrupt routing across the APIC. These are called *I/O entry fields*. Let's use the following excerpt from the output for example:

```
io int.    intr   po=1 el=1, srcbus 02 irq 04 dst apic 01 intin 04
```

The first column, `io int.`, indicates that this entry describes an I/O interrupt. An I/O interrupt is an interrupt that is connected to the APIC interrupt input line. The other type of supported interrupt is a local interrupt. A local interrupt is one that is directly connected to a local interrupt input line on the APIC. The sample output above describes both types of interrupts.

The second column indicates the interrupt type described by this entry. The valid values for this field are `INTR` (a vectored interrupt, with the vector supplied by the APIC redirection table), `NMI` (nonmaskable interrupt), `SMI` (system management interrupt), and `ExtINT` (vectored interrupt from an external PIC).

The next column is labeled po. This describes the polarity of the underlying interrupt. The valid values are 0 for interrupts that conform to the underlying bus specification (e.g., active low for EISA, etc), 1 for active high, and 11 for active low.

Following the polarity, the `el` column indicates the trigger mode of the APIC signal input. The only valid values are 0 for bus-conforming interrupt levels, 1 for edge-triggered, and 11 for level-triggered interrupts.

The remaining columns deal with the routing of the interrupt. The `src-bus` column indicates the bus that the interrupt is coming from. This bus number corresponds directly to the list of buses that was printed just prior to these I/O interrupt entry fields. The `irq` field provides the Interrupt Request on the source bus.

The next column, `dst apic`, tells the system which I/O APIC the signal is connected to. An important note is that if this value is `FF`, the signal is connected to all I/O APICs. The final column identifies the actual interrupt pin to which the signal is connected.

The chosen example illustrates the following: an I/O interrupt is connected from IRQ 4 on the system's ISA bus through I/O APIC number 1 into INT4 pin on the CPU. This is an active high, edge-triggered interrupt.

## Address Space Mapping Entry Fields

The system address space mapping entries define the system addresses that are visible on a particular bus. Each bus defined can have any number of address space mapping entries included in the extended MPS table. This provides the ability for individual buses to support different address ranges for increased system performance. The address mapping fields in the above example are excerpted below:

```
address.   bus 00 io port                        0 len 10000
address.   bus 00 memory                   4000000 len f9000000
address.   bus 00 prefetch mem            fd000000 len 1dff000
address.   bus 00 memory                  fedff000 len 1201000
address.   bus 00 memory                     a0000 len 20000
address.   bus 00 memory                     d0000 len 18000
```

As in all entry fields, the first column describes the type of entry field. In this case, it is `address..` This is followed by a bus identifier for this entry. In this example, all of the address mappings apply to bus 00, which is the first PCI bus.

After the bus ID is the address type being mapped. The valid types are I/O ports, memory, and prefetch memory. The address type is followed by a starting address and a length.

## Bus Hierarchy Description Entry

If this is present, the entries define how I/O buses are connected, relative to one another. Entries of this type are required for each bus that is connected to the system hierarchically below another bus. In this example:

```
child bus. bus 02 is child of bus 00 subtractive
```

Bus 02, the ISA bus, is a child of bus 00, one of the PCI buses. Given that there is only one entry, the following assumptions can be made about the configuration of the system: There are two PCI buses that are peers, one of which contains a PCI–ISA bridge. The ISA bus is subservient to this PCI bus.

The indicator that the bus is "subtractive" indicates that all addresses visible on the parent bus are useable on this bus.

### Compatibility Bus Address Space Modifier Entry

This area defines a set of predefined address ranges that should be either added or removed from the supported address map ranges for a given bug. Combined with the system address space mapping entries, a complete description of the memory and I/O ranges for a given bus can be derived. The example follows:

```
bus comp.  bus 00 include ISA ranges
bus comp.  bus 00 include VGA ranges
```

These entries offer up that bus 00, the PCI bus that has the ISA bus hanging off of it, includes all I/O port addresses that are valid for ISA and VGA cards. For more detail on these ranges, consult the MPS version 1.4.

## Peering into Interrupt Controllers (PIC and APIC)

The MPS table describes how interrupts are routed through the interrupt controllers. The `!apic` and `!pic` debugger extension commands provide insight directly into the interrupt controllers on Intel platforms. On most Intel-based platforms, there are two different types of interrupt controllers: the Programmable Interrupt Controller (PIC), and the Advanced Programmable Interrupt Controller (APIC). Usually, you will find only APICs on multiprocessor systems where interrupts must be routed from multiple sources to multiple CPUs.

### The !apic Command

The `!apic` command provides detail as to the status and configuration of the APIC:

```
 > !apicApic @ fffe0000  ID:0 (40011)  LogDesc:01000000  DestFmt:fffffff
TPR D1
TimeCnt: 03f8ff90clk  SpurVec:1f  FaultVec:e3  error:0
Ipi Cmd: 00040041  Vec:41  FixedDel    Dest=Self      edg
Timer..: 000300fd  Vec:FD  FixedDel    Dest=Self      edg        masked
Linti0.: 0001001f  Vec:1F  FixedDel    Dest=Self      edg        masked
Linti1.: 000084ff  Vec:FF  NMI         Dest=Self      lvl
TMR: 52, 72
IRR: 41, 92, d1, e3
ISR: d1
```

There are a couple of things that can be gleaned from this output. First, the base address of the APIC is 0xfffe0000. You can use this information to read directly from and write directly to the APIC. This is dangerous and not recommended, but if you know what you are doing, this it is certainly doable. The APIC is under the direct control of the operating system. You should control interrupt behavior only through the appropriate kernel and HAL calls.

Most of the remaining output refers to the vector mapping of the various interrupts supported by the APIC. The `IPi` refers to the interprocessor interrupt. This interrupt is issued if a local CPU writes to the interrupt command register in the local unit of the APIC. The contents of that status register are detailed, and the example shows that the `IPi` is vectored to interrupt 41. It is an edge-triggered interrupt.

In addition, there are a timer interrupt and two local interrupts that are detailed in the same manner as the `IPi`. The local interrupts are interrupts that are always passed to the local processor. The mnemonic `Linti0` and `Linti1` indicate these local interrupts. One of these is wired to an NMI for catastrophic errors; the other is in general use.

For more information about the meaning of the various fields within the APIC data output, refer to an APIC manual. Search the Intel documentation web site for data on an 82489 or later-model APIC.

## The !pic Command

The `!pic` command provides detail as to the status and configuration of this simple interrupt controller device:

```
> !pic
----- IRQ Number ----- 00 01 02 03 04 05 06 07 08 09 0A 0B 0C 0D 0E 0F
Physically in service:  .  .  .  .  .  .  .  .  .  .  .  .  .  .  .  .
Physically masked:      Y  Y  Y  Y  Y  Y  Y  Y  Y  Y  Y  Y  Y  Y  Y  Y
Physically requested:   .  .  .  Y  .  .  .  .  Y  .  .  .  Y  .  .  .
```

You can see from the output that there are three interrupts pending (3, 8, and 0xc). All interrupts appear masked. This is because they are all masked when the debugger has control of the machine. An important thing to note about servicing interrupts with the `!pic` command is that the interrupts are serviced from the highest number to the lowest. Also, keep in mind that the pending interrupts were most likely cascaded up from the APICs in the system (if any).

# Examining Power Management Structures

Windows 2000 introduces the concept of power management to the NT world for the first time. Windows 2000 is supported on laptop and portable computers and is friendly toward "green" computers. To that end, Microsoft has provided within the kernel debugging extensions shipping with Windows 2000 commands that offer up a view of the power management features within the operating system.

These commands will be of interest to developers of hardware device drivers who must now honor the power management policies set forth by the user and the operating system. The commands address power capabilities (`!pocaps`), power management policies (`!popolicy`), and power management data structures (`!polist` and `!ponode`).

This section will not explain how power management features work in Windows 2000. For detailed information about what power management means in the Windows 2000 world, you are encouraged to visit the Microsoft hardware development site at *http://www.microsoft.com/hwdev*. There are many links to papers and web sites written by Microsoft and its partners, describing the inner workings of power management functionality.

## Power Management Capabilities

The power management capabilities structure maintained by the operating system is populated in conjunction with ACPI BIOS. This structure describes the hardware capabilities present for implementing power management functionality. It is displayed with the `!pocaps` command, as follows:

```
> !pocapsPopCapabilities @ 0x8046f680  Misc Supported Features:  S4
FullWake  Processor Features:        Disk Features:            SpinDown
Battery Features:           Wake Caps    Ac OnLine Wake:         Sx    Soft
Lid Wake:           Sx
    RTC Wake:               Sx
    Min Device Wake:        Sx
    Default Wake:           Sx
```

Examination of the output yields information about the power management capabilities of the underlying hardware. The first thing to note is that the structure address is 0x8046f680. Armed with this information, you can either view a raw display of the structure (you never know what Microsoft includes or excludes from its formatted views) or modify the structure as needed for your development and testing purposes.

The output is separated into four distinct sections: Miscellaneous Power Management Features, Processor Power Management Features, Disk Power Management Features, and Battery Features.

## Power Management Policies

Given a set of power management capabilities from the BIOS and hardware, the operating system can set the appropriate power management policies. These policies are viewed with the `!popolicy` extension command, as follows:

```
> !popolicy
SYSTEM_POWER_POLICY (R.1) @ 0x80469bc0
  PowerButton:        Shutdown  Flags: 00000003   Event: 00000000   Query UI
  SleepButton:            None  Flags: 00000003   Event: 00000000   Query UI
  LidClose:               None  Flags: 00000001   Event: 00000000   Query
  Idle:                   None  Flags: 00000001   Event: 00000000   Query
  OverThrottled:          None  Flags: c0000004   Event: 00000000   Override
NoWakes Critical
  IdleTimeout:        00000000  IdleSensitivity:          32
  MinSleep:                 S0  MaxSleep:                 S0
  LidOpenWake:              S0  FastSleep:                S0
  WinLogonFlags:      00000001  S4Timeout:          00000000
  VideoTimeout:       000004b0  VideoDim:                 02
  SpinTimeout:        00000000  OptForPower:              00
  FanTolerance:             64  ForcedThrottle:           64
  MinThrottle:              5a
```

As you can see from the output, the features of the underlying hardware that have an impact on the power management system are detailed. Enumerated for each item are the state, any flags, and the event associated with the feature.

Following the detail on the power management features is a set of thresholds and timeouts governing the behavior of the power management system. Note that the address of the structure is provided (in this example, the policy structure lives at 0x80469bc0). Knowing the address of this structure allows for the ability to go in and modify the values directly with the kernel debugger.

## Power Management IRPs

The debugger extensions supplied with Windows 2000 provide a command that lists out in a formatted view any I/O Request Packets (IRPs) queued to the power management system. This same information can be found by performing an `!irpfind` and filtering out those IRPs destined for the power management system. The `!polist` command will filter out only those IRPs that are related to power management:

```
> !polist
All entries in Power Irp Serial List
PopIrpSerialListLength = 0
```

## Examining SCSI Requests

There are no built-in commands for examining SCSI requests. Microsoft has provided with Windows 2000 a new debugger extension DLL just for looking at SCSI detail. This extension is called *scsikd.dll* and is found on the Windows 2000 Support Tools CD.

This extension DLL, like all debugger extension libraries, can coexist with the other loaded DLLs. Chapter 9 provides information about the restrictions of using and manipulating debugger extensions.

To load the SCSI debugger extension from within the kernel debugger, you simply issue the `!load` command:

```
> !load scsikd.dll
```

That's all there is to it. You now have access to three new commands:

- `!scsiext` dumps a specified SCSI port extension.
- `!classext` provides a formatted view into a class extension.
- `!srbdata` details the contents of a specified SCSI Request Block.

## Summary

This chapter has shown that it is possible to use the kernel debuggers to provide a view into the underlying hardware of your system. This is useful if you are either debugging device drive code that directly manipulates hardware (such as USB or SCSI physical drivers) or debugging suspected hardware problems.

SEVEN

# Working with Memory Dumps

**CHAPTER OBJECTIVES**

- Crash Dump Management
- Triggering Dumps
- dumpchk
- dumpexam

*Debugging and understanding crash dumps is a common chore of many support development engineers. A dump file is a snapshot of a system's memory taken at the time of a catastrophic failure that is written to persistent storage for later analysis. The ability to generate a dump file may be enabled or disabled at will. The behavior of the system at the time of a bug check is governed by a number of system policies. These will be discussed in this chapter.*

*Most of the techniques developed throughout this book are valid on both crash dump files and live systems alike. The focus of this chapter is on issues that are particular only to dump files, not on general debugging issues. The chapter will discuss the various policies governing the behavior of dump files and the tools provided by Microsoft.*

# Crash Dump Management

Crash dumps occur only at the time that a system encounters a bug check. There is a set of policies that govern whether or not the dumps actually occur at the time of a system failure and, if so, how the dumps occur. There are considerations for examining and storing dump files in a support environment where various flavors and service packs of Windows 2000 will be encountered. All of these issues are addressed in this section.

## Setting Crash Dump Policies

Chapter 3 discusses the various policies related to handling bug checks and system failures. It provides instruction on how to configure these items through the control panel, as well as directly with the registry editor. Please refer back to Chapter 3 for this detail. In this section, the policies governing crash dumps will be reviewed.

### ENABLING DUMP FILE CREATION

One of the options in the control panel allows for the computer to "write debugging information" to a specified file when the system bug checks. This is the crash dump file. With this option selected, the system will save a copy of the system memory to the dump file specified. There are a couple of caveats that you must be aware of.

When the operating system attempts to create a crash dump, it does not immediately open the dump file and begin writing data. Remember that the system is in an unstable state, and opening files and writing to a file system can compromise the integrity of the data that you're attempting to save. If you're diagnosing a crash dump with a file system error, you want the file system data structures intact—not necessarily the state they'll be in if you start creating new files. Instead, the operating system will copy the contents of memory to the system's page file. For this to work, your page file must be configured to match or exceed the size of main memory.

As the system is rebooting, it will detect that there is crash dump information stored in the page file. This isn't a good thing from the perspective of the operating system because it needs the page file to perform its virtual memory functions. The data must be moved as quickly as possible to an area of the disk that is less critical to system operation. This is accomplished with a background process called *dumpsave*. You don't need to do anything to make this happen. Dumpsave will run whenever a dump is detected in the paging file and transfer the contents of the dump into the dump file that you specified in the configuration screen.

Be aware that, as the system is coming up, you may receive a message that you are running low on virtual memory. This will correct itself as the available paging file is emptied of the dump information. To avoid this scenario, you can create either a very large paging file or an alternate paging file on a separate disk drive large enough to contain the dump information (the Microsoft suggested solution). This will keep enough page file space to manage normal operating system stress adequately during the boot cycle while allowing dump files to be created at the same time.

Again, the size of the memory image can be quite large (up to 4 Gbytes on a 32-bit NT system). Ensure that, when you select the location of the system dump file, there is enough space on the selected volume. There are no restrictions on where you can locate the dump file in your system. Choose a location that will maintain enough free space.

#### OVERWRITING PREVIOUS FILES

There is an operation that allows the overwriting of previous dump files. If this is set, a new dump will overwrite a previous file. If this is not set, you must always take care to save the crash dump file to another location so that subsequent failures will have a place to write their information. The only real reason not to select this is if you are having a continuing failure and want to save the original dump file without the overhead of continuous dumps.

#### KERNEL ADDRESS-ONLY DUMPS

Windows 2000 gives you an option that isn't present in Windows 2000 4.0. This is the option to save only kernel information. When this option is enabled, the dump file will contain only images of memory assigned to kernel address spaces. In many cases, this is enough to understand the failure when doing later analysis. There are also many cases when it will not be enough, for example, when debugging traces into user-mode code

#### WHERE'S THE INFORMATION?

The actual configuration information set by the Startup and Recovery dialog box is stored, like most things in Windows 2000, in the system registry. The recovery options are stored under the registry key HKEY_LOCAL_MACHINE\CurrentControlSet\Control\CrashControl. The subkeys used to govern recovery behavior are enumerated in Table 3-1.

## Triggering Dumps: The Dump Switch

There are times when a system misbehaves and the cause cannot be immediately determined through normal mechanisms. The system may be in a hung, nonresponsive state or may be behaving erratically. In these instances, it is useful to be able to stop the system and generate a crash dump for later analysis.

Beginning with Service Pack 4, Windows 2000 supports the concept of dump switch cards. These are simple cards that plug into a PCI bus that generate a nonmaskable interrupt (NMI). Some computer manufacturers (such as NCR) include NMI buttons on their servers, because their Unix implementations have long supported the ability to trigger a crash dump on NMI.

Ordinarily, in the NT world, an NMI from the hardware would indicate a hardware failure. When hardware dump switch support is enabled, that NMI will generate a bug check, and a crash dump will occur (if dumps are enabled!). When dump switch support is not enabled, the NMI would be treated as it normally would by the hardware application layer (HAL)—you will see a HAL stop screen (as discussed in Chapter 3).

### ENABLING DUMP SWITCH SUPPORT

To enable dump switch support, use the registry editor to edit the HKLM\System\CurrentControlSet\Control\CrashControl registry key. Add a subkey called *NMICrashDump* as a DWORD. If NMICrashDump is set to 1, an NMI will trigger a bug check. If it is set to 0, it will be treated as a hardware failure. This value is read at boot time into the global variable HalpNMIDumpFlag. You can edit this value directly with the kernel debugger.

This change works by changing the `HalHandleNMI()` routine to perform the check. As a result of the HAL needing modification, not all HALs are enabled to support this facility. The most common HALs have been modified to support dump switch cards. For an up-to-date list, consult the Microsoft web page *http://www.microsoft.com/HWDEV/debugging/dmpsw.htm*.

### WHERE TO GET THE DUMP SWITCH

Many servers from vendors that support both Windows 2000 and Unix flavors will provide the necessary functionality to generate an NMI at will. Ask your vendor, because it may be enabled or shipped by default only on servers preloaded with Unix. Failing that, there are third-party vendors that provide diagnostic plug-in cards with NMI functionality.

You can also build a PCI dump switch card. Microsoft provides a reference design in its application note, describing dump switch support in Windows 2000. See the web page at *http://www.microsoft.com/HWDEV/debugging/dmpsw.htm*. Because web sites tend to reorganize, I also encourage you to do a web search for "dump switch" or "NMI switch" on Microsoft's search engine (and external web search engines).

# Validating the Dump File with dumpchk

The *dumpchk.exe* utility is used to validate the integrity of a given dump file. *dumpchk* is provided as a part of the support tools and ships as a part of the Windows 2000 Device Driver Kit (DDK). It provides information about the validity of the dump file. It also provides a basic level of detail regarding the actual failure that generated the dump.

## Usage

*dumpchk* is strictly a command-line-based tool—it must be run from a command window. It is controlled by a number of command-line arguments. Table 7–1 details the command-line arguments supported by *dumpchk*.

**TABLE 7–1** *dumpchk.exe Command-Line Arguments*

| Argument | Description |
|---|---|
| `-?` | Prints a list of supported command line arguments. |
| `-p` | Displays the header information for the dump file only; provides NO validation. |
| `-q` | Performs a quick validation of the dump file. |
| `-r` | Lists the service pack level present on the machine that caused the memory dump. This is new in Windows 2000. |
| `-v` | Enables verbose mode. Prints extra detail about the job that *dumpchk* is performing. |
| `-x` | Enables extra verbose mode. |

## Output

The *dumpchk* command prints out a summary of the contents of the dump file, along with some validation information. It prints this information to the standard output (usually your command window). If you wish to save this information, you must redirect it to a file.

### VERSION INFORMATION

The first section that is displayed is the header file. It prints out information as follows:

```
Filename . . . . . . .memory.dmp
Signature. . . . . . .PAGE
ValidDump. . . . . . .DUMP
MajorVersion . . . . .free system
MinorVersion . . . . .1381
```

As you can see, the first part of the header indicates that it is a memory dump file from a free build. The dump file name is *memory.dmp*. The build number is 1381. This is a Windows 2000 system. This is enough information to locate a set of symbol files that match the dump, so that more complex analysis can be run against the file.

Following the informational part of the header comes a list of indexes into the dump file. These are strictly informational—this detail is available from within the debugger when opening a dump file. For completeness, however, the next lines of output look like this:

```
DirectoryTableBase . .0x00030000
PfnDataBase. . . . . .0x83f9f000
PsLoadedModuleList . .0x8014eab0
PsActiveProcessHead. .0x8014e9a8
```

The next two lines begin to provide useful information that will assist in setting up for diagnosing the underlying problem:

```
MachineImageType . . .i386
NumberProcessors . . .1
```

You can tell that this is an Intel-based uniprocessor. This, in combination with the major and minor version information in the first part of the header, will allow you to locate the proper symbol files. If this had been a multiprocessor machine, you would need to point to a symbol tree containing a multiprocessor version of the NT kernel and HAL.

### BUG CHECK DATA

Now that you understand what kind of system you are debugging, it is time to figure out what the exception is. If you did not see the blue screen as it occurred, this is your first opportunity to understand the problem. The next several lines detail the problem that caused the crash dump:

```
BugCheckCode . . . . .0x0000000a
BugCheckParameter1 . .0x47380891
BugCheckParameter2 . .0x0000001c
BugCheckParameter3 . .0x00000000
BugCheckParameter4 . .0x80115cdd
```

The dump header indicates that the system stopped because it encountered the bug check code 0xA. This bug check, as a quick glance in Appendix B will point out, is IRQL_NOT_LESS_OR_EQUAL. Some device driver performed an operation at the wrong interrupt request level (IRQL).

The parameters to the bug check call are then detailed in the following four items. The meanings of these can also be gleaned from Appendix B, which indicates the following meanings for each of these parameters:

1. The virtual address of the memory being referenced.
2. The interrupt request level (IRQL) at which the access was attempted.
3. Value indicating whether the operation was a read operation or write operation. Zero (0) indicates a read operation, and a one (1) indicates a write operation.
4. The virtual address of the executable code that caused the exception.

So, what is understood about the bug check at this point? The device driver living at virtual address 0x8013fe6c (parameter 4) attempted to read (parameter 3) the virtual address 0x47380891 (parameter 1) while at IRQL 0x1C (parameter 2). The IRQL was too high to take a page fault, so the system bug checked. But which driver is responsible?

If *dumpchk* provided a listing of loaded modules, you could figure out very quickly which driver was the offending driver. It doesn't, so it is necessary to run *dumpexam.exe* and maybe even to use the debugger to dig deeper into the problem.

### EXCEPTION INFORMATION

Following the bug check data, the exception record from the failing operating system is printed. Given the bug check code that was displayed, this information is actually meaningless. If the bug check had been related to an exception, this would have been more useful.

```
ExceptionCode. . . . .0x80000003
ExceptionFlags . . . .0x00000001
ExceptionAddress . . .0x8013fe6c
```

This exception record indicates that the last exception was a code of 0x80000003. Appendix C resolves that to STATUS_BREAKPOINT. Indeed, when this dump was generated, active debugging was going on and breakpoints were being hit and set.

If the bug check code had been a KMODE_EXCEPTION_NOT_HANDLED, the exception information in this record would have matched the parameters to the bug check.

### DUMP VALIDATION DETAIL

The final section in the output from running *dumpchk* on a normal dump file doesn't really provide useful information. This section says simply "the dump file is correct." A status message is displayed as each stage of the validation occurs. If there had been anomalies in the dump file, the messages in this section would indicate that.

```
**************
**************--> Validating the integrity of the PsLoadedModuleList
**************
```

What's actually validated? First, the list of loaded modules is examined for corruption. This check says that the data structures are intact and that it is safe to use the debugger to walk through them. If these structures are not intact, proceeding will be a waste of time. It is too unpredictable to attempt to walk lists that are known to be invalid.

```
**************
**************--> Performing a complete check (^C to end)
**************
```

What happens next is dependent on whether you selected a quick check or a complete check (the default option). The status message indicates the method chosen. A quick check would inhibit the *dumpchk* tool from actually reading each page of memory in the following steps. A complete check, as in this example, would cause the *dumpchk* utility to read and verify each page as it validates the physical and virtual memory contents of the dump file. Note that a complete check can take a couple of minutes, depending on the size of the dump file.

```
**************
**************--> Validating all physical addresses
**************
```

The next step is to validate all physical addresses. The *dumpchk* utility reads the starting and ending physical address range for the dump file. It then walks through the dump file, ensuring that every page of physical memory is matched up with a page in the dump file.

This check will fail if the dump was truncated for some reason (e.g., there wasn't space for the entire contents of memory). Even if this check fails, the dump may be usable. It depends on where the address range for the bad pages lay. All you really need to perform effective crash dump analysis are kernel mode-pages.

```
*************
*************--> Validating all virtual addresses
*************
```

A similar procedure is run against virtual addresses as was taken against the physical addresses: Each virtual address is validated against the contents of the dump file. The big difference is that, whereas physical pages are expected to be present, virtual addresses are not. If pages in the virtual address space were paged out at the time the dump was taken, those pages may not be represented in the system dump. You will see only a warning of these cases when *dumpchk* is run in verbose or extra verbose modes.

```
**************
**************--> This dump file is good!
**************
```

The verdict in this example is that there is a valid dump. The user should feel free to move on to the next step and perform some analysis to understand what went wrong. Before hooking up the debugger and reading the crash dump file, you should first try *dumpexam*.

## Examining the Dump with dumpexam

Just as *dumpchk* validates a dump, *dumpexam.exe* will perform a level of analysis on the dump file. *dumpexam* will load the appropriate debugger extension dynamic linked library (DLL) for the version of the operating system contained in the dump and run a sequence of kernel debugging extension commands on it.

These commands are, unfortunately, hard-coded into the *dumpexam* utility. This is the output that Microsoft wants to see first when examining a problem. Very often, it is enough information to provide a diagnosis. It is almost always enough to isolate an errant device driver.

After printing the information contained in the dump header, *dumpexam* runs a series of kernel debugger extension commands against the dump file. The sequence of commands that are executed is very straightforward. First, the following kernel debugging extension commands are executed:

- `!drivers` to list the loaded modules in the kernel at the time of the failure.
- `!locks` to provide detail as to the outstanding lock situation in the kernel at the time of the failure.
- `!memusage` to give a snap-shot of the overall memory situation.
- `!vm` provides detail about the actual allocations of memory among the drivers and memory pools.
- `!errlog` dumps the contents of the system error log.
- `!process 0 0` is run to provide a summary listing of all the processes in the system.
- `!process 0 7` is then run to provide a detailed listing of the system's processes.

Once this global information is collected, the *dumpexam* utility drills down a little further. On a multiprocessor machine, the following list of commands is run on each CPU. If the machine is a single processor, they are executed against only the current processor:

1. The currently active process is displayed with the output of the `!process` command.
2. The thread that is currently being executed is also displayed, using the `!thread` command.

3. The registers of the current processor are displayed.
4. Following the register display, a stack trace is generated.
5. A disassembly of the return address from the top of the stack is printed.
6. If there are issues that *dumpexam* can pinpoint, some heuristics are printed to aid you in your diagnosis.

If the underlying problem cannot be determined by following these steps, it will be necessary to perform a more advanced level of interpretation with the debugging tools. If you are the driver writer, you might also want to use the driver tools to drill down in discovering the actual cause of the failure.

## Usage

*dumpchk*, like many of the diagnostic tools, is a command-line-based utility that is configured and driven with command-line options. These arguments are detailed in Table 7-2.

The usage is straightforward:

```
dumpexam [arguments] [dump_file]
```

If no dump file is specified, the default location for a system dump file is used. This is the same dump file location that is configured through the System Applet in the control panel. The file name is read from the controlling registry key, HKLM\CurrentControlSet\System\CrashControl\DumpFile. If you are examining the dump file on a machine other than the one it crashed on, it is a good idea to specify explicitly the name of the dump file.

**TABLE 7–2** *dumpexam.exe Command-Line Arguments*

| Argument | Description |
|---|---|
| `-?` | Displays a message describing the command line arguments. |
| `-v` | Adds an extra level of verbosity to the output. |
| `-p` | Displays only the dump header, performing no analysis on the dump file. |
| `-f File_Name` | Writes the output of the examination to the specified file. If not present, the output will go to standard output. |
| `-y Path` | Points to the path for the symbol tree. If this is not specified, the CD ROM drive is used. |

## Output

The *dumpexam* utility outputs the results of the analysis steps that have already been described. This section will walk through a dump file, and the root cause of the problem will be ferreted out.

Because most of the information presented is the same as the output of the kernel debugging extension commands in WinDbg and KD that were covered earlier in this book, there will not be a lot of attention paid to the detail of the output. The focus in this section is twofold: an understanding of what to expect as output when running this command and an understanding of what might have caused the failure in this example.

### DUMP HEADER

The first thing you see when viewing the output of *dumpexam* is the header from the dump file. This is the same header that was described in the discussion of *dumpchk* previously. It is displayed as follows:

```
*************************************************************
**
** Windows 2000 Crash Dump Analysis
**
*************************************************************
*
Filename . . . . . . .f:memory.dmp
Signature. . . . . . .PAGE
ValidDump. . . . . . .DUMP
MajorVersion . . . . .free system
MinorVersion . . . . .1381
DirectoryTableBase . .0x00030000
PfnDataBase. . . . . .0xff5de000
PsLoadedModuleList . .0x801523c0
PsActiveProcessHead. .0x801522b8
MachineImageType . . .i386
NumberProcessors . . .4
BugCheckCode . . . . .0x0000000a
BugCheckParameter1 . .0x01000006
BugCheckParameter2 . .0x00000002
BugCheckParameter3 . .0x00000000
BugCheckParameter4 . .0x8023971c
ExceptionCode. . . . .0x80000003
ExceptionFlags . . . .0x00000001
ExceptionAddress . . .0x80142c88
```

The dump header indicates that the failing system was running a free build of Windows 2000 (build 1381). It was a multiprocessor machine with four Intel-based CPUs. The stop code was IRQL_NOT_LESS_OR_EQUAL (0xA).

The failing device driver code, as derived from bug check parameter 4 with this particular bug check (see Appendix B for detail on bug check parameters), lives at the virtual address 0x8023971C. This can be related back to a specific device driver, once the symbol files have been loaded and the addresses of the device drivers are known.

### SYMBOL FILE LOADING

Once the header for the dump file has been read and displayed, *dumpexam* attempts to load the symbols associated with the dump file. It takes these symbols from the symbol path provided when the utility was started. This section of output indicates that the symbols are being loaded and lists any errors or warnings that occurred while loading the symbols:

```
*******************************************************************
** Symbol File Load Log
*******************************************************
***** Warning: Checksum mismatch (SYMCHK=0000a5bc, SYSCHK=000205ec) for
J:\Debug\Debug4.0\sp3\symbols\sys\aic78xx.dbg
```

As you can see from this output, there was a problem loading the symbol file for the device driver AIC78XX. The error indicates a "checksum mismatch." This error occurs when the symbol file does not match the loaded device driver. This will be a problem only if the AIX78XX driver is implicated as a part of the failure. In that case, tracking down the correct symbol file would be a necessary step.

This error is also a warning that the device driver in question may not be the one supplied by Microsoft. A little off-line investigation in this example (I asked the system administrator!) showed that the AIX78XX device driver is the Adaptec SCSI driver. It was replaced by a hot-fix after the system was initially loaded. This is why the symbol file doesn't match the symbol file on the debugging machine. If the symbol file is used in any stack traces, you must locate and install into the symbol tree the appropriate symbol file and rerun *dumpexam*.

### LOADED DRIVERS LISTING

Following the loading of the symbol files comes the first of the kernel debugging extension commands. The `!drivers` command is run to list the loaded drivers and their build dates. The output from this command is shown below:

```
***************************************************************
** !drivers
***************************************************************
*
Loaded System Driver Summary

Base        Code Size       Data Size        Driver Name       Creation Time
80100000  c1540 ( 773 kb)  227c0 ( 137 kb) ntoskrnl.exe   Sun May 11 00:11:27 1997
80001000   dae0 (  54 kb)   2cc0 (  11 kb)       hal.dll   Mon Mar 10 16:40:06 1997
80062000   ec60 (  59 kb)   2000 (   8 kb)   aic78xx.sys   Fri Jun 12 17:32:24 1998
80012000   6bc0 (  26 kb)   1480 (   5 kb)  SCSIPORT.SYS   Mon Mar 10 16:42:27 1997
801ff000   ba00 (  46 kb)   8d40 (  35 kb)    ncr875.sys   Tue Jun 30 20:11:31 1998
80073000   3320 (  12 kb)    600 (   1 kb) dac960nt.sys   Tue Mar 24 20:16:27 1998
8001a000   2ee0 (  11 kb)    900 (   2 kb)      Disk.sys   Thu Apr 24 22:27:46 1997
80214000   2660 (   9 kb)    a20 (   2 kb)    CLASS2.SYS   Thu Apr 24 22:23:43 1997
80218000   7920 (  30 kb)  16860 (  90 kb)    gamdrv.sys   Fri Feb 21 16:15:05 1997
80236000   5d80 (  23 kb)   4540 (  17 kb)   ExtMirr.sys   Mon Nov 03 16:57:22 1997
80240000  54980 ( 338 kb)   5a20 (  22 kb)      Ntfs.sys   Thu Apr 17 22:02:31 1997
f1ee0000   3b40 (  14 kb)    b00 (   2 kb)    Floppy.SYS   Wed Jul 17 00:31:09 1996
f2094000   1c00 (   7 kb)    680 (   1 kb)  Scsiscan.SYS   Wed Jul 17 00:32:00 1996
```

```
f1ef0000    4960 (  18 kb)     960 (   2 kb)      Cdrom.SYS   Wed Jul 17 00:31:29 1996
f21e1000     2c0 (   0 kb)     4a0 (   1 kb)       Null.SYS   Wed Jul 17 00:31:21 1996
f209c000    1680 (   5 kb)     a40 (   2 kb)     KSecDD.SYS   Wed Jul 17 20:34:19 1996
f21e2000     760 (   1 kb)     560 (   1 kb)       Beep.SYS   Wed Apr 23 15:19:43 1997
f1f20000    5500 (  21 kb)    1ba0 (   6 kb) i8042prt.sys   Mon Apr 21 16:03:54 1997
f20a4000    1740 (   5 kb)     a60 (   2 kb) mouclass.sys   Mon Mar 10 16:43:11 1997
f20ac000    16a0 (   5 kb)     a60 (   2 kb) kbdclass.sys   Wed Jul 17 00:31:16 1996
f1f38000    3f00 (  15 kb)    1220 (   4 kb) VIDEOPRT.SYS   Mon Mar 10 16:41:37 1997
f1c20000    5560 (  21 kb)    6680 (  25 kb)     cirrus.SYS   Mon Mar 10 16:41:46 1997
f1f68000    45c0 (  17 kb)     e40 (   3 kb)       Msfs.SYS   Mon Mar 10 16:45:01 1997
f1c30000    7e80 (  31 kb)    1240 (   4 kb)       Npfs.SYS   Mon Mar 10 16:44:48 1997
f1b68000   1ba00 ( 110 kb)    3e80 (  15 kb)       NDIS.SYS   Thu Apr 17 22:19:45 1997
f20cc000    1600 (   5 kb)     7a0 (   1 kb) ndistapi.sys   Wed Apr 23 17:31:08 1997
a0000000 11d680 (1141 kb)   1d4e0 ( 117 kb)    win32k.sys   Fri Apr 25 21:17:32 1997
f1cd0000    b240 (  44 kb)    1720 (   5 kb)    vga256.dll   Wed Apr 02 15:39:56 1997
f1ad5000   1f720 ( 125 kb)    2920 (  10 kb)   Fastfat.SYS   Mon Apr 21 16:50:22 1997
f228b000     620 (   1 kb)     400 (   1 kb) smpmgrdrv.sys   Tue Oct 07 10:06:11 1997
f213c000    1300 (   4 kb)     900 (   2 kb)     rasacd.sys   Wed Apr 23 17:19:14 1997
f20ec000    1620 (   5 kb)     c00 (   3 kb)        TDI.SYS   Wed Jul 17 00:39:08 1996
f1a89000    1fb00 ( 126 kb)   3fc0 (  15 kb)     tcpip.sys   Fri May 09 17:02:39 1997
f1a6c000    1a6e0 ( 105 kb)   25e0 (   9 kb)     netbt.sys   Sat Apr 26 21:00:42 1997
f1ac9000    26e0 (   9 kb)     820 (   2 kb)     rasarp.sys   Fri Apr 11 19:21:53 1997
f1d50000    8780 (  33 kb)     e20 (   3 kb)  asyncmac.sys   Wed Jul 17 01:03:39 1996
f1d60000    bda0 (  47 kb)     d80 (   3 kb)   smcpwrn.sys   Tue Dec 31 07:06:49 1996
f1e60000    bc60 (  47 kb)    1e20 (   7 kb)   ndiswan.sys   Wed Apr 23 15:02:57 1997
f1e70000    d900 (  54 kb)    1c20 (   7 kb)       afd.sys   Thu Apr 10 15:09:17 1997
f1e90000    62c0 (  24 kb)     b40 (   2 kb)   netbios.sys   Mon Mar 10 16:56:01 1997
f20bc000    19a0 (   6 kb)     a20 (   2 kb)   Parport.SYS   Wed Jul 17 00:31:23 1996
f1ad1000    2ca0 (  11 kb)     9e0 (   2 kb)  Parallel.SYS   Wed Jul 17 00:31:23 1996
f218e000     d80 (   3 kb)     780 (   1 kb)    ParVdm.SYS   Wed Jul 17 00:31:25 1996
f1c70000    9340 (  36 kb)    1a00 (   6 kb)    Serial.SYS   Mon Mar 10 16:44:11 1997
f193b000   3a480 ( 233 kb)    5be0 (  22 kb)       rdr.sys   Wed Mar 26 14:22:36 1997
f192a000    d220 (  52 kb)    3220 (  12 kb)       mup.sys   Mon Mar 10 16:57:09 1997
f1788000   33e60 ( 207 kb)    59a0 (  22 kb)       srv.sys   Fri Apr 25 13:59:31 1997
f1ff8000    3940 (  14 kb)     9c0 (   2 kb)     Modem.SYS   Mon Mar 10 16:43:09 1997
f14d8000    d700 (  53 kb)    1520 (   5 kb)      Cdfs.SYS   Mon Mar 10 16:57:04 1997
TOTAL:    3f78e0 (4062 kb)   aaee0 ( 683 kb) (     0 kb      0 kb)
```

The format should look familiar, because it is identical to the output of the `!drivers` command detailed in Chapter 5. Please refer to that section for information on reading this output. This is also well documented in the Windows 2000 DDK documentation.

Assuming that we know how to read the columns, what does the output tell us about this dump and the failure that caused the dump? First, examining the date on the driver AIC78XX shows that it is the newest driver in the machine. This is also the driver that had the symbol mismatch when the symbols loaded. This could be a suspect in the cause of the failure. Or, it might not be relevant to understanding the failure. The stop code needs closer examination, and the stacks need to be examined before that judgment can be made.

Refer back to the stop code from this dump. It was IRQL_NOT_LESS_OR_EQUAL, with the faulting address in parameter 4 as 0x8023971C. Now that the symbols are loaded, it is possible to determine the device driver that caused the failure.

Recall that the column labeled `BASE` contains the load addresses of each driver in the system. The entries are sorted by address. This makes it an easy matter to place the failing address between two drivers. In this case, the failing address of 0x8023971C falls after the load address of *extmirr.sys* (which is loaded at 0x80236000) and before the starting address of the next driver in the list, *ntfs.sysS* (which is loaded at 80240000). The address belongs to *extmirr.sys*.

On the surface, it looks as though the *extmirr.sys* driver attempted to read either from a bad address or from paged memory while at an elevated IRQL. Did the *extmirr.sys* driver cause the problem? Or was it acting on an invalid pointer that was passed to it by another driver? Either situation would cause the failure.

What is required at this point is more examination. Looking at the stack should show whether the faulting address, shown in bug check parameter 1 as 0x01000006 (again, referring to the bug check parameter description in Appendix B), is being passed as an argument to the *extmirr.sys* driver. If it is being passed into *extmirr.sys*, the focus should shift to the calling driver. If it isn't, the focus should probably remain on the *extmirr.sys* device driver.

Given a linker map file for the *extmirr.sys*, the function within the *extmirr.sys* driver that caused the failure can be determined. To use the map file, subtract the base address of the driver from the failing address. The result is the offset into the driver. In this example, the base address of *extmirr.sys* is 0x80236000, and the failing address is 0x8023971C. This gives us an offset into the *extmirr.sys* driver of 0z3713. Given this offset, the map file should indicate the function within the driver that is failing. Unfortunately, in this example, we do not have a map file for this driver. Regardless, the stack trace later in the *dumpexam* output should yield the same information.

The information contained within the bug check data, coupled with the information contained in the loaded driver list, has provided very good clues as to the culprit, if not the cause of the failure. To further isolate the problem, the analysis must continue.

### LOCK RESOURCES

The kernel debugging extension `!locks` is executed against the crash dump file. In this example, the output is minimal and not useful to diagnosing the problem:

```
*****************************************************************
** !locks -p -v -d
****************************************************************
**** Dump Resource Performance Data ****
0012fec8: No resource performance data available
```

The expected output and the format of this command are discussed in Chapter 5. The command is also well documented in the Windows 2000 DDK.

### MEMORY USAGE STATISTICS

General statistics concerning memory usage within the failed system are provided by the `!memusage` debugger extension. The output from this dump is as follows:

```
*****************************************************************
** !memusage
*****************************************************************
Zeroed:    1106 (  4424 kb)
               Free:        0 (      0 kb)
            Standby: 132262 (529048 kb)
           Modified:     595 (  2380 kb)
    ModifiedNoWrite:       0 (      0 kb)
       Active/Valid: 128180 (512720 kb)
         Transition:       0 (      0 kb)
            Unknown:       0 (      0 kb)
              TOTAL: 262143 (1048572 kb)
```

There is nothing obvious in the output from this command. There is a relatively normal amount of memory being used in a 1-Gbyte system.

Following the memory usage summary comes a more detailed view of memory allocations. It is provided courtesy of the !vm debugger extension command. The output from this example dump is as follows:

```
*****************************************************************
** !vm
*****************************************************************
*** Virtual Memory Usage ***
      Physical Memory:    261996    (1047984 Kb)
      Available Pages:    133368    (533472 Kb)
      Modified Pages:        595    (   2380 Kb)
      NonPagedPool Usage:  2153    (   8612 Kb)
      PagedPool 0 Usage:   1437    (   5748 Kb)
      PagedPool 1 Usage:    672    (   2688 Kb)
      PagedPool 2 Usage:    711    (   2844 Kb)
      PagedPool 3 Usage:    683    (   2732 Kb)
      PagedPool 4 Usage:    720    (   2880 Kb)
      PagedPool Usage:     4223    ( 16892 Kb)
      Shared Commit:        400    (   1600 Kb)
      Shared Process:      2562    ( 10248 Kb)
      Total Private:     199105    (796420 Kb)

            ORACLE73.EXE       71710 (286840 Kb)
            ORACLE73.EXE       56936 (227744 Kb)
            ORACLE73.EXE       55176 (220704 Kb)
            NCRMasterMinder     1848 (   7392 Kb)
            TAPEENG.EXE         1005 (   4020 Kb)
            RDS.EXE              665 (   2660 Kb)
            TNSLSNR.EXE          550 (   2200 Kb)
            TNSLSNR.EXE          543 (   2172 Kb)
            TNSLSNR.EXE          540 (   2160 Kb)
            lcd.exe              483 (   1932 Kb)
            SPOOLSS.EXE          461 (   1844 Kb)
            eismservice.exe      406 (   1624 Kb)
            lksvc.exe            399 (   1596 Kb)
            lkresmon.exe         397 (   1588 Kb)
            csrss.exe            386 (   1544 Kb)
            ASDscSvc.exe         369 (   1476 Kb)
            LcmLcdInt.exe        367 (   1468 Kb)
            DBENG.EXE            321 (   1284 Kb)
            SERVICES.EXE         313 (   1252 Kb)
            dbabrd.exe           306 (   1224 Kb)
            LSASS.EXE            277 (   1108 Kb)
            SOCKCA.exe           276 (   1104 Kb)
            MSGENG.EXE           271 (   1084 Kb)
            LKCMServer.exe       267 (   1068 Kb)
```

```
        JOBENG.EXE           266 (   1064 Kb)
        TTYCA.exe            260 (   1040 Kb)
        DISKCA.exe           257 (   1028 Kb)
        lcm.exe              251 (   1004 Kb)
        WINLOGON.EXE         246 (    984 Kb)
        SNMP.EXE             219 (    876 Kb)
        RPCSS.EXE            209 (    836 Kb)
        TAPISRV.EXE          206 (    824 Kb)
        RASMAN.EXE           197 (    788 Kb)
        EXPLORER.EXE         196 (    784 Kb)
        ExtMirrSvc.exe       169 (    676 Kb)
        RASSRV.EXE           162 (    648 Kb)
        Interactive.exe      146 (    584 Kb)
        LLSSRV.EXE           134 (    536 Kb)
        LOCATOR.EXE          125 (    500 Kb)
        sh.exe               123 (    492 Kb)
        sh.exe               122 (    488 Kb)
        sh.exe               120 (    480 Kb)
        sh.exe               120 (    480 Kb)
        sh.exe               119 (    476 Kb)
        sh.exe               118 (    472 Kb)
        GAMEVENT.EXE         112 (    448 Kb)
        smpmgrsr.exe         104 (    416 Kb)
        GAMSERV.EXE           99 (    396 Kb)
        STRTDB73.EXE          94 (    376 Kb)
        STRTDB73.EXE          94 (    376 Kb)
        STRTDB73.EXE          94 (    376 Kb)
        dbasvr.exe            67 (    268 Kb)
        GAMSCM.EXE            58 (    232 Kb)
        sc.exe                44 (    176 Kb)
        smss.exe              41 (    164 Kb)
        GAMEVLOG.EXE          36 (    144 Kb)
        sh.exe                36 (    144 Kb)
        sh.exe                36 (    144 Kb)
        sh.exe                36 (    144 Kb)
        sh.exe                36 (    144 Kb)
        sh.exe                36 (    144 Kb)
        sh.exe                36 (    144 Kb)
        System                 9 (     36 Kb)

PagedPool Commit:     4223     ( 16892 Kb)
Driver Commit:         412     (  1648 Kb)
Committed pages:    207128     (828512 Kb)
Commit limit:       512028     (2048112 Kb)
```

Examining the output of this command does not show any allocation abuses from the running processes. The big memory consumers seem to be Oracle and NCR Master Minder. Given the nature of each of these applications, this does not seem out of line. There are no obvious clues here for this dump.

Had the memory statistics indicated extremely low amounts of free paged or nonpaged pool memory, you might need to worry about how the various device drivers are handling failures from the allocation requests. These are error paths that are not normally well tested as a part of device driver development (although this is changing—see the description of the driver verifier in Chapter 11).

### ERROR LOG

The system error log is then dumped. In this case, there are no entries:

```
****************************************************************
** !errlog
****************************************************************
*
errorlog is empty
```

### PROCESS AND THREAD INFORMATION

Following the error log information, variations on the `!process` command are run. First, a summary list of all of the currently running processes is displayed (the output here is edited for brevity):

```
****************************************************************
** !process 0 0
****************************************************************
**** NT ACTIVE PROCESS DUMP ****
PROCESS 80f96820  Cid: 0002    Peb: 00000000  ParentCid: 0000
    DirBase: 00030000  ObjectTable: 80fbfae8  TableSize: 814.
    Image: System

… [process list dramatically shortened]…

PROCESS 808fc920  Cid: 01f1    Peb: 7ffdf000  ParentCid: 0166
    DirBase: 3b1ce000  ObjectTable: 808f9828  TableSize:  14.
    Image: sh.exe
```

This information will not point to any failure directly. It tells about the load of the system, the locations of each process, and what was running at the time of the failure.

Drilling down deeper, the `!process 0 7` command is run. This provides complete detail about every process in the system. It lists the process information, along with detail on each process's threads and the stack owned by each thread (see Chapter 5 for a complete description of these commands and their output). For clarity, the output has been truncated to a single process:

```
****************************************************************
** !process 0 7
****************************************************************
*
**** NT ACTIVE PROCESS DUMP ****
PROCESS 80f96820  Cid: 0002    Peb: 00000000  ParentCid: 0000
    DirBase: 00030000  ObjectTable: 80fbfae8  TableSize: 814.
    Image: System
    VadRoot 80f80b88 Clone 0 Private 5. Modified 715367. Locked 0.
    80F969DC MutantState Signalled OwningThread 0
    Token                             e1002a70
    ElapsedTime                       15:11:10.0281
    UserTime                          0:00:00.0000
    KernelTime                        1:18:31.0562
    QuotaPoolUsage[PagedPool]         0
    QuotaPoolUsage[NonPagedPool]      0
    Working Set Sizes (now,min,max)  (50, 50, 345) (200KB, 200KB, 1380KB)
    PeakWorkingSetSize                130
    VirtualSize                       1 Mb
```

```
    PeakVirtualSize                      1 Mb
    PageFaultCount                       12563
    MemoryPriority                       BACKGROUND
    BasePriority                         8
    CommitCharge                         9

        THREAD 80f965c0  Cid 2.1  Teb: 00000000  Win32Thread: 00000000 WAIT:
(WrFreePage) KernelMode Non-Alertable
            801517b0  SynchronizationEvent
        Not impersonating
        Owning Process 80f96820
        WaitTime (seconds)        53952281
        Context Switch Count      2507507
        UserTime                    0:00:00.0000
        KernelTime                  1:03:15.0453
        Start Address Phase1Initialization (0x801c77cc)
        Stack Init f2014000 Current f2013cf8 Base f2014000 Limit f2011000 Call 0
        Priority 0 BasePriority 0 PriorityDecrement 0 DecrementCount 0

        ChildEBP RetAddr  Args to Child
        f2013d10 80118260 c0502000 000394c0 00000000 KiSwapThread+0x1b1
        f2013d34 8012d178 801517b0 00000008 00000000 KeWaitForSingleObject+0x1b8
        f2013d68 801c8002 00000000 00000000 00000000 MmZeroPageThread+0x48
        f2013f4c 80138824 80087000 00000000 00000000 Phase1Initialization+0x836
        f2013f7c 8014427e 801c77cc 80087000 00000000 PspSystemThreadStartup+0x54
        00000000 00000000 00000000 00000000 00000000 KiThreadStartup+0x16
```

This type of output is useful in cases where the computer might be in deadlock. Given the output of this command, as was discussed in Chapter 6, you can see the synchronization event that every thread in the system is waiting on. The stacks for threads are also displayed.

### PER-PROCESSOR INFORMATION

After the global information is collected, the state of each processor is queried. A register dump, stack trace, and the current process and thread are all displayed. If the problem hasn't shown up in the global information described above, there may be further clues in this output.

For the sake of brevity, the *dumpexam* output for this section is limited in this example to a single CPU. Recall from the dump header that the failing machine in this example has four processors. The same sequence of commands described here was run on all four processors. The first piece of information presented is a dump of the processor's current register set:

```
****************************************************************
** Register Dump For Processor #0
****************************************************************
*
eax=00000000 ebx=f0d12c58 ecx=00000002 edx=00000000 esi=00000020 edi=00000020
eip=801407a3 esp=f0d12c44 ebp=f0d12c98 iopl=0         nv up di pl nz na pe nc
cs=0008  ss=0010  ds=0023  es=0023  fs=0030  gs=0000             efl=00000202
cr0=8001003b cr2=00000020 cr3=29bf9000 dr0=00000000 dr1=00000000 dr2=00000000
dr3=00000000 dr6=ffff0ff0 dr7=00000400 cr4=000000d1
gdtr=80036000   gdtl=03ff idtr=80036400   idtl=07ff tr=0028  ldtr=0000
```

In the case of the bug check that is being tracked, the register information does not provide much useful information. If the investigation required using the disassembly information provided in the next section, the register information may be of value. It may also be of value if the dump being examined is from a hung system, forced to halt with a dump switch card.

Following the register display, the *dumpexam* utility provides a modified stack trace on the current processor. It prints the first couple of elements in the stack, then provides a disassembly of the return address for the topmost element on the stack. This is illustrated as follows:

```
****************************************************************
** Stack Trace
****************************************************************
*
ChildEBP RetAddr  Args to Child
f0d12c90 8014077d ffffffff b593a76c 000007aa CommonDispatchException+0x23 (FPO:
[0,0,0])
f0d12c98 b593a76c 000007aa f0d12dd8 00000246 KiUnexpectedInterruptTail+0x1ee

    80140753: FF 15 F4 54 14 80  call        dword ptr
[KiUnexpectedInterruptTail+1C6h]
    80140759: E9 0E FC FF FF     jmp         KiUnexpectedInterruptTail+1CBh
    8014075E: 33 C9              xor         ecx,ecx
    80140760: E8 1B 00 00 00     call        KiUnexpectedInterruptTail+1D2h
    80140765: 33 D2              xor         edx,edx
    80140767: B9 01 00 00 00     mov         ecx,offset
KiUnexpectedInterruptTail+1D9h
    8014076C: E8 0F 00 00 00     call        KiUnexpectedInterruptTail+1DEh
    80140771: 33 D2              xor         edx,edx
    80140773: B9 02 00 00 00     mov         ecx,offset
KiUnexpectedInterruptTail+1E5h
    80140778: E8 03 00 00 00     call        KiUnexpectedInterruptTail+1EAh
    8014077D: 2E 8B C0           mov         eax,eax
    80140780: 83 EC 50           sub         esp,50h
    80140783: 89 04 24           mov         dword ptr [esp],eax
    80140786: 33 C0              xor         eax,eax
    80140788: 89 44 24 04        mov         dword ptr [esp+4],eax
    8014078C: 89 44 24 08        mov         dword ptr [esp+8],eax
    80140790: 89 5C 24 0C        mov         dword ptr [esp+0Ch],ebx
    80140794: 89 4C 24 10        mov         dword ptr [esp+10h],ecx
    80140798: 83 F9 00           cmp         ecx,0
    8014079B: 74 0C              je          CommonDispatchException+29h
    8014079D: 8D 5C 24 14        lea         ebx,dword ptr [esp+14h]
    801407A1: 89 13              mov         dword ptr [ebx],edx
--->801407A3: 89 73 04           mov         dword ptr [ebx+4],esi
    801407A6: 89 7B 08           mov         dword ptr [ebx+8],edi
    801407A9: 8B CC              mov         ecx,esp
    801407AB: F7 45 70 00 00 02  test        dword ptr [ebp+70h],offset
CommonDispatchException+2Eh
              00
    801407B2: 74 07              je          CommonDispatchException+3Bh
    801407B4: B8 FF FF 00 00     mov         eax,offset
```

The first thing that you should notice is that the address pointer for the return address of the topmost element of the stack is marked in the disassembly with a "---->" notation. The second thing that you should notice is that the topmost elements on the stack are the routines that are called to handle the exception raised by the failure. This is very often the case—if a bug check occurred, the then-topmost two or three routines on the stack are either the bug check itself or the exception routines that called it. This part of the output is of dubious value in all but dump-switch-generated crash dumps.

Now that the register display, stack trace, and disassembly have been executed and provided no clues to the bug check, it is time for *dumpexam* to look at the currently active process and thread. The currently executing process is displayed first:

```
****************************************************************
** !process
****************************************************************
*
PROCESS 80bb5ce0  Cid: 009c    Peb: 7ffdf000  ParentCid: 002d
    DirBase: 07450000  ObjectTable: 80bf3288  TableSize:  46.
    Image: ExtMirrSvc.exe
    VadRoot 80bb5288 Clone 0 Private 149. Modified 32721. Locked 0.
    80BB5E9C MutantState Signalled OwningThread 0
    Token                             e1677cb0
    ElapsedTime                       18:08:13.0609
    UserTime                          0:00:00.0078
    KernelTime                        0:55:01.0359
    QuotaPoolUsage[PagedPool]         12807
    QuotaPoolUsage[NonPagedPool]      34836
    Working Set Sizes (now,min,max)  (60, 50, 345) (240KB, 200KB, 1380KB)
    PeakWorkingSetSize                444
    VirtualSize                       25 Mb
    PeakVirtualSize                   27 Mb
    PageFaultCount                    71480
    MemoryPriority                    BACKGROUND
    BasePriority                      8
    CommitCharge                      169

  THREAD 80bb5a00  Cid 9c.9b  Teb: 7ffde000  Win32Thread: e16a0ea8 WAIT:
(Executive) UserMode Non-Alertable
            80bb43a4  NotificationEvent

        THREAD 80bb3ba0  Cid 9c.9e  Teb: 7ffdd000  Win32Thread: 00000000 WAIT:
(UserRequest) UserMode Non-Alertable
            80bb3160  NotificationEvent

        THREAD 80bb1020  Cid 9c.a0  Teb: 7ffdb000  Win32Thread: 00000000 WAIT:
(UserRequest) UserMode Non-Alertable
            80aadcc4  NotificationEvent

        THREAD 80bb1dc0  Cid 9c.a1  Teb: 7ffda000  Win32Thread: 00000000 WAIT:
(UserRequest) UserMode Non-Alertable
            80bf0424  NotificationEvent

        THREAD 80bb1b60  Cid 9c.a4  Teb: 7ffdc000  Win32Thread: 00000000 WAIT:
(Executive) UserMode Non-Alertable
            80bb3444  NotificationEvent

        THREAD 809d1dc0  Cid 9c.141  Teb: 00000000  Win32Thread: 00000000
RUNNING
```

Examining the currently executing process yields a number of things that are interesting. First, notice the name of the currently running process. It's on the line that begins with the label `Image:` (refer to Chapter 5 for a complete description of how to read this output). The process name is *ExtMirrSvc.exe*. Recall that the name of the suspect device driver from the investigation above in this example is *ExtMirr.sys*—is this a coincidence? Or are they related? Without additional information, one is forced to continue with the analysis. However, this seems like a promising lead.

Another item of interest is the state of the process's threads. You can see that the process owns six threads, all of which are sleeping on an event except one. The currently executing thread is detailed with *dumpexam*'s next item:

```
****************************************************************
** !thread
****************************************************************
*
THREAD 809d1dc0  Cid 9c.141  Teb: 00000000  Win32Thread: 00000000 RUNNING
Not impersonating
Owning Process 80bb5ce0
WaitTime (seconds)       53952466
Context Switch Count     19038639
UserTime                   0:00:00.0000
KernelTime                 0:55:00.0765
Start Address 0x80238738
Stack Init f1730000 Current f172f71c Base f1730000 Limit f172d000 Call 0
Priority 9 BasePriority 8 PriorityDecrement 0 DecrementCount 0

ChildEBP RetAddr  Args to Child
f0d12c90 8014077d ffffffff b593a76c 000007aa CommonDispatchException+0x23
f0d12c98 b593a76c 000007aa f0d12dd8 00000246 KiUnexpectedInterruptTail+0x1ee
f172fcdc 80239704 00000001 00310033 00000031 KiTrap0E+0x25c
f172fef8 802387cf 80d77c48 f172ff1c 00000000 ExtMirrQueryDevice+0x30
c0000008 00000000 00000000 00000000 00000000 IoCallDriver+0x2df
00000000 00000000 00000000 00000000 00000000 +0x25c
```

The stack on the currently executing thread seems to be the culprit. Looking at the stack, you will note that the `ExtMirrQueryDevice` function in the *ExtMirr.sys* device driver took an exception that ultimately triggered the bug check. The failing address does not seem to be passed into the function, although if the function has more than three arguments, it may not appear on the stack trace. Even so, this does not mean that the problem is absolutely the fault of the *ExtMirr.sys* device driver, but the evidence looks fairly daunting. The device driver was doing work on behalf of the *ExtMirrSvc.exe* service. This seems to be enough information to contact the vendor of this device driver.

Determining the origin of the failure within the device driver requires more detective work than is available with the *dumpchk* utility. To probe deeper, you must have proper symbols to the driver and an understanding of what the driver is doing. Often, the best that can be hoped for is that there is enough information available to allow the vendor to isolate and find a fix.

In this example, which was taken from a real-world problem, the development team for the *ExtMirr.sys* driver isolated the failure and provided a hot-fix within a few days. The problem isolation was provided with only the output of the *dumpchk* utility. There was never a need to fire up the debugger.

**Whose Device Driver Is It?**

There will be cases where you do not know the vendor of the device driver, or it isn't intuitively obvious. The first step in isolating the owner of a suspect device driver is determining whether the driver is a part of the NT distribution. If it is, the appropriate path is through Microsoft Support Channels. Failing that, there may be information embedded within the device driver itself. Most of the current crop of development tools provide for embedding resource information into the file.

You can access the version resource information by opening an exploring window in the directory that contains the questionable device driver. Highlight the file name of the device driver, then depress the right mouse button. From the pop-up menu, choose Properties. On the resulting dialog, select the Version tab. The elements associated with the version are enumerated at the bottom of the box. The elements may include the company name, copyright information, etc. All of this can be used to identify the source of the driver file.

## Summary

This chapter discussed memory dumps. It showed that a dump file is a snapshot of a system at the time of a failure. The chapter talked about what's in this dump file and how to validate it. There was discussion on the various dump validation tools. The reader should walk away from the chapter with a good understanding of what dump files are and how they are to be used effectively.

E I G H T

# Remote Debugging

**CHAPTER OBJECTIVES**

- What Is Remote Debugging?
- Debugging over a Modem
- Debugging across a Network

*Okay, so we can debug a machine that's directly connected to ours. This is useful in a development environment. But what about in a support environment where the troubled machine may be thousands of miles away? The answer is remote debugging. Microsoft provides some support of this with WinDbg and KD. This chapter will describe the hows and whys of remote debugging.*

*This chapter will discuss the limitations in a remote debugging environment and the strengths it provides. You will walk away with an understanding of remote kernel debugging in a Windows 2000 environment. The chapter will discuss both on-line and crash dump debugging from a remote location.*

# What Is Remote Debugging?

Remote debugging is an extension of the local debugging model. The simple NULL-modem serial connection that was discussed in Chapter 2 is replaced with a real modem connection to a remote location. In another case, the traditional host machine that is connected by a NULL-modem cable turns instead into a proxy computer, simply relaying commands from a computer elsewhere on the computer network.

Remote debugging is critical in diagnosing failures that occur in remote locations. With main memory sizes growing in excess of 4 Gbytes, crash dump file sizes follow suit. It becomes unmanageable to move these dump files around. With stand-alone data centers connected over ever-cheaper and ever-faster communication links, it becomes the norm to not have on-site debugging expertise. In all of these instances, remote debugging is key.

Setting up a debugging session either over either a modem (the simplest case) or across a machine acting as a proxy for the kernel debugger is not a hard task. It is, however, ridden by details that are easy to overlook. The following sections explain all that is involved in setting up these remote debugging sessions.

The steps in configuring for remote debugging are remarkably similar to those steps taken for local debugging. The host and target are prepared as described in Chapter 2 for local debugging. In a modem debugging scenario, the modems must be configured on each side. The target's modem must have auto-answer enabled, so that it knows to answer the phone when the host calls. In network debugging, a new component is introduced—that of the remote shell.

Once the remote debugging session is connected, the rules remain the same as when performing local debugging tasks. All of the commands that you are used to entering for local debugging are still valid in a remote environment. The data may move a little slower than local debugging would provide, especially if the debugging is occurring over a dialup modem line. Over a network, the NULL-modem cable becomes the bottleneck, and you will not notice any difference from a local debugging session.

# Debugging over a Modem

Debugging over a modem connection is the easiest case of remote debugging. It is simply the replacement of the NULL-modem cable with a properly configured modem. The model of host/target debugging assumed throughout this book so far holds. Figure 8-1 demonstrates this relationship.

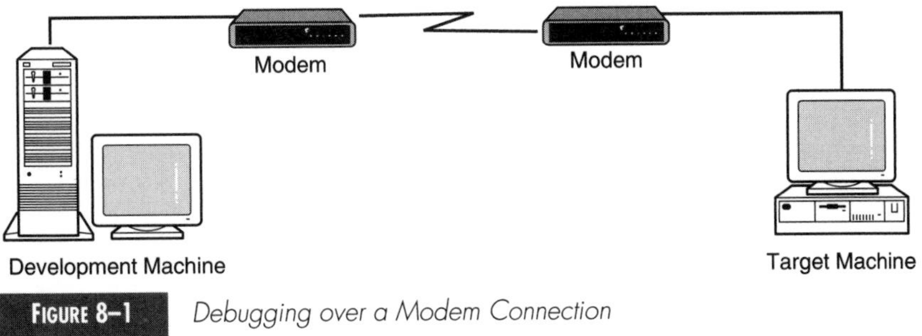


FIGURE 8–1 *Debugging over a Modem Connection*

To do kernel debugging over a modem connection, the modems must be properly configured. This is a different process on the host than on the target machine. The target machine, for example, must be configured to answer automatically when the phone line rings. The host must dial out on the modem, then let the debugger have control of the serial connection (the debugger has no inherent support for dialing the phone). These tasks are all explained in this section.

## Preparing the Target Modem

To perform any sort of kernel mode debugging on a target machine, that machine must first be configured for kernel debugging. Chapter 2 in this book covers all of the details of that configuration. Ensure that it is complete before attempting to debug remotely. Configure for kernel debugging on an open serial port or to a serial port already configured with a modem attached. It doesn't matter which, so long as any attached modem is configured to the parameters presented in this section.

The first step to preparing any machine for remote modem debugging is the setup of the modem. On the target side, there are two basic choices. You can configure the modem directly on the target machine. This requires that the target machine actually be up and running—something that may not be the case if you are troubleshooting stop screens. You can also configure the modem on another computer and move it to the target machine. It's important to note that the operating system does not need to have the modem configured as it would if you were actually using the modem device from within Windows—after all, we're simply using this as an extension of the serial port.

The requirements for using a modem with KD or WinDbg are as follows:

- All hardware compression must be disabled.
- Error detection must be disabled.
- Flow control must be turned off.
- Auto-answer should be enabled.

The reason for disabling all of the flow control, compression, and error detection is that the host debuggers are expecting a pure serial stream of binary data. If these features were left on, they could be inadvertently triggered by the data flowing across the connection. The Microsoft documentation (in the form of a knowledge base article) suggests running the modem at 9600 bps. It works at higher rates, but choose one that doesn't require compression to achieve. I suggest 19200 bps.

To configure the target modem, connect it to a machine with an open serial port. This can be the actual target machine, if that computer is up and available. Start HyperTerminal (from the Windows Start menu, it is on the Accessories/Communication submenu). If you do not have this option installed, insert your Windows 2000 installation CD and load it.

The following commands are used to configure a Hayes-compatible modem for proper operation. Enter them in sequence:

```
ATE1     ← Allows you to see what you type
AT&F     ← Restore the factory defaults to the modem
AT&H0    ← Disable flow control when transmitting data
AT&I0    ← Disable flow control when receiving data
AT&K0    ← Disable data compression when exchanging data
AT&M0    ← Disable error control
ATS0=1   ← Enable the auto-answer feature on the modem
AT&D0    ← Disable the reset of the modem on lost DTR
AT&W     ← Write the newly configured parameters to NVRAM
```

The command `AT&D0` is used to tell the modem not to reset the connection when it loses the Data Terminal Ready signal on the cable to the target computer. This signal may be erroneously and inadvertently lost while debugging. You don't want it interfering in the debugging session.

The final command, `AT&W`, tells the modem to store the configuration in nonvolatile memory (NVRAM). This allows the configuration to remain, even in the case of power loss to the modem. It allows you to configure the modem on one machine, unplug it, and move it to the target machine.

Once the newly configured modem is connected to the same serial port that was specified in the *boot.ini* file for kernel debugging and kernel debugging is enabled on the target machine, the system is ready to be debugged. Once the host is set up, debugging can commence.

## Connecting the Host Debugger

Operating WinDbg or KD for remote modem debugging is the same as with local debugging. The same advice given throughout this book for local debugging is valid for remote debugging sessions across a modem line. Remote debugging necessitates that a modem be attached to the host computer. This modem should be connected to the target machine before starting the debugger. The debugger should also be configured to perform kernel debugging across the serial port that the modem is connected to, at the same speed for which the target is configured to talk to its modem.

To configure a modem on the host debugging system, use the normal procedures for adding a modem in a Windows 2000 environment. Selecting the Phone/Modem Options icon in the system control panel brings up the modem configuration wizard. Follow the prompts to configure the modem appropriately for your environment.

There are no restrictions imposed on the host configuration, as there are on the target side. When the host and target modems negotiate, the connection will be established with the more restrictive settings of the modem on the target computer.

To connect to the target system, you must enter into a terminal program and have the modem dial the phone number for the line to which the target modem is connected. You can use the HyperTerminal program supplied with Windows to do this, or your favorite terminal emulation program can be used. The important point is that, when exiting from the terminal emulation program, you should not hang up the modem. If you are prompted to hang up, choose "No."

You must exit out of the terminal emulation program before you can use the debugger. If you open the debugger first or attempt to open the debugger while the terminal emulation program is open, this process will not work correctly. Only one process can have the serial port active at a time. The proper order is to dial the phone with the terminal emulation program, exit that program, then start the debugger.

## Debugging over a Network (or RAS) Link

Debugging over a computer network or RAS (Microsoft's remote access services) connection is a useful method to perform remote debugging. This allows debugging machines in a lab environment from a desktop. It also allows debugging over the Internet. Any place that a network connection can be established, so can a debugging session. Remote debugging can be achieved without the work required to debug across a normal modem connection.

The processes for debugging over a network with KD and WinDbg are remarkably similar. In each case, the host machine's debugger functionality is proxied to a remote computer, where the actual debugger interface will be displayed and debugging will occur. The communication between the host machine and the remote machine occurs across named pipes. This scenario is illustrated in Figure 8-2.

An important point to note when debugging across a network is that the actual debugger still lives on the host machine. It is only the interface to the debugger that is being sent to the remote machine. This means that any sym-

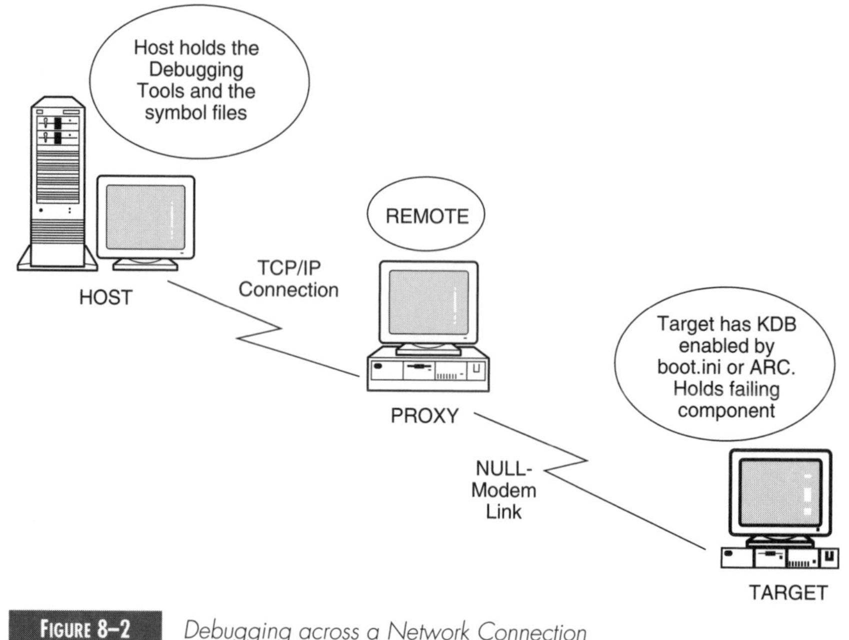


FIGURE 8–2 *Debugging across a Network Connection*

bol configuration, workspace files, log files, etc., will all remain on the host system, not on the remote system. It may be an obvious point, but it's one that is easily overlooked in practice.

Before setting up a remote pipe server for remote debugging, you must decide on the pipe name that you want to use. I use *WDBPIPE*. The only restriction on the name you choose is that it must not be *STOP*—that is a keyword used by WinDbg to terminate the remote session. The name must also be unique. If one name doesn't work, try another.

The flows of execution for both KD and WinDbg are very similar. A named pipe server is started on the host machine, while the remote client interacts with it across a named pipe via the `remote` command. What is different between the two debuggers is the basic setup and operation of the various pieces. The steps to set up a remote debugging scenario are executed as follows:

1. The target machine must be configured for debugging.
2. The host machine must be connected to the target machine via a NULL-modem cable.
3. The debugger must be started and configured for kernel debugging.
4. A named pipe server must be created to allow the debugger to be operated remotely.
5. The user runs the appropriate *remote.exe* on the remote system to operate the debugger.

**The `remote` Command**

Using the debuggers across a network requires the use of the `remote` utility. `remote` provides command-line output of data flowing across a named pipe. It opens a new Windows command window for the input/output of the session. This utility does not ship as a standard part of Windows 2000, but rather as a component within the support tools directory on the Windows 2000 distribution CD. It is also available as a part of the Windows 2000 Resource kit.

To start a server connection on the named pipe, `remote` is started with the `/S` option. The arguments with the server are:

**`/F`** ***`<foreground color>`***—sets the foreground color of the window
**`/B`** ***`<background color>`***—sets the background color of the window
**`/U`** ***`<username or groupname>`***—provides credentials to the named pipe server, if needed
**`/V`**—allows this session to be visible to queries with the `/Q` option
**`/-V`**—hides this session from queries

A client connection is started with the `/C` option. The options on a client are:

**`/L`** ***`<number of lines>`***—buffers the specified number of lines of traffic
**`/F`** ***`<foreground color>`***—sets the foreground color of the window
**`/B`** ***`<background color>`***—sets the background color of the window

The first three steps are well explained in Chapter 2 of this book and will not be repeated here. Instead, the focus will be on the process to actually access the debugger remotely. Basic configuration steps of the debugger itself are unchanged.

## Remote WinDbg

Running WinDbg across a network link is possible, but it sacrifices a great deal of the functionality inherent in the debugger. The only part of WinDbg that is truly available across a network link is the command window. This is enough in most cases but can severely limit the ability to do source-level debugging. It also forces the operator of the debugger to sacrifice the graphical user interface that makes WinDbg so easy to use. Given these restrictions, it is still better to have the option of remote debugging than not to have the option.

Once WinDbg is running, you must cause it to create a named pipe server. This is done by entering the following command in the WinDbg command window on the host machine:

```
> remote pipename
```

In this command, replace the `pipename` argument with the name of the pipe that you've chosen to communicate across. Remember, this should be a unique name. If there is a conflict, choose another name. At this point, you have created a named pipe server. You will see a Windows command window open that echoes what is being done on the remote session.

To use the debugger on the remote machine, you must use the `remote` command to connect to the established named pipe server. Remote is a console application, which means that it must be executed from a command window. Once you have a command window open on the remote machine, enter the following command at the command prompt:

```
remote /c hostname pipename
```

With this command, you will replace the `hostname` argument with the name of the machine that is hosting the debugger. You will also replace `pipename` with the name of the pipe chosen when you enabled the named pipe server from within WinDbg. At this point, the remote machine can execute commands as though they were being typed directly into the WinDbg command window. There are no restrictions. Again, you will not see the familiar WinDbg user interface. Instead, you will see just what would be displayed on the WinDbg command window.

To end the session, execute the following command in the remote window:

```
> @K
```

This will cause the named pipe server to shut down, and the session will be terminated.

**The Documentation Is Wrong!**

**The WinDbg documentation and knowledge base articles will tell you that the proper way to terminate a remote session from within WinDbg is to issue the `remote stop` command. This does not work and results in an error message being displayed. Terminate the named pipe session with the `@K` command.**

## Remote KD

Operating KD remotely over a network is remarkably similar to the operation of WinDbg. In each case, a named pipe server is created on the host machine. The difference is that WinDbg has built-in functionality for creating the named pipe server, whereas KD relies on the `remote` command on the host machine.

Recall that KD requires certain environment variables to set before it can be successfully run. Remote operation is no different. The `remote` command assumes that these variables are set for the proper operation of KD.

To cause KD to operate in the context of a named pipe server, the following command must be run:

```
>remote -v "i386kd -v -m" debug
```

At this point, KD is executing within the context of a named pipe server. When a named pipe client connects, it will be able to operate KD as though the user were on the host machine. The remote machine connects to this named pipe server with the `remote` command.

On the remote machine, the debugger can be connected with the following command:

```
remote /c hostname pipename
```

With this command, you will replace the `hostname` argument with the name of the machine that is hosting the debugger. You will also replace `pipename` with the name of the pipe chosen when you enabled the named pipe server on the host machine.

To end the session, execute the following command in the remote window:

```
> @K
```

This will cause the named pipe server to shut down, and the session will be terminated. To terminate the pipe connection without stopping the debugger (which will allow you to reconnect at some point), enter a **@Q** command.

### Remote Dump Analysis

Remote dump analysis is possible, using one of two methods. The drive containing the dump file can be mapped as a logical drive to the analysis machine, in which case normal analysis methods can be employed with no additional work. Additionally, a debugging session can be executed across the network, with the host connected to the dump file (instead of to a target machine). In either case, normal analysis techniques can be employed.

## Summary

This chapter has shown you how to perform remote debugging with the kernel debuggers. It has demonstrated that this is not a difficult feat to achieve. There are many details that must be paid attention to, and those have been explained. The concept of remote shell and debugging proxies has been introduced and explained. Remote debugging is a very useful function in a support environment. It is a task that can be achieved over both a modem line and a network link. It becomes an invaluable tool as support organizations become centralized and data centers spread out across the planet.

N I N E

# Debugger Extensions

**CHAPTER OBJECTIVES**

- What Is an Extension DLL?
- Using Debugger Extensions
- Writing a Debugger Extension

*A powerful but little used feature of the kernel debugger is the debugger extension. It's possible to write a dynamic link library (DLL) that the debugger will load to provide commands of the user's own devise. These extensions are not hard to write, and pointers are given to the appropriate documentation and samples provided by Microsoft.*

*This chapter develops a simple debugger extension to provide easier access into the kernel running on a target machine. You are shown how to control debugger extensions from within the debuggers—the helper functions provided by the toolkits. You should walk away with a basic understanding of how to develop your own debugger extension commands to solve debugging problems while developing device drivers.*

Debugger extensions are, simply stated, loadable DLLs that follow the protocol defined by Microsoft for talking to its debuggers. The kernel debugging commands that have been demonstrated throughout this book are a part of a loadable extension DLL. Microsoft provides excellent documentation on the construction and support routines used to build your own extensions.

Debugger extensions become useful and, in some cases, indispensable for the device driver developer. This class of user is one who performs rote functions in the debugger (such as always looking at the device extension of his or her driver after a blue screen), who has a need to examine data structures not defined as a part of Windows NT, or who simply needs to do something not explicitly provided for by the existing tools.

These extensions are usually tied to the specific version of the software with which they are defined to work. As an example, the kernel debugger extensions provided with each build of NT must be used with only that specific build of the operating system. Likewise, a debugger extension that has knowledge of a specific device driver's data structures (through a shared header file) or of a driver's symbols should be built when those items change.

## Using Debugger Extensions

The debuggers were designed from the ground up with support for extensions in mind. The Microsoft kernel development teams make extensive use of extensions to debug each of their components. As such, there is integrated support within both WinDbg and KD for managing the use of a debugger extension.

### Loading and Unloading Extensions

The debuggers support both explicit and implicit loading of debugger extensions. If the debugger can infer from the usage that a command is being executed that lives in an extension DLL that is not loaded, it will attempt to load that DLL.

#### IMPLICIT LOADING

There are two options for executing commands within an extension DLL. The first is by entering a command and letting the debugger resolve it to the appropriate, already loaded DLL. That method is discussed later in this chapter. The other method is to specify the DLL in which the command you want to execute resides. This implicitly forces the specified extension DLL to be loaded if it isn't already loaded.

The syntax for executing a command within an unloaded extension DLL is as follows:

```
!<DLL_NAME>.<COMMAND> <ARGUMENTS>
```

To execute commands that live in extension DLLs, you must always precede them with the "`!`" symbol (recall the more general case of kernel debugger extensions). There are some built-in commands that begin with this symbol, but those are all related to managing extension DLLs, as will be demonstrated.

The syntax then allows for the name of the DLL (without the .DLL file extension), a delimiting period ("`.`"), then a command within that extension. When the debugger parses this, it first attempts to locate the DLL in its list of loaded extensions (it allows up to 255 to be loaded simultaneously). If the extension is not loaded, the debugger searches its path for the DLL and attempts to load it.

Once the debugger is able to establish a linkage to the DLL, it searches the DLL for the command entered. It executes the command.

### EXPLICIT LOADING AND UNLOADING

Explicit loading of an extension DLL is almost trivial. There is a single command, `!load`, that causes a DLL to be loaded into the debugger. The argument that this command expects is one of two items:

1. The name of the DLL with no file extension or path, e.g.,
   **`!load`** *mydll*
2. A fully qualified path name, ending with the DLL, e.g.,
   **`!load`** *d:\testprog\mydll.DLL*

If the path is not explicitly qualified, the directory that the debugger was executed from will be searched for the extension DLL. In Windows 2000, the subdirectory corresponding to the build of the operating system will be searched as well.

To unload a debugger extension, the `!unload` command is used. There is no implicit unloading of a debugger extension.

### EXECUTING EXTENSION COMMANDS

Commands within debugger extensions are executed in the same manner as the kernel debugging extensions that have been dealt with throughout this book. They are preceded with the "`!`" symbol. These commands are always lowercase. There are some issues with the execution of these commands that you should be aware of.

If the command that you want to execute within an extension is not unique, there are only two ways to guarantee that the command entered will result in yours being used. You can explicitly name your extension when entering the command with the syntax described above, i.e., *dllname.command*. This removes all ambiguity.

Commands that are entered without specifying the extension name are resolved by first looking in the default DLL. If the command is not found in the default DLL, the debugger will scan the list of exported functions (commands) by each DLL *in the order in which they were loaded*. When the first occurrence of the command is found, it is executed. To minimize ambiguity, it is recommended that you prefix commands in your extension with a unique identifier.

The default extension for the debugger can be set. The command to do this is `!default`. Setting the default will force the debugger always to search this extension first to resolve any entered commands. The kernel debugger extension DLL (*kdextx86.dll* or *kdextalpha.dll*) is always the default until overridden.

# Writing a Debugger Extension

There is no magic involved in writing a debugger extension. It follows the same basic rules as any other DLL, with a very few caveats. Writing an extension DLL forces you into a basic structure that eases the task of integrating with the debugger. There are macros that wrap those functions that you want exported as commands; there are a few mandatory functions and some basic requirements on functionality that must be there.

Microsoft supplies you (as a part of the Device Driver Kit [DDK]) with a number of tools to assist in the development of extension DLLs. There are numerous *helper functions* that allow the extension DLL to probe the target machine. This frees you from having to understand debugger protocol, so that you can focus on solving the problem at hand. Microsoft also supplies a couple of well-written sample extension DLLs. I recommend that, before writing your own extension, you examine and leverage what you can from these samples.

## Requirements of a Debugger Extension

There is no defined structure of a debugger extension, but there are some basic requirements.

The first of these is that you must include the header file *wdbgexts.h* in your DLL. This header file is found in the *include* subdirectory in the Microsoft Windows 2000 Software Development Kit (SDK).

The next requirement is that all of the commands that you want to export must be defined in a *.def* file. This is a very simple file—just a list of exported functions. An example of this file can be found in the Microsoft DDK.

All functions in the DLL that you want to access from the debugger must be wrapped in a macro, `DECLARE_API()`.

The last of these requirements is that there are three functions that must be exported by the DLL: `WinDbgExtensionDllInit()`, `ExtensionAPIVersion()`, and `CheckVersion()`.

### WINDBGEXTENSIONDLLINIT()

This is the first function that is called by the debugger when the extension DLL is loaded. This function is passed an API structure that provides callbacks to functions that are useful from within the DLL (such as printing to the command window). Use these callback pointers to employ the functionality provided by the debugger. This structure is similar to the following (consult the *wdbgexts.h* that you are building against for the latest version):

```
struct  {
    DWORD nSize;
    PNTKD_OUTPUT_ROUTINE lpOutputRoutine;
    PNTKD_GET_EXPRESSION lpGetExpressionRoutine;
    PNTKD_GET_SYMBOL lpGetSymbolRoutine;
    PNTKD_DISASM lpDisasmRoutine;
    PNTKD_CHECK_CONTROL_C lpCheckControlCRoutine;
    PNTKD_READ_VIRTUAL_MEMORY lpReadVirtualMemRoutine;
    PNTKD_WRITE_VIRTUAL_MEMORY lpWriteVirtualMemRoutine;
    PNTKD_READ_PHYSICAL_MEMORY lpReadPhysicalMemRoutine;
    PNTKD_WRITE_PHYSICAL_MEMORY lpWritePhysicalMemRoutine;
} NTKD_EXTENSION_APIS
```

Also passed into the `WinDbgExtensionDllInit()` function are variables indicating the major and minor numbers of the machine being debugged. The major number tells you whether the target machine is a checked or a free build (by returning 0x0c or 0x0f, respectively). The minor number provides the build number.

### EXTENSIONAPIVERSION()

WinDbg calls this function to validate the version of your extensions. The debugger expects this function to return a pointer to an API_VERSION structure. This structure is defined as:

```
struct {
      USHORT MajorVersion;
      USHORT MinorVersion;
      USHORT Revision;
      USHORT Reserved;
} API_VERSION
```

Your extension must match the version of WinDbg for which it was built.

**CHECKVERSION()**

This is an optional function that the extension DLL can provide to allow the debugger to validate the extension against the version of the target system. Even if you provide the function, you can override its use with the `!noversion` command in WinDbg.

### DECLARING YOUR COMMANDS IN THE DLL

There are some functions within the extension DLL that you will want exported as commands that you can enter from within the debugger. There are also functions within the DLL that are there just for the use by the other functions within the DLL. The functions that are for internal DLL use only have no special requirements outside of the normal restrictions present in a DLL environment.

When writing functions that are exported as commands, there is the minor restriction that declaration of the function be wrapped within a macro, supplied as a part of *windbgext.h*. This macro is called *DECLARE_API*. It is used as follows:

```
DECLARE_API( function1 )
{
… normal function C code here
}
```

The macro wraps a C++ style try/except mechanism around the function. This keeps an extension DLL from corrupting a debugging session or from causing the debugger to fail with an exception. Most exceptions, such as bad pointer references, are trapped within this structure. When this occurs, a message is displayed on the debugger command window.

## Helper Functions

There are many helper functions provided by the DDK that allow the debugger extension to access the hosting debugger's functionality for its own use. These functions also allow for accessing the target machine through the debugger. This frees the extension developer from having to understand the internal workings of the debugger.

The helper functions are well documented in the DDK documentation and within the Microsoft Developer Network (MSDN) library. They are summarized in Table 9-1.

TABLE 9-1 *Debugger Helper Functions*

| Function | Use |
|---|---|
| `CheckControlC()` | A Boolean function that tells whether the user has entered a Ctrl-C key sequence on the command line. It may be useful to poll this function periodically during particularly long operations. |
| `Disassm()` | A function that disassembles instructions. It takes in a pointer to the address that is to be disassembled and returns the disassembled string to an output buffer. |
| `dprintf()` | A function that displays a message on the debugger command windows. This takes `DbgPrint()` style arguments. |
| `GetExpression()` | A function that takes a character string as an input argument and extracts the expression. |
| `GetSetSympath` | A function that retrieves a pointer to the path defined for locating symbols. |
| `GetSymbol` | A function that returns the virtual address of a given symbol or the most similar symbol, if there isn't an exact match. |
| `ReadIoSpace`, `ReadIoSpaceEx` | Functions that read from the target's I/O port locations. |
| `ReadMemory`, `ReadMemoryEx` | Functions that read from the target machine's virtual address space. |
| `ReadMsr` | A function that reads the machine state from the target's MSR register (consult Intel's documentation for a description of the MSR register). |
| `ReadPhysical` | A function that reads values from a physical address on the target. |
| `SetContext` | A function that sets the processor context in which the debugger commands should be executed. |
| `SetThreadForOperation` | A function that causes the described thread to be scheduled to run. |
| `StackTrace` | A function that retrieves a pointer to a listing of the target's stack. |
| `WriteIoSpace`, `WriteIoSpaceEx` | Functions that write into the target's I/O port space. |
| `WriteMemory` | A function that allows the extension to write values into a virtual address on the target machine. |
| `WritePhysical` | A function that writes a buffer into a physical address on the target machine. |

## A Sample Debugger Extension

In this section, a debugger extension is written and explained. It provides the simple functionality of printing out the contents of a structure defined in a header file. The assumption is that a device driver developed by the user uses the same structure. This sample is easily adapted to any device driver development environment.

Recalling the discussion above, the extension DLL maintains certain requirements. It contains the `WinDbgExtensionDllInit()`, `ExtensionApiVersion()`, and `CheckVersion()` functions. It wraps its commands with the `DECLARE_API` macro. It also uses the helper functions to retrieve data from the target machine.

While describing the implementation of this simple debugger extension, some basic error checking will be ignored. Also, items such as include files and global variables, which are usually included in the prologue of the code, are left out for the sake of readability. If you would like to see and download the complete extension DLL, please visit this book's web site at *http://www.aint-it-good.com/kerneldebug.htm*.

### GLOBAL VARIABLES

There are many variables in the extension DLL that must be maintained across the various functions. These include the WINDBG_EXTENSION_APIS structure, which is populated during the DLL's initialization and contains pointers to functions within the actual debugger. Also, version information must be maintained. Here are the declarations for these global variables, which will be used in the code fragments that follow:

```
PWINDBG_EXTENSION_APIS lpExtensionApis;    // List of callback functions
USHORT SavedMajorVersion;      // The build type of the target
USHORT SavedMinorVersion;      // The build number of the machine being debugged.
BOOLEAN ChkTarget;     // Boolean indicating whether the target is a checked build.
EXT_API_VERSION ApiVersion = {3, 5, EXT_API_VERSION_NUMBER, 0);
```

### INITIALIZING THE EXTENSION

Recall from the discussion above that the debugger immediately searches for and calls a function named `WinDbgExtensionDllInit()` within the extension DLL being loaded. It is passed in a structure containing callback pointers for commonly used functions and version information. As you can see, very little work is actually performed within this function. It is used primarily to save the variables given to it by the debugger.

Here is the initialization function for the sample DLL:

```
VOID WinDbgExtensionDllInit(
    PWINDBG_EXTENSION_APIS lpExtensionApis,
    USHORT MajorVersion,
    USHORT MinorVersion
    )
{
```

```
    ExtensionApis = *lpExtensionApis;

    SavedMajorVersion = MajorVersion;
    SavedMinorVersion = MinorVersion;

    ChkTarget = SavedMajorVersion == 0x0c ? TRUE : FALSE;
}
```

#### VALIDATING THE VERSION

After the initialization function is called by the debugger, the ExtensionApiVersion() function is called. This function is required only to return a pointer to a structure defining the minimum build of the debugger with which it can function. We derive this global variable (which we defined above) with the numbers that WinDbg expects.

```
LPEXT_API_VERSION ExtensionApiVersion(VOID)
{
   Return &ApiVersion;
}
```

The MajorVersion and MinorVersion variables within the structure being populated have different meanings from the similarly named variables in the initialization function. In this case, Majorversion is actually the major version number of the operating system (4 for NT 4.0, and 5 for Windows 2000). The minor version is not used in this context, and should be set to zero. The constant EXT_API_VERSION_NUMBER is defined in the *windbgext.h* header file.

Once the debugger has validated that the extension DLL can work with the version of the debugger, it allows the DLL to decide whether it can work with the target. The debugger calls the DLL function CheckVersion() to allow the DLL to validate whether it can work with the debugger.

```
VOID CheckVersion( VOID )
{
    if (ChkTarget != TRUE)
        dprintf("\n\r *** Extension DLL is only designed
to be used with Checked Build..\r\n");
    return;
}
```

In this case, the function validated only that it was being used on a checked build of Windows NT. No action occurred except that a message was printed. It could have just as easily set a flag that disabled certain functions, based on the build type or version. The functionality of this routine is completely dependent on your needs.

### IMPLEMENTING A COMMAND

At this point, all of the mandatory commands have been implemented. The rest of the DLL is yours to populate to suit your needs. The sample DLL will implement a command named *sample* that does nothing more than dump the contents of a structure named *samplestruct*. This structure is defined in an external header file that is shared between the device driver being debugged and this extension DLL. For the purposes of this example, the structure is defined as follows:

```
Typedef struct SAMPLE_STRUCT {
   ULONG element1;
   ULONG element2;
   BOOLEAN flag1;
} SAMPLE_STRUCT, *PSAMPLE_STRUCT;
```

Recall that commands designed to be called from the debugger command line must be wrapped in the macro `DECLARE_API` and that no return value is expected from the function. Here is the sample function:

```
DECLARE_API( sample )
{
   PSAMPLE_STRUCT pSampleStruct;
   SAMPLE_STRUCT SampleStructIn;
   ULONG bytesin;

   if(!args || *args) {
         dprintf("Usage: sample <pointer to sample structure>\n");
         return;
   }

   pSampleStruct = (PSAMPLE_STRUCT) GetExpression(args);

   if(!pSampleStruct){
          dprintf("invalid address for structure\n");
          return;
   }
   dprintf(" SampleStruct 0x%x: ", pSampleStruct );

   ReadMemory(pSampleStruct,  &SampleStructIn, sizeof(SAMPLE_STRUCT), &bytesin);
   if(bytesin != sizeof(SAMPLE_STRUCT))
   {
         dprintf("Incorrect length read\n");
         return;
   }

   PrintSampleStructDetails(&SampleStructIn);
   return;
}
```

This function illustrates good usage of the helper functions. After validating that there are arguments, it uses `GetExpressions()` to retrieve the pointer to `SampleStruct` that was passed in. It then uses that address in the call to `GetData()`. The `GetData()` helper function copies a range of data from the target's virtual address space into a pointer supplied by the caller (in the first argument). Finally, this function calls another routine within the DLL, `printSampleStructDetails()`:

```
PrintSampleStructDetails( IN PSAMPLE_STRUCT pSampleStruct )
{
   dprintf("Dumping SampleStruct at 0x%x\n", pSampleStruct);
   dprintf("  → element 1: 0x%x\n", pSampleStruct->element1);
   dprintf(" → element 2: 0x%x\n", pSampleStruct->element2);
   dprintf(" → flag: 0x%x\n", pSampleStruct->flag);
   return;
}
```

This is a simple example of what a function can do, but it is often enough. There are many times when all you want is a formatted display of a data structure. This code will provide that. It could also be as complex as you need it to be—following points through a linked list, for example. The point is that the extension DLL model is infinitely moldable and flexible to the needs of the device driver developer.

## Summary

This chapter described what debugger extensions are and how you can use them in your environment. A sample debugger extension was presented and dissected. You should take away from this discussion that debugger extensions are useful and do not require a large amount of development time. The effort expended in constructing an extension DLL will likely be recouped in saved debugging time.

TEN

# Driver Verifier

**CHAPTER OBJECTIVES**

- Overview
- Configuration
- Using the Tool

*Microsoft has provided a tool to assist device driver writers in addressing the number one maxim of software quality assurance: Proactive detection of bugs will reduce after-shipment costs and drive up customer satisfaction. The driver verifier utility supplied with Windows 2000 unobtrusively detects many of the most common mistakes made by device driver writers—mistakes that may not manifest themselves in errors until well into the life of the driver.*

## What Is the Driver Verifier?

The driver verifier exists as a number of extra checks that are enabled in the critical subsystems of the Windows 2000 kernel. These are there to assist in exposing errors in kernel-mode code. Because of the lack of strict protection afforded kernel-mode code, problems often lie undetected and dormant until circumstances converge to force symptoms to occur that can be catastrophic to the underlying system. These issues may be as complex as mismanagement of allocated memory or as simple as not following the rules as to what code can execute at which interrupt request level (IRQL). The driver verifier helps in exposing such failures in device drivers before they manifest themselves as something more serious.

The current version of the driver verifier uses the following techniques to ensure that the underlying device drivers do not break the rules:

- Using a special memory pool, buffer overruns and underruns are detected.
- All pageable memory is unmapped prior to raising the IRQL to DISPATCH_LEVEL or higher.
- Fault injection is achieved by simulating low memory conditions.
- Pool tracking is enabled to provide memory leak detection.
- I/O verification is achieved by performing strict validation on IRPs as they're being processed.
- Read-only memory is enforced.

These techniques can be used either separately or in combination with one another to provide fuller coverage of the device driver being debugged. These techniques are usually applied on a per-driver basis to minimize confusion during the debugging process. It's important to note that these techniques are applied *without* modifying the driver under test.

Before discussing how to use the driver verifier, you should understand what each of the various techniques actually does. This will be covered in the following sections.

## Detecting Buffer Underruns and Overruns

One of the more common errors that programmers make is also one of the hardest to detect after the fact: mismanagement of allocated memory pools. Errant pointers can push data beyond the limits of allocated memory, resulting in a buffer overrun, or subtract a pointer to an area "beneath" the allocated memory, resulting in a buffer underrun.

Using the driver verifier, memory allocations can come from a special memory pool designed to catch these types of errors. Memory allocated from this special pool is aligned so that any accesses beyond the allocation result in an informative bug check.

Allocation from the special pool causes the virtual addresses pointing to memory pages above the allocated page to be marked as inaccessible. In an overrun situation, as illustrated in Figure 10-1, an attempt to write to an address above the allocated memory range is immediately caught by the built-in protection mechanisms. In this case, an immediate bug check occurs.

Figure 10-1 shows overrun detection, where the system returns the highest possible address, aligning the memory to the end of the page. Any access beyond the allocation request will result in an immediate bug check because the access would occur on the following page, which will be marked as inac-

| Border Page Access Causes Exception | Allocated Page Unprotected | Border Page Access Causes Exception |
|---|---|---|

FIGURE 10–1 *Special Pool Detects Overruns*

cessible. Likewise, if the driver attempts to write before the beginning of the buffer, the system will issue a bug check at the time the buffer is freed, because the free routine will detect that one or more of the fill bytes has changed.

Buffer underruns are handled a little differently. The addresses prior to the starting address of the memory pool are filled with a special fill pattern. This pattern is verified at the time that the buffer is freed. If the free routine detects that one or more of these fill bytes is invalid, a bug check is triggered.

Because of the way that these checks are implemented, allocations from the special pool require a large number of memory resources. It is entirely possible that the special pool can be exhausted in a driver with a large number of allocations. If the special pool becomes exhausted, the memory manager will revert back to normal behavior and allocate memory from the normal paged and nonpaged pools. In such a case, those allocations will not be protected, and no notice will be given to the user. Also, any allocation larger than the system page size will be allocated from the normal system pools.

The amount of memory allocated to the special pool is based in part on the amount of physical memory available in the machine. Because of this fact, Microsoft recommends performing special pool testing on systems with large amounts of physical memory. The company further recommends that you stress your driver over long periods of time to verify that there are no long-term problems that may not be detected with only quick tests.

Because the special pool size increases with the amount of physical memory a machine has, it is important to do special pool testing on systems with large amounts of physical memory. Be sure to stress your driver thoroughly over long periods of time and to use the Verifier *.exe* program to make sure you have enough physical and virtual memory to use the special pool.

Another important consideration when using this feature of the driver verifier is ensuring that you are running with as much kernel-mode memory available as is possible. Booting the operating system without the /3GB *boot.ini* switch on Intel-based machines is highly desirable, because this frees up more memory for the operating system. Understandably, there are times when this is not acceptable to the applications—in these cases, leave the /3GB switch enabled.

## Unmapping Memory before Raising the IRQL

Interrupt level constraints force kernel mode programmers to choose the most appropriate type of memory pool allocations for the code being operated on. For example, the system cannot handle page faults at DISPATCH_LEVEL or above. When using allocated memory at these IRQLs, that memory must be allocated from the nonpaged pool. Because the nonpaged pool is a finite resource within the NT kernel, programmers are chided to use this pool only when absolutely necessary.

It is a very common error to allocate paged memory and to then access it at DISPATCH_LEVEL or above. Depending on the behavior of your system, it may work most of the time. Accessing paged memory at elevated IRQLs fails only when the page is paged out of memory and a paged fault must be incurred to bring it back in. When a page fault is incurred at DISPATCH_LEVEL, a bug check occurs.

To catch these types of sporadic errors, the driver verifier provides the ability to unmap all pageable memory before raising to an IRQL of DISPATH_LEVEL or above. This includes all pageable system and driver code, and pageable system and driver data segments. There is a performance penalty for all of this mapping and unmapping, but it will catch these types of violations every time.

## Fault Injection to Simulate Low Memory Conditions

Many device drivers fail in unexpected ways when memory allocation requests to the memory manager fail. Because this is a relatively rare occurrence, it often does not come up in general testing of the driver. The driver verifier can change that. It makes it easy to verify the behavior of your driver when memory allocation requests fail.

When the Allocation Fault Injection option in the driver verifier is enabled, the memory manager will randomly fail requests to allocate memory (using the `ExAllocatePool` function). This simulates an environment with low memory conditions present. It's important to note that this behavior does not begin until seven minutes after the machine is booted—after all, injecting memory manager faults during the system boot process might just leave your NT system in an unusable state. The developers of the driver verifier recognized this and provided accordingly. Unfortunately, this seven minutes does not seem to be a tunable value.

## Pool Tracking to Detect Memory Leaks

Pool tracking will cause the system to bug check if memory allocated by the driver under test does not free all of its memory at the time the driver is unloaded. Also, pool tracking provides for extensive allocation information from within the kernel debugger with the command `!verifier 3` in WinDbg and KD.

## I/O Verification to Validate IRP Processing

The driver verifier IRPs are strictly validated in a couple of ways. First, all IRPs allocated with a call to `IoAllocateIRP` are taken from the special pool. These IRPs are governed by the behavior described above for memory allocated from the special pool.

Second, the system applies an extra level of rigor in validating IRP integrity during calls to `IoCallDriver`, `IoCompleteRequest`, and `IoFreeIrp`. If the driver verifier detects a problem with the IRP, it will cause a bug check describing the inconsistency.

## Enforcing Read-Only Memory Protection

In Windows 2000, the memory manager enforces read-only access of pages that are not marked as writeable. If a driver attempts to write to a read-only memory segment, the system will force a bug check with a stop code of 0xC4.

This has a couple of implications for misbehaving drivers. First, it prevents a bad driver from overwriting code. Likewise, drivers that attempt to intercept various system calls by inserting jump instructions will no longer work. This is because all pages containing code are flagged as read-only. The memory manager will catch the driver when it attempts to add the jump instruction.

# Configuring the Driver Verifier

The driver verifier is not a stand-alone piece of software. Rather, elements of the driver verifier exist within the NT kernel. The behavior of these components is configured and controlled through the driver verifier manager. To start the driver verifier manager, you must execute the executable file *VERIFIER.EXE*. This executable is installed automatically as a part of the Windows 2000 Device Driver Kit (DDK) and should be accessible from the Start menu.

It's important to note that, unlike most of the other debugging tools, the verifier program must be run on the target machine, not the source. This is because we are configuring behavior in the environment of the device driver under test. Once the driver verifier manager is running, click on the Modify Setting tab to select the driver that you want to verify. It's important to consider that running the driver verifier on multiple device drivers simultaneously

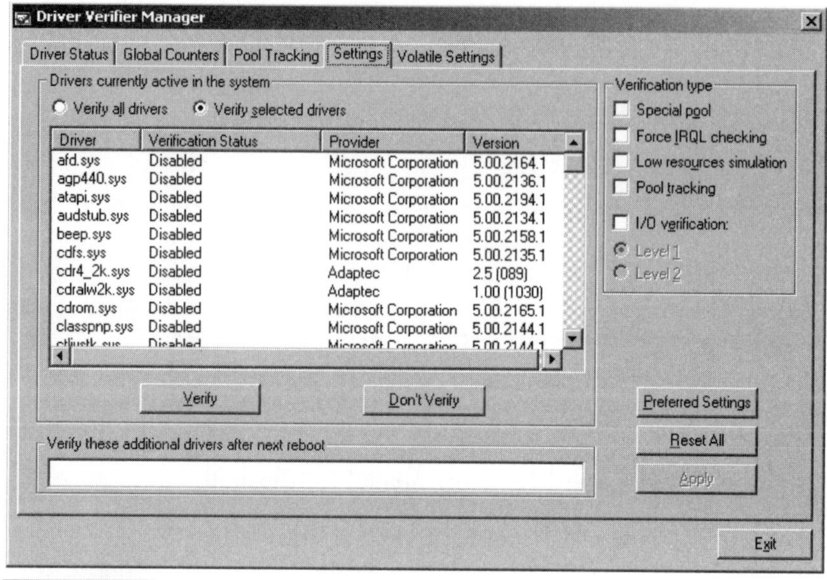


FIGURE 10-2 *Driver Verifier Manager*

increases the burden in understanding the bug checks as they occur. Microsoft recommends that you restrict the use of the driver verifier to a single driver at a time. The verifier manager is illustrated in Figure 10-2.

The driver verifier manager allows you to select and enable each of the available techniques. The only one that is not recommended for everyday testing of your driver is the Allocation Fault Injection—you do not want to be continuously testing the failure paths in your driver's allocation error path code!

You will notice that there is not an option describing the read-only memory enforcement. This is because with Windows 2000, enforcing read-only memory pages is always enabled. There is no way to disable the behavior.

Once you have selected the techniques that you want to apply against your driver, select Apply, then Exit. The changes will take effect after the next reboot cycle on the target machine.

After you reboot the machine, the driver verifier manager will show that the driver you verified is under test. It will also indicate if you do not have enough memory to service the special pool for memory checking. If this is indicated, you will need more memory resources to test your driver effectively. See Figure 10-3 for an example of counters available for on-line viewing.

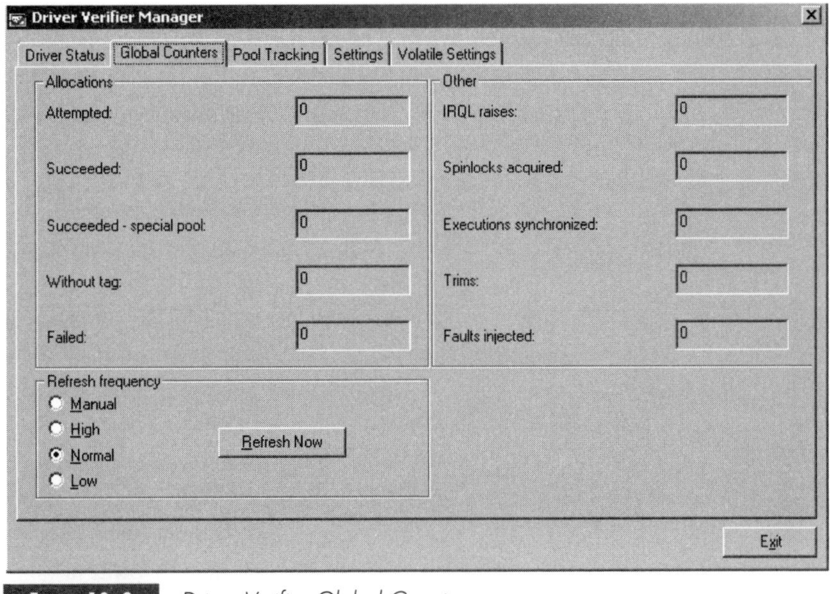


**FIGURE 10-3** *Driver Verifier Global Counters*

# Verifier Stop Codes

The driver verifier work in the Windows 2000 kernel added two new stop codes. These stop codes make it easy to identify the problems encountered with a driver under test. The first of these new stop codes is DRIVER_VERIFIER_DETECTED_VIOLATION (0xC4). The parameters of this stop code are detailed in Table 10-1.

The second new stop code that was introduced into Windows 2000 as a part of the driver verifier work is the DRIVER_VERIFIER_IOMANAGER_VIOLATION stop code. The valid parameters for this stop code are detailed in Table 10-2.

**TABLE 10–1** *DRIVER_VERIFIER_DETECTED_VIOLATION Bug Check Parameters*

| Parameter 1 | Parameter 2 | Parameter 3 | Parameter 4 | Description |
|---|---|---|---|---|
| 0x0 | N/A | Pool Type | 0 | Call to allocate 0 bytes; must allocate at least 1 byte. |
| 0x1 | Current IRQL | Pool Type | Number of bytes | Attempt to allocate paged memory at IRQL >= DISPATCH_LEVEL. |
| 0x2 | Current IRQL | Pool Type | Number of bytes | Attempt to allocate nonpaged memory at IRQL > DISPATCH. |
| 0x10 | Bad Address | N/A | N/A | Attempt to free from an address that was not returned from an allocate call. |
| 0x11 | Current IRQL | Pool Type | Number of bytes | Attempt to free paged pool at IRQL >= DISPATCH. |
| 0x12 | Current IRQL | Pool Type | Number of bytes | Attempt to free nonpaged pool at IRQL > DISPATH. |
| 0x14 | N/A | N/A | N/A | Attempt to free memory already freed. |
| 0x30 | Current IRQL | Requested IRQL | N/A | Attempt to lower IRQL in KeRaiseIrql. |
| 0x31 | Current IRQL | Requested IRQL | N/A | Attempt to raise IRQL in KeLowerIrql. |
| 0x32 | Current IRQL | Spinlock Address | N/A | Call to `KeReleaseSpinlock()` at IRQL != DISPATCH. |
| 0x33 | Current IRQL | Fast Mutex address | N/A | Attempt to acquire fast mutex at IRQL > APC. |
| 0x34 | Current IRQL | Fast Mutex address | N/A | Attempt to release fast mutex at IRQL > APC. |
| 0x40 | Current IRQL | Spinlock Address | N/A | Attempt to acquire spinlock at IRQL != DISPATCH. |
| 0x60 | # of bytes still allocated from paged pool | # bytes still allocated from nonpaged pool | # of allocations not freed | Driver was unloaded with memory still allocated. |

TABLE 10–2 *DRIVER_VERIFIER_IOMANAGER_VIOLATION Bug Check Parameters*

| Parameter 1 | Parameter 2 | Parameter 3 | Parameter 4 | Description |
|---|---|---|---|---|
| 0x1 | Address of IRP being freed | 0 | 0 | Attempt to free an object whose type is not IO_TYPE_IRP. |
| 0x2 | Address of IRP being freed | 0 | 0 | Attempt to free an IRP not associated with a thread (ThreadListEntry list is empty). |
| 0x3 | Address of IRP being sent | 0 | 0 | Call to IoCallDriver with IRP type not equal to IRP_TYPE. |
| 0x4 | Address of DeviceObject | 0 | 0 | Call to IoCallDriver with invalid device object. |
| 0x5 | IRQ level before IoCallDriver | IRQ level after IoCallDriver | 0 | Return from IoCallDriver at different IRQL. |
| 0x6 | IRP Status | Address of IRP being completed | 0 | Call to IoCompleteRequest with status marked pending. |
| 0x7 | Address of cancel routine | Address of IRP being completed | 0 | Call to IoCompleteRequest with cancel routine still set. |
| 0x8 | Address of DeviceObject | Major function | 0 | Invalid buffer passed to IoBuildAsynchronousFsdRequest. |
| 0x9 | Address of DeviceObject | IoControlCod e | 0 | Invalid buffer passed to IoBuildDeviceIoControlRequest |
| 0xA | Address of DeviceObject | 0 | 0 | Call to IoInitializeTimer with a DeviceObject having an already-initialized timer. |
| 0xC | Address of IO status block passed in the IRP | 0 | 0 | IO status block passed to IRP is allocated on stack that has already unwound past that point. |
| 0xD | Address of event object passed in the IRP | 0 | 0 | Event passed in the IRP is allocated on stack that has already unwound past that point. |

## Driver Verifier Debugger Extension Command

The driver verifier statistics can be captured and displayed from within the kernel debuggers. As a part of the Windows 2000 kernel debugging extensions, the `!verifier` command is provided.

## Summary

This chapter has demonstrated that the driver verifier performs an amazing amount of analysis that is not easy to achieve in any other manner. It should become an indispensable tool in your arsenal of debugging tools. It is more proactive than any of the other tools that Microsoft has provided and has the potential to be the most important.

E L E V E N

# Debugging Resources

**CHAPTER OBJECTIVES**

- Web Sites
- Knowledge Base
- Training
- Newsgroups
- Books

*There are many resources available to aid in the debugging and development of device drivers. There is a number of web sites, newsgroups, training programs, and consultants dedicated to assisting you in learning how to debug kernel-mode software. This chapter will attempt to shed some light on what is available and what is useful.*

*Because this type of information changes, the reader is pointed to the web site for the book for the most current resource information. The web site for this book is http://www.aint-it-good.com/kerneldebug.htm.*

# Web Sites

There is a multitude of web sites offering up information that is useful to both the kernel-mode developer and the kernel-mode debugger. The sites listed here cover everything from hardware specifications and information to undocumented Windows 2000 calls to useful utilities. I strongly encourage the kernel-mode developer to visit each of these sites as least once to get a feel for what is available for the asking.

## Microsoft Corporation

It may seem obvious, but the best place to find Windows 2000 debugging information is at Microsoft. Microsoft may be less than forthcoming about how the operating system works or in providing unsupported diagnostic utilities, as do some of the other web sites in this category, but it is the undisputed expert at Windows 2000 kernel debugging.

The latest release of WinDbg can always be found on the Software Development Kit (SDK) home page. This is located at *http://msdn.microsoft.com/developer/sdk*.

Microsoft has also put up an excellent debugging resource page that contains links to both internal and external information about debugging in the Windows environment, as well as debugging in general. This page is *http://www.microsoft.com/hwdev/driver/ntdebugging.htm*.

Device driver developers would be remiss to not check in on the Microsoft Hardware Development page. There are links from there to technology whitepapers and specifications describing most aspects of running Windows 2000/NT on any hardware platform. The link there is *http://www.microsoft.com/hwdev*.

## System Internals

There are several web sites catering to the NT kernel-mode community, but the most famous is the System Internals web site. The folks who run this site provide a seemingly endless stream of diagnostic utilities exploiting undocumented NT functions. Most of this software is freeware, but there is some software for sale there. In addition to the software on the System Internals site, there are numerous informational articles. This site should be in the bookmarks of any serious driver developer. The address is *www.sysinternals.com*.

## Open Systems Research

Another valuable source of third-party information about Windows 2000 internals is the Open Systems Research (OSR) web site at *www.osr.com*.

These guys are the industry-acknowledged experts in Windows 2000 internals. They provide consulting, training, and even put out a newsletter. Browsing this web site periodically is a good idea for those who work in NT kernel mode.

### x86.org

This is the granddaddy of hardware hacking sites for Intel Platforms—the Dr. Dobbs Microprocessor Center. It contains information on the undocumented features of the various chipsets and processors. The articles there explain the inner workings of the electronics in the computers that driver developers write for. The address is *www.x86.org*.

### Intel Corporation

Intel maintains a site geared toward driver-level developers and hardware engineers. Point your web browser to *developer.intel.com*. You will find numerous specifications there. There is on-line documentation to most of the processors and chipsets that Intel sells and supports. If you are doing low-level hardware integration work, this web site becomes invaluable.

## Knowledge Base Articles

Contained within a Microsoft Developer Network (MSDN) subscription from Microsoft and available directly on the web, the Microsoft Knowledge Base brings forth Microsoft's expertise in kernel debugging matters. You can access the knowledge base on the web at *support.microsoft.com*. Even if using the web-based search tool, I encourage every developer to subscribe to the MSDN. It is an invaluable resource that will pay for itself again and again.

When searching through the knowledge base, search for keywords such as DEBUGREF, WINDBG, KD, and DEBUGGING. A sampling of some current articles that relate to kernel debugging follows in Table 11-1. Note that the knowledge base will allow you to query on the knowledge base article number.

TABLE 11–1 *Sampling of Kernel Debugging-Related KB Articles*

| Article No. | Title |
|---|---|
| Q121366 | INFO: PDB and DBG Files—What They Are and How They Work |
| Q103059 | Descriptions of Bug Codes for Windows NT |
| Q121543 | Setting Up for Remote Debugging |
| Q121652 | List of Debuggers Supported with Windows NT |
| Q129845 | Blue Screen Preparation before Calling Microsoft |
| Q141470 | How to Use the Kernel Debugger to Debug Driver Initialization |
| Q148659 | How to Set Up Windows NT Debug Symbols |
| Q148954 | How to Set Up a Remote Debug Session Using a Modem |
| Q151981 | How to Set Up a Remote Debug Session Using a NULL-Modem Cable |
| Q128372 | How to Remove Symbols from Device Drivers |
| Q155011 | Error Codes in Windows NT Part 1 of 2 |
| Q155012 | Error Codes in Windows NT Part 2 of 2 |
| Q106066 | Additional Remote Debugging Requirement |
| Q97858 | CTRL+C Exception Handling under WinDbg |
| Q102873 | BOOT.INI and ARC Path Naming Conventions and Usage |
| Q105677 | Debugging the Win32 Subsystem |
| Q115760 | Kernel Debugging Using WinDbg |
| Q103862 | Symbolic Information for System DLLs |
| Q98288 | Watching Local Variables That Are Also Globally Declared |
| Q99953 | WinDbg Message "Breakpoint Not Instantiated" |
| Q102430 | HOWTO: Debugging 32-Bit Applications under Win32s |
| Q128372 | HOWTO: Remove Symbols from Device Drivers |
| Q159455 | Assembly Language Conventions on DEC Alpha Systems |
| Q157472 | Debugging Windows NT Kernel STOPs on RISC-Based Platforms |

# Training

There is not a lot of activity in the area of training people to be effective kernel-mode debuggers. Nonetheless, the training arena for debugging skills is growing. The community is beginning to recognize the value of effective debugging resources.

### Microsoft

Microsoft has an internal course geared toward support people that it occasionally makes available to its partners. It is called the *Windows 2000 Kernel-Debugging Workshop*. If you are part of an organization with a relationship with Microsoft, pursue that option through your Microsoft representative.

Another option available through Microsoft is the *Supporting Windows 2000 in the Enterprise* course. This course is a part of the Microsoft Certified Engineer program. Even so, it is a good course and spends a couple of modules talking about diagnosing failures from crash dumps and blue screens.

### Open Systems Research

Open Systems Research, found at *www.osr.com*, is a consulting and training firm specializing in Windows NT internals. OSR is a recognized leader in the NT consulting and training world. It has just introduced a four-day workshop and class specifically geared toward Windows NT kernel debugging. If you have a need to understand these issues, call OSR.

### USENIX Association

The USENIX Association sponsors workshops and conferences throughout the year. While traditionally focused on UNIX and open systems in general, it has recently begun to focus more and more on Windows 2000. It has, in the past, had tutorials geared toward the kernel-mode developer. This has included tutorials on kernel debugging and crash dump analysis. Contact the association through its web site at *www.usenix.org*.

## Newsgroups and Mailing Lists

There are a couple of relevant newsgroups and mailing lists dedicated to the kernel-mode developer. These are focused on kernel-mode issues, but questions of debugging arise periodically. There is no better forum to ask these questions.

### USENET Newsgroups

The primary gathering place in the USENET newsgroups for NT kernel mode developers is *news:comp.os.ms-windows.programmer.nt.kernel-mode*. If you develop device drivers on NT and you have USENET access, you should be reading this group. It is archived on *www.dejanews.com*.

Another newsgroup that periodically has kernel-mode information posted to it is *news:microsoft.public.win32.programmer.kernel*. Although chartered to serve the Win32 community, the word *kernel* in the name has attracted scores of kernel-mode dialog. It features an eclectic mix of topics.

Finally, the newsgroup *news:microsoft.public.msdn.general* serves the MSDN subscriber base. If you have questions about the DDK or other tools that come with MSDN, this is the place for you.

### NTDEV and NTFSD Mailing Lists

There are two mailing lists that serve the kernel-mode community. The first is NTDEV, which focuses on generic NT development issues. The second is NTFSD, which is a discussion area for Windows NT file systems developers. Each of these lists is hosted by Open Systems Research, and can be subscribed to from its web site *www.osr.com*.

## Books and Newsletters

There are many books that describe kernel-mode development in the Windows 2000 environment. Each has its own various strengths and weaknesses. Most of them have at least some information about debugging in a kernel-mode environment. A sampling of titles is found in Table 11-2.

**Table 11–2** *Books Related to Windows NT Kernel-Mode Topics*

| Title | Author | Publisher/ISBN |
|---|---|---|
| *The Windows NT Device Driver Book: A Guide for Programmers* | Art Baker | Prentice Hall/0131844741 |
| *Windows NT Device Driver Development* | Peter Viscarola and Tony Mason | Macmillan Technical Publishing/ 1578700582 |
| *Developing Windows NT Device Drivers* | Edward Dekker and Joseph Newcomer | Addison-Wesley/0201695901 |
| *Windows NT File System Internals: A Developer's Guide* | Rajeev Nagar | O'Reilly & Associates/1565922492 |
| *Inside Microsoft Windows 2000, Third Edition* | David Solomon and Mark Russinovich | Microsoft Press/0735610215 |

In addition to the books listed, there is a newsletter put out by OSR called the *NT Insider*. This is a "mostly monthly" publication that is free of charge. This is full of information and tips. Everyone should subscribe. Contact OSR through its web site *www.osr.com*. There are selected articles from back issues available on-line.

## Summary

There is a multitude of resources available for the resourceful developer. This chapter has pointed toward many of those. A web search will undoubtedly turn up yet more. Check out this book's web site, *http://www.aint-it-good.com/kerneldebug.htm*, from time to time for an up-to-date listing of this information.

APPENDIX A

# WinDbg Reference

*This appendix details all of the supported commands and options used by WinDbg in its kernel debugging and crash dump analysis modes. These are separated into the "built-in" commands, the "dot" commands, and the "bang" or "kernel extension" commands. The arguments presented within angle brackets (<>) are required for the proper operation of the command, and those contained within regular brackets ([arg]) are optional.*

## WinDbg Command Line Options

There are many options that can be issued on the WinDbg debugger command line to control the execution and environment of your debugging session. This section describes these options.

### USAGE

windbg [-a] [-g] [-h] [-i] [-k [platform port speed]] [-l[text]] [-m] [-s[pipe]] [-v] [-w name] [-y path] [-z crashfile] [filename[.ext] [arguments]]

### PARAMETERS

-a

This instructs the debugger only to print warning messages when encountering bad symbols but not to take any other action.

-g

The debugger should immediately attach to the target system and begin executing. The default behavior is to wait until the "g" command has been issued from the user interface.

-h

Allows any children processes to access WinDbg's handles.

-i

Starts the debugger and ignores the saved common workspace.

-k [platform port speed]

This option overrides any previously stored configuration options for communicating with the debugger target machine. The valid values are:

Platform: x86 or *alpha* determines whether debugging an Intel-based or Alpha-based target.

Port: *COM1* or *COM2* determines which port the cable to the target machine is connected to.

Speed: *9600, 19200, 57600, 115200* determines the speed of the debugging connection.

-l text

The window title bar for the debugging session is set to [text].

-m

When the debugger starts, this option minimizes it.

-s pipe

Starts a remote server using the named pipe specified in [pipe].

-v

Runs in verbose mode. This will cause WinDbg to print extra messages indicating what it is doing, not just the default of printing the results.

-w name

When the debugging begins, it should load the previously saved workspace indicated by *name*.

-y path

Sets the path that the debugger uses to search when attempting to resolve symbols. You can use multiple paths if they are separated with a semicolon.

-z crashfile

Instead of connecting to a target, the debugger will be used to examine the crash file specified in *crashfile*.

## Built-In Commands

The built-in commands offer basic functionality for controlling and configuring the debugger. They also provide some basic debugging commands. These commands are entered directly from the command window, the prompt from the KD interface, or from a script file that can be read in from either of these interfaces. They are listed here alphabetically.

---

## ~[processor]

Sets or displays the processor context on a multiprocessor system. All commands entered in the debugger are executed in the context of the current processor context. This is invalid on a single-processor system. If this command is issued with no parameters, the current processor context is displayed.

#### PARAMETERS

Processor
: Indicates the number of the processor to use.

---

## ? <expression>

Evaluates a C-style expression and prints the output to the console.

#### PARAMETERS

<expression> is a C-style expression.

---

## #<expression>

Searches for an expression within the disassembled range of virtual addresses.

#### PARAMETERS

Expression
: The regular expression to be evaluated.

---

## % <stackframe>

Changes the current stack frame.

#### PARAMETERS

Stackframe
: The virtual address of the stack frame to use. Valid stack frames can be derived from the output of the "k" commands.

## BC <bplist>

Clears the specified breakpoints. This completely disables and eliminates the breakpoint. If you want to disable a breakpoint temporarily, you should use the "BD" option.

### PARAMETERS

bplist

A list of the breakpoint numbers to clear. This is the number of the breakpoint (derived from the output of the "BL" command) and not the address or breakpoint expression.

## BD <bplist>

Disables the specified breakpoints. This keeps the breakpoint condition from occurring but does not eliminate the breakpoint from the breakpoint list. It can be re-enabled with the "BE" command.

### PARAMETERS

bplist

A list of the breakpoint numbers to disable. This is the number of the breakpoint and not the address of the breakpoint expression.

## BL [bplist]

Lists the breakpoints, their current status (e.g., disabled, etc.), and the breakpoint condition for the current debugging session. Given no arguments, this lists all of the breakpoints that are currently set.

### PARAMETERS

bplist

A list of the breakpoint numbers that you want to examine.

## BP [id] <breakpoint> [options]

Sets a breakpoint at a given location. Once set, the breakpoint is automatically enabled. This also allows you to specify the conditions under which a breakpoint can be set.

#### PARAMETERS

Id

The breakpoint number to assign to the breakpoint. If not specified, the next available number is assigned.

Breakpoint

This specifies the address upon which the debugger should break. It can be issued in one of several formats. These are as follows:

[file]@line

Sets a breakpoint at the line number specified in the given source file. If no file is specified, the last file referenced is used.

?expression

Assigns the breakpoint if the given C-style expression is true.

=addr[/R<size>]

Assigns a breakpoint if contents within the virtual address change. The "/R" option specifies the range within the memory to watch.

[context]<address>

Assigns a breakpoint at the given virtual address in the specified context. If no context is specified, the current context is assumed. Addresses in the kernel address space do not require a context, because all contexts share the address space assigned to kernel mode.

Options

/P<count>

Skips the first <count> occurrences of this breakpoint.

/Q

Suppresses the dialog box message that occurs when a breakpoint is unable to be resolved.

/C<command list>

Executes the list of debugger commands specified in <command list> when the breakpoint occurs.

## C <start address> <end address>

Compares a range of virtual addresses.

#### PARAMETERS

Start address

This is the starting virtual address to examine.

End address

This is the end of the range of virtual addresses that you wish to compare.

## D<mode> <address>|<range>

Decodes and displays a range of memory.

#### PARAMETERS

Mode

The "D" must be followed by a mode for this command to be valid. The supported modes are:

| | |
|---|---|
| C | Provides disassembled output of the addresses. |
| A | Provides an ASCII dump of the memory range. |
| U | Decodes the specified addresses as a UNICODE string. |
| B | Displays the addresses as a series of bytes. |
| W | Displays the address range as a series of 16-bit words. |
| D | Decodes the addresses as a series of 32-bit words. |
| S | Provides the output as a 4-byte Real number. |
| I | Provides the output as an 8-byte Real number. |
| T | Provides the output as a 10-byte Real number. |

Address

A valid address expression. If no address is specified, the display of memory will continue from the last point at which memory was accessed. In this way, a series of this command will require only that the address be entered the first time.

Range

A valid address range expression. This is mutually exclusive of the address parameter.

## E<mode> <address> [value-list]

Enters a value into memory.

### PARAMETERS

Mode

The "E" must be followed by a mode for this command to be valid. The supported modes are:

| | |
|---|---|
| A | Enters the values as ASCII characters. |
| U | Enters the values as UNICODE characters. |
| B | The values entered are interpreted as discrete BYTES. |
| W | Interprets the values entered as 16-bit WORDS. |
| D | Enters the values as 32-bit DWORDS. |
| S | The values are entered as 4-byte Real numbers. |
| I | Interprets the values as 8-byte Real numbers. |
| T | Enters the values as 10-byte Real numbers. |

Address

The virtual address at which to begin entered values. If not provided, the debugger will assume a continuation from the last address used.

Value-list

Specifies a list of values to enter at the specified address. If this isn't specified, the debugger will resume from the last address accessed. If this list isn't provided, you will be prompted to enter the values. Using the carriage return instead of entering a value will terminate entry.

## FI<mode> <begin-address> <end-address> <value>

Fills a range of memory with specified values.

### PARAMETERS

Mode

The "FI" must be followed by a mode for this command to be valid. The supported modes are:

| | |
|---|---|
| A | Enters the values as ASCII characters. |
| U | Enters the values as UNICODE characters. |
| B | The values entered are interpreted as discrete BYTES. |
| W | Interprets the values entered as 16-bit WORDS. |
| D | Enters the values as 32-bit DWORDS. |

S The values are entered as 4-byte Real numbers.
I Interprets the values as 8-byte Real numbers.
T Enters the values as 10-byte Real numbers.

Begin Address
: The address expression at which to begin the fill.

End Address
: The last address that the fill will affect.

Value
: The value that should be used to fill the specified range of addresses.

## FR [<register>[=<value>]]

Sets or displays the values in floating point registers. When run with no arguments, this command will display the contents of the registers.

### PARAMETERS

Register
: The floating point register to display or set.

Value
: The value to populate into the floating point register.

## G[mode] [=<address>] [breakpoint]

Continues execution of the target machine being debugged.

### PARAMETERS

Mode
: This optional parameter specifies that a pending exception be marked as either handled or ignored. The value for marking the exception handled is "H" and the value for not handling the exception is "N."

Address
: Sets the program counter to this address and resumes execution at that point.

Breakpoint
: Execution will resume until the breakpoint address is encountered. Note that this is the address to continue execution through, not necessarily a defined breakpoint as used by the "Bx" commands.

## Help

Displays a short list of supported built-in debugger commands. This does not display the "dot" commands or the commands supported by the kernel debugging extensions.

## K[option] [=Frame Stack PC] [Frame]

Displays the contents of the current call stack.

#### PARAMETERS

Option

Specifies options that modify the output of the stack display. This immediately follows the "K," with no space in between. The valid options are:

| | |
|---|---|
| B | Displays the first three DWORDS from each entry in the call stack. |
| S | Includes the source file and line number information, if any. |
| V | Includes in the display any runtime information that may be available. |
| N | Displays the stack frame number of each stack location. |

Frame

Displays the stack entry for the given stack frame, where the stack frame is an address expression. This parameter can be used either by itself or in conjunction with the "Stack" and "PC" arguments.

Stack

Displays the stack entry whose stack pointer matches the specified address expression. This is used in conjunction with the "Frame" and "PC" parameters.

PC

Displays the stack entry whose Program Counter matches the specified address expression. This is used in conjunction with the "Stack" and "Frame" arguments.

## LD <module>

Loads the symbols for a given module. The default behavior when initially loading symbol files is to defer the symbol loading. This overrides that behavior.

#### PARAMETERS

Module
: Provides the mode name of the binary file from which to load symbols.

## LM [module-name]

Lists the modules loaded in a given debugging session. If no arguments are specified, all of the modules are listed. The on-line help will list options other than the ones described here. These are not applicable to kernel debugging.

#### PARAMETERS

Module-name
: Lists the information for just this module.

## LN <address>

Scans the kernel memory and lists the symbol nearest the specified address expression.

#### PARAMETERS

Address
: Valid address expression that you wish to map to a symbol and offset.

## M <start-address> <end-address> <new-address>

Moves the contents of memory from one location to another.

#### PARAMETERS

Start-address
: This is the first source address in the range to be moved.

End-address

The end address in the range to be moved. The range is inclusive of this address.

New-address

This is the starting address of destination of the move. The ending destination address is not required, because the length is determined by the start and end addresses specified for the source of the move.

## N [radix]

Sets or displays the radix used in data entry and display. If no argument is provided, the current radix is displayed. Otherwise, it is set.

### PARAMETERS

Radix

The number to use as the new radix. The valid values are 8, 10, and 16 for octal, decimal, and hexadecimal.

## P [repeat]

Performs a single program step.

### PARAMETERS

Repeat

The number of times to repeat the single step.

## Q

Exits (or Quits) the debugger.

## R [<register>=<value>]

Displays or sets a processor register. With no arguments, the value of all the processor registers for the current processor context are displayed.

### PARAMETERS

Register

The register to set or display.

Value

The value to which to set the register.

## S <start-address> <end-address> <value-list>

Searches memory for a value. The starting address that matches the pattern will be displayed.

### PARAMETERS

Start-address

This is the address at which to begin the search.

End-address

This is the ending boundary for the search.

Value-list

This is the byte pattern to search the specified memory range for.

## S<+/->

Controls source-level debugging.

## SX[option] [exception number] [exception name]

Displays or modifies the behavior of the debugger when an exception is encountered.

### PARAMETERS

Option

The option that controls the behavior of the "SX" command. The valid values are:

| | |
|---|---|
| D | Disables the specified exception or displays those that are disabled. |
| N | Causes the exception to notify the debugger or lists those that do. |
| E | Enables the specified exception or displays those that are enabled. |

When no option is provided, the list of exceptions that the debugger ignores is provided.

Exception Number
    The numerical value of the exception to ignore.

Exception Name
    Provides a name with which to tag the exception.

---

## T <repeat>

Traces into a function when single-stepping. The default behavior is to single-step over a function call.

### PARAMETERS

Repeat
    The number of times to repeat this command.

---

## U [address]

Unassembles the bytes, starting at the specified address.

### PARAMETERS

Address
    The starting address of the disassembly. If no address is specified, the command uses the last address accessed as its starting point.

---

## X[scope] [context] [pattern]

Searches the symbol table and locates a symbol within the debug target. If provided with no arguments, all of the symbol information being maintained by the debugger will be listed.

### PARAMETERS

Scope
    Defines the scope of the search. The valid parameters in kernel debugging are:

| | |
|---|---|
| L | Lexical |
| F | Function |
| C | Class |
| M | Module |
| E | Executable |
| P | Public |

| | |
|---|---|
| G | Global |
| * | All |

Context

The execution context in which to perform the search.

Pattern

The pattern that is being searched for.

## Dot Commands

The "dot" commands provide basic control over the debugging session. They are distinguished by having to be entered with a period in front of the actual command.

---

### .break

In kernel-debugging mode, the "break" command causes the debugger to stop the target computer from executing so that it can be debugged.

---

### .list [address]

Lists on the command window the source or disassembled output of either the current program counter position or the address specified. If source information is available and the *S+* option has been enabled (which it is by default), source code will be displayed. If there is no source available or the *S-* option has been set, only disassembled output will be provided.

#### PARAMETERS

Address

The address at which the listing will begin.

---

### .logopen [filename]

This command allows all of the command window commands and output to be saved to a text file. This is useful for saving the information obtained during a session for later analysis. Unless overridden by an argument, the default log file name is "wndbg.LOG." You can start and stop logging at any time during your debugging session.

#### PARAMETERS

filename
This is the name of the file that you will log to.

---

## .logappend [filename]

The output of the debugging session command window will be appended to the end of an existing log file.

#### PARAMETERS

filename
The name of the log file that you wish to append.

---

## .logclose

Closes the open log files.

---

## .opt [args]

This command allows you to control the various operating parameters of the kernel debugger from the command line or from within a script file.

#### PARAMETERS

AsmSymbols {on/off}
When disassembling output, the debugger should attempt to resolve addresses back to their symbols when this is set to *on* (its default state).

AsmRaw {on/off}
If this option is set to *on,* a column containing the raw byte information will be included when disassembling code. The default is *off.*

BackgroundSym {on/off}
When set to *on,* this allows symbol loading in the background.

CaseSensitive {on/off}
The debugger applies case sensitivity to input when this is set to *on.*

CommandRepeat {on/off}
When set to *on,* the last command entered will be executed when you press the Enter key.

DllEE <filename>

This is the DLL that the debugger uses to evaluate entered expressions. This should be modified only if you have a new expression evaluator DLL from Microsoft.

DllEm <filename>

This is the DLL that the debugger uses to handle its execution model. This should be modified only if you have a DLL from Microsoft.

DllSh <filename>

This is the DLL that the debugger uses for symbol handling. This should be modified only if you have a new DLL from Microsoft.

DllTl <filename [args]>

This is the DLL that the debugger uses for its transport layer. This should be modified only if you have a new DLL from Microsoft.

DllPath <path>

This is the path that the debugger searches for the DLLs that it uses or loads. This is a semicolon-separated list of directories.

IgnoreAll {on/off}

When set to *on,* the debugger will ignore any error or warning messages encountered regarding symbol errors.

KdInitialBp {on/off}

If this option is set to *on,* the debugger will force the target machine to break whenever the debugger first attempts to attach to that machine.

KdEnable {on/off}

This option enables kernel debugging mode. It should always be set to *on* for kernel debugging.

KdGoExit {on/off}

Tells the target to resume execution whenever the debugger exits. This will keep you from exiting the debugger while the target machine is still locked.

KdUseModem {on/off}

Uses modem control signals while communicating over the serial link between the debugger and the target machine.

KdBaudRate <baudrate>

Sets the baudrate on the serial connection between the debugger and the target machine. The valid values are 9600, 19200, 56800, and 115200.

KdPort <port#>

Sets the COM port over which the debugger communicates with the target. The format is "COMx," where *x* is the COM port number to use.

KdCacheSize <cachesize>

Sets the size of the cache used by the command window to store previous input and output. This determines the depth at which you can traverse the history of your debugging session.

KdPlatform <platform>

The platform architecture that you are debugging is specified here. The valid values for NT4 and NT5 are *x86* for Intel architecture platforms and *alpha* for Digital/Compaq Alpha platforms.

MasmEval {on/off}

When set to *on*, the debugger will evaluate expressions using the MASM style of expressions. The default is *off*.

Verbose {on/off}

With this option, the debugger will print information about what it is doing to execute the command you issued. This is actually useful only in debugging the debugger and is not recommended for everyday use.

## .reload [module]

The "reload" command causes the specified symbol files to be reread and the symbols to be reloaded. If no argument is specified, all of the symbols will be reloaded.

### PARAMETERS

Module

A list of driver or DLL modules that you wish to have reloaded. Use the complete file name (e.g., ntfs.sys) to reload ntfs.

## .resync

Attempts to resynchronize the communication between the debugger and the target machine. This is useful if you get into a situation where the debugger doesn't know whether the target is running or at a breakpoint.

## .sleep <seconds>

This command causes the debugger to stop responding for some number of seconds. It may be useful when writing debugger scripts.

#### PARAMETERS

Seconds
: The number of seconds to sleep.

## .source<scriptfile>

This command causes the debugger to accept the contents of the specified file as input to the command window. This essentially allows you to write debugging scripts or macros of common debugging sequences.

#### PARAMETERS

Scriptfile
: The filename containing the debugger commands. Note that there is *no* space between the ".source" command and the name of the script file.

## .title <window-title>

Sets the text in the main window's title bar. If no argument is specified, it sets it back to the default title.

#### PARAMETERS

Window-title
: The text string to insert into the window title bar.

## .trace <option>

This command traces the internal execution of the debugger. It is useful not for debugging the target machine, but rather for troubleshooting a debugging session or communication problems.

### .unload <module>

This command will remove the symbols included in the specified module from the debugger. With no parameters specified, it will cause all of the currently loaded symbol and module information to be unloaded.

#### PARAMETERS

Module

The driver or DLL module that you wish to have unloaded.

### .waitforstr <string>

This command will pause the debugger until the specified debug print string is received from the debugged target machine.

#### PARAMETERS

String

The string to wait for.

## Built-In Extension Commands

Although almost all commands that begin with a bang ("!") are externally loaded debugger extensions, there are a number of commands that begin with a "!" that are built directly into the debugger. These are used to control the loading and execution of the loaded extensions. These will be detailed here.

### !?

Lists both the built-in extension commands and those of every loaded kernel extension.

### !default <extension>

This command sets the default debugger extension to that specified. The default extension is the one that is searched first when attempting to resolve commands entered. If the command is not found in the default extension, any other extensions are searched in the order in which they were loaded.

#### PARAMETERS

Extension

This is the name of the debugger extension to set as the default. If the kernel extension was loaded with its full path specified, you must use the full path here.

---

### !load <extension>

Loads an additional debugger extension for use in your debugging session.

#### PARAMETERS

Extension

This is the name of the extension that you want to load. If it is not in your current path, you must specify the full path to the extension.

---

### !noversion

By default, the version of Windows NT that you are debugging is compared with the version information in a debugger extension. If the versions do not match, you will get a warning message every time you attempt to use that extension. This command disables that checking.

---

### !pagein <address>

This extension command causes the virtual address to be paged in from the system paging file.

#### PARAMETERS

Address

The virtual address of the page to retrieve from backing store.

---

### !reload [module]

This has the same behavior as the ".reload" command. It will reload all the modules used by the debugged system.

#### PARAMETERS

Module

If specified, the debugger will reload only this module.

### !sympath [path]

This command specifies the path that the debugger should search when attempting to resolve symbols. Given no arguments, it will display the current symbol path.

#### PARAMETERS

Path

The path that should be searched to resolve symbols. This is a semicolon-separated list of directories.

### !unload

Forces the specified debugger extension to be unloaded and made unavailable to the debugger.

#### PARAMETERS

Extension

The name of the extension to unload. If it was loaded with its full path specified, you must use the full path here.

## Kernel Debugging Extension Commands

The kernel debugger ships with a set of predefined extensions designed for examining kernel structures and objects. These are the kernel debugger extensions. Like all sets of extensions, these commands are all accessed with a preceding "!" character. Windows NT 5.0 has introduced a number of extensions, corresponding to some of the newer features of the NT 5.0 kernel, and it has eliminated some of the older ones. Where there are differences or commands that work only on NT 5.0 or later, you will see a notation made.

## !?

This command displays the help information for the kernel extensions.

## !apic <address>

Formats and displays information about the local APIC in an Intel-based system. Documentation for the meanings of the fields displayed can be found in the corresponding documentation from Intel on their APIC chips. This is an Intel-only command.

### PARAMETERS

Address

The virtual address of the local APIC in the target system.

## !arbiter [flags]

This command displays information about the "arbiter" arbitration locks in the Windows NT PCI driver. This command is supported only in Windows NT 5.0 and later.

### PARAMETERS

Flags

The flags indicate which types of arbiters to examine. If no flag is specified, all arbiters are dumped. The meanings of the bits of the flag are as follows (you can OR the flags to show multiple arbiter types):

1: Shows I/O port arbiters
2: Shows PCI memory arbiters
3: Shows IRQ arbiters
4: Shows DMA arbiters

## !atom <address>

Formats and displays the information contained in the atom table located at the specified address.

#### PARAMETERS

Address

The virtual address of the atom table to display.

---

## !bugdump [component]

Formats and displays the information contained within the various system bug check buffers. If an argument is specified, the debugger will display only the information contained within the specified module.

#### PARAMETERS

Component

The component whose bug dump data you want to examine. The default is to display all bug dump data.

---

## !callback

This command displays the callback data related to the current system trap. If the system has not experienced a system trap, this command is invalid. This is valid only on Intel-based systems NT 5.0 and later.

---

## !calldata <tablename>

Displays performance information in the form of procedure call statistics from the named table.

#### PARAMETERS

Tablename

The name of the table into which the call data is being collected.

---

## !ccb <ccb-address>

Given an NTFS CCB address, this command will format and display that information. The CCB address can be derived from a valid NTFS file object.

#### PARAMETERS

Ccb-address

The virtual address of the CCB that you want decoded.

## !cmreslist <device-object>

Formats and displays the Configuration Manager resource list for the specified device object. This is valid only on Windows NT 5.0 or later systems.

#### PARAMETERS

Device-object

The address of the device object whose resource list you wish to examine.

## !cxr <address>

Displays the processor context saved at the specified address.

#### PARAMETERS

Address

The address of the process context.

## !db <physical-address>

This command displays the contents of the *physical* address in byte form. This is one of the few commands that takes a physical address instead of a virtual address.

#### PARAMETERS

Physical-address

The absolute physical address of the memory that you wish to examine.

## !dd <physical-address>

This command displays the contents of the *physical* address in 32-bit doubleword form. This is one of the few commands that takes a physical address instead of a virtual address.

#### PARAMETERS

Physical-address

The absolute physical address of the memory that you wish to examine.

## !dblink <address> [count]

Given a list entry, this routine will walk the list's backward pointer and display previous list entries. This walk is bounded by a given count or will stop when it encounters a list whose back pointer is NULL.

#### PARAMETERS

Address
: The address of the list entry that should serve as the starting point.

Count
: The number of list entries to step through. If this count is not specified, the traversal will continue until a list entry whose back pointer is NULL is encountered.

## !dbgprint

This command displays any information that may be stored in the kernel's debug print buffers. This is valid only on NT 5.0 and later systems.

## !devnode <device-object>

Given a device object, this command will display the fields of the corresponding device node. This is valid only on NT 5.0 and later systems.

#### PARAMETERS

Device-object
: The address of the device object whose device node you want to examine.

## !devobj <device-address>

This command displays a formatted view of fields within the device object, given its address.

#### PARAMETERS

Device-address
: The address of the device object that you want to examine.

## !dflink <list-address> [count]

Given a list entry, this routine will walk the list's forward pointer and display next list entries. This walk is bounded by a given count or will stop when it encounters a list whose back pointer is NULL. This is valid only on NT 5.0 or later systems (while its corresponding command, "dblink," is valid on NT 4.0 and later systems).

#### PARAMETERS

Address

The address of the list entry that should serve as the starting point.

Count

The number of list entries to step through. If this count is not specified, the traversal will continue until a list entry whose forward pointer is NULL is encountered.

## !dh <address>

Given the address of a NTFS file object, this command will display the fields of that file object's header.

#### PARAMETERS

Address

The address of a valid NTFS file object.

## !dlls <process-address>

This command scans the given process or thread and lists the modules that the thread is using, along with the entry points into that module.

#### PARAMETERS

Process-address

The address of the process or thread that you want to examine.

## !drvobj <driver-address>

Formats and displays the fields of a given driver object.

#### PARAMETERS

Driver-address
: The address of the driver object.

---

## !drivers [flags]

This command lists all of the drivers currently loaded into the system or crash dump that you are debugging.

#### PARAMETERS

Flags
: The flags can be logically OR'd together to provide alternate or additional output formats. The flags are as follows:

  1: Causes the command to output working set sizes for each driver.

  6: Forces base, header, and section information to also be displayed.

---

## !eb <physical-address> [byte-list]

Enters a list of values into the specified physical address. The values are entered as a series of bytes. If the values are not listed on the command line, you will be prompted to enter them. Strike the return key with no value entered to terminate the process.

#### PARAMETERS

Physical-address
: The physical address that you wish to modify.

Byte-list
: This is a space-separated list of bytes to enter into the memory locations specified.

---

## !ed <physical-address> [word-list]

Enters a list of values into the specified physical address. The values are entered as a series of 32-bit double-words. If the values are not listed on the command line, you will be prompted to enter them. Strike the return key with no value entered to terminate the process.

#### PARAMETERS

Physical-address
: The physical address that you wish to modify.

Word-list
: This is a space-separated list of double-words to enter into the memory locations specified.

---

### !errlog

This command displays data from the system error log.

---

### !exr <address>

Formats and displays the processor exception record stored at the specified address. The EXR address can be derived from the output of the "!pcr" command. This is most useful following a trap.

#### PARAMETERS

Address
: The virtual address of the EXR record.

---

### !exrlog

Formats and prints the system exception log.

---

### !fcb <fcb-address>

This command displays the fields of an NTFS file control block (FCB) for an active and valid file object. The FCB address can be easily derived from the file object, which can be displayed with the "!file" command.

#### PARAMETERS

Fcb-address
: The address of the file control block.

## !fcbtable <address>

This command displays the entries in the NTFS file control block table. This command is valid only in Windows NT 5.0 and later.

#### PARAMETERS

Address
   The address of the FCB table maintained by NTFS.

## !file <fileobject-address>

Displays the relevant fields and information from a valid NTFS file object.

#### PARAMETERS

Fileobject-address
   The address of the file object that you wish to examine.

## !filecache

Formats and displays information about the system's file cache.

## !filelock <file-object>

Provides detail of information relating to any file locks that may be in effect for the given file object.

#### PARAMETERS

File-object
   The address of the file object that you want to examine.

## !foirp <irp-address>

Given an IRP that is related to a file operation, this command will format and print the relevant file object details of that IRP.

#### PARAMETERS

Irp-address
   The address of the file operation IRP that is being examined.

## !frag [flags] [pool-address]

This displays information about the relative fragmentation of the various memory pools.

#### PARAMETERS

Flags

This indicates the type of information that you want displayed. The values are defined as follows (these flag values are logically ORable):

1: Displays all fragmentation information.
2: Includes information about memory allocation, including any tag information.

## !handle [address] [flags] [process] [typename]

Displays the per-process handle table information. If no process address is given, the command will assume the context of the currently executing process.

#### PARAMETERS

Address

The address of the handle. If present, this will return only information about this handle.

Flags

Describes the information you want to see in the output. These flags are defined as follows (and may be logically OR'd together):

2: Shows only handles to objects that are allocated from the nonpaged pool.
4: Shows only free handles for the process.
8: Shows only directory or symbolic link objects.

Process

The address of a process or thread whose handle table you wish to traverse. If not provided, the current process is assumed.

Typename

The type of handle you want to examine.

## !heap [address] [flags] [process]

Displays information about the system's heap usage.

#### PARAMETERS

Address

Address of a specific heap that you would like to examine. If zero, then all heaps are displayed.

Process

This parameter specfies either the ID or the address of the process whose heap you would like to examine.

Flags

Flags specify the quanitity of information that you would like displayed. These are:

- -v Verbose, provides the most information available on each entry.
- -f Displays only information on the items in the free list.
- -a Displays information on all heap types.
- -x Forces the system to attempt to dump data, even if the heap data structures seem invalid.

---

## !help

Provides a listing of some of the valid kernel extension commands.

---

## !icthread <thread-address>

Provides detail on the IRP context for a specified thread.

#### PARAMETERS

Thread-address

The address of the thread that you want to examine.

---

## !ib <port>

This command reads and displays a byte from the specified I/O port. You should be careful that reading the I/O port will not affect the behavior of the device that you are reading from. Some devices change state once a read-only port has been read.

#### PARAMETERS

Port

The port in the system I/O address space that you want to examine.

---

### !id <port>

This command reads and displays a 32-bit double-word from the specified I/O port. You should be careful that reading the I/O port will not affect the behavior of the device that you are reading from. Some devices change state once a read-only port has been read. You should also take care that the port you are reading from is capable of returning a 32-bit value.

#### PARAMETERS

Port

The port in the system I/O address space that you want to examine.

---

### !igrep <pattern> <start-address> <bounding-address>

Searches the specified address range for a pattern in the disassembled output.

#### PARAMETERS

Pattern

The string that you want to search the disassembled memory locations for.

Start-address

The starting address of the search.

Bounding-address

The final address to use for the search.

## !ioapic <address>

Formats and displays information from one of the system IOAPICs found at the specified address. This command is valid only on Intel-architecture systems.

#### PARAMETERS

Address
: The virtual address of the IOAPIC in the system's memory space.

## !ioreslist <device-object>

Displays the I/O Resource List, if any, for the specified device object. This is valid only on Windows NT 5.0 and later systems.

#### PARAMETERS

Device-object
: The address of the device object that you are querying.

## !iw <port>

This command reads and displays a 16-bit word from the specified I/O port. You should be careful that reading the I/O port will not affect the behavior of the device that you are reading from. Some devices change state once a read-only port has been read. You should also take care that the port you are reading from is capable of returning a 16-bit value.

#### PARAMETERS

Port
: The port in the system I/O address space that you want to examine.

## !irp [address] [flags]

Displays the important fields of the specified IRP.

#### PARAMETERS

Address
: Address of the IRP to examine.

Flags

If set to a nonzero number (regardless of value), the output will include verbose information about the IRP.

---

## !irpcontext <irp-address>

Don't know. Run it and see.

---

## !irpfind [flags]

This command will locate and print information about any currently outstanding or pending IRPs at the time either the debugger stopped the target or the crash occurred.

#### PARAMETERS

Flags

If set to *1*, full detail about the IRP will be printed.

---

## !job <address>

Displays resource and other information about the job associated with the given process or thread. This is valid only on Windows NT 5.0 and later systems.

#### PARAMETERS

Address

The address of either a process or thread that you wish to examine.

---

## !kb

Displays a formatted stack trace from the last trap frame used by the debugger. Use this command after a "!trap" or a "!cxr" command, so that it will use that stack frame.

---

## !kuser

Displays resource and other information about the currently logged-on user.

## !lcb <lcb-address>

Displays the fields of the specified NTFS LCB.

#### PARAMETERS

Lcb-address
: The address of the LCB that you wish to examine.

## !locks [-v] [address]

Displays information about ERESOURCE locks held by the system.

#### PARAMETERS

Flags
: Indicates which information the command should produce. The valid values are:

- -D: Displays all locks, not just those with contention.
- -P: Provides performance statistics on locks.
- -V: Provides a full accounting of lock information.

Address
: The address of a particular lock that you might want to examine.

## !lookaside [address] [options] [depth]

Displays information about the lookaside lists maintained by the operating system.

#### PARAMETERS

Address
: If specified, this parameter points to a specific list that you wish to examine. If absent, the debugger will display all lookaside list information.

Options
: Allows the user to either reset list counters or set the depth. The valid values are:

- 1: Resets the list counters.
- 2: Resets the depth of the lookaside list.

Depth

If option *2* was invoked, this parameter determines the depth of the lookaside list.

## !lpc

Provides detail on any outstanding local procedure calls that may be pending.

## !mcb <address>

Displays the fields of the specified NTFS MCB structure.

### PARAMETERS

Address

The address of the MCB structure to decode.

## !memusage

Provides summary statistics on the system's virtual memory usage.

## !mtrr

Displays the contents of the MTRR register. This is valid only on Intel-based platforms.

## !npx <address>

Displays the contents of the floating point register save area. This is valid only on Intel-based systems.

### PARAMETERS

Address

The address of the location of the NPX area.

## !ob <port> <value>

This command will write a byte of data to the specified I/O port. It will prompt you for the value to write.

### PARAMETERS

Port

The address in the I/O address space of the port that you want to write to.

Value

The byte value that you wish to output to the specified I/O port location.

## !obja <address>

Provides detail on the specific attributes of the specified object.

### PARAMETERS

Address

The address of the object under investigation.

## !object <address>

Displays the values of the object header at the specified address.

### PARAMETERS

Address

The address of the object header that you wish to examine.

## !od <port> <value>

This command will write a 32-bit double-word of data to the specified I/O port. It will prompt you for the value to write. You should take care to ensure that the port you are writing to has the ability to handle 32-bit values.

#### PARAMETERS

Port

The address in the I/O address space of the port that you want to write to.

Value

The double-word value that you wish to output to the specified I/O port location.

---

### !ow <port> <value>

This command will write a 16-bit word of data to the specified I/O port. It will prompt you for the value to write. You should take care to ensure that the port you are writing to has the ability to handle 16-bit write values.

#### PARAMETERS

Port

The address in the I/O address space of the port that you want to write to.

Value

The word value that you wish to output to the specified I/O port location.

---

### !pci [address]

Displays a formatted view of the PCI Type 2 configuration data that exists for the system's PCI busses. This is valid only on Intel-based platforms running Windows NT 5.0 or later.

#### PARAMETERS

Address

If provided, the debugger will display only information relating to this PCI address.

---

### !pcr [processor]

Displays the information contained within the process context register for the given processor. If no processor is specified, the current processor context is assumed.

#### PARAMETERS

Processor

The processor number in a multiprocessor computer that you want to examine.

## !peb <Address>

Displays a formatted view of the information contained within a process environment block. Note that this command does not assume the currently executing process, unlike most thread- and process-related commands.

#### PARAMETERS

Address

This is the address of the process that you want to examine. This is not the address of a PEB as derived from the kernel process block for the process.

## !pfn [entry] [flags]

Displays information about the specified page frame number database entry.

#### PARAMETERS

Entry

This specifies the entry number of the PFN that you want to examine. This number can be obtained by looking at the page table entry for the desired virtual address (using the !pte command).

Flags

If non-zero, the command will display the entire contents of the PFN structure. If zero, then only summary information is displayed.

## !podev <device-object>

Displays any relevant information about the power subsystem contained within the specified device object.

#### PARAMETERS

Device-object
: The device object whose power-related fields you wish to examine.

---

## !polist [device-object]

Provides a listing of power-related IRPs that are outstanding or pending in the system. This is valid only on Windows NT 5.0 or later platforms.

#### PARAMETERS

Device-object
: If specified, displays power-related IRPs associated with only this device.

---

## !ponode [flags]

Lists the elements in the device node table created by the power-management subsystem. This command is valid only on Windows NT 5.0 or later platforms.

#### PARAMETERS

Flags
: If set to a nonzero value, the devices will be listed in PNP enumeration order. The default is power-management ordering.

---

## !pool <address> [flags]

Provides statistics about the specified memory pool.

#### PARAMETERS

Address
: The address within the pool for which you wish statistics.

Flags
: A value indicating the level of detail you wish to see about this pool. The valid values are:

    0: Provides only summary information.
    1: Provides both summary information and allocation information.
    2: Includes the free-list information in the output.

## !poolfind <tag> [pooltype]

Searches through the various memory pools for a region that is allocated with the given tag. This is valid only on checked builds, because tags are not allocated on free builds.

#### PARAMETERS

Tag

The 4-byte tag that was given when the memory buffer was allocated .

Pooltype

The type of memory pool to search. The valid values for this are:

0: Searches only nonpaged pool memory for the tag.
1: Searches the paged pool for the given tag.

## !poolused [flags]

This command will display various information about memory pool usage.

#### PARAMETERS

Flags

The flags will determine how information is sorted and will determine the level of detail to display. The valid values are:

0: Sorts the information by tag, and provides summary information only. This is the default behavior.
1: Sorts the information by tag, and displays a verbose level of information.
2: Sorts the information by nonpaged memory usage, providing summary output only.
3: Sorts the information by nonpaged pool usage, providing verbose output.
4: Sorts by paged pool usage, providing summary information.
5: Sorts by paged pool usage, and provides verbose output.

## !process [address] [flags]

Displays a formatted view of the process state information for the requested process. This is the process information stored in the kernel process block. If no process address is provided, the currently executing thread is assumed.

#### PARAMETERS

Address

The address of the thread that is to be examined. A value of –1 (0xffffffff) defaults to the current process; this is necessary to use the flags field.

Flags

Bit-field of flags indicating which information about the process is to be displayed. The definition of the bit follows:

1: Displays complete process information, including virtual address usage and scheduling information.

## !processfields

This command displays the names and offsets of the various fields within a kernel thread block. This is useful when attempting to decode thread information.

## !pte <address>

Displays the page table entry (PTE) for the given address.

#### PARAMETERS

Address

The virtual address whose PTE you want to examine.

## !ptov <physical-address>

Translates a physical address into its corresponding virtual address.

#### PARAMETERS

Physical-address

The physical address to translate.

## !ready

Lists all threads that are marked as "ready to execute."

## !regkcb

Provides a display of the registry key control blocks (KCB).

## !scb <scb-address> [flags]

Displays information about the stream control block (SCB) on an open stream-type file in NTFS. This is valid only for debugging issues with NTFS.

### PARAMETERS

Scb-address

The address of the SCB to decode.

Flags

Controls the level of information displayed. The valid values are:

1: Includes information about the related FCB and VCB.
2: Includes information about the related FCB, VCB, and FCB tables.
4: Displays information for each stream file opened by the filesystem.
8: Displays information about each element in the FCB table.

## !sel [selector]

Displays information about the given processor selector. If no argument is given, the values for all current selectors will be displayed. This command is valid only on Intel-based architectures.

### PARAMETERS

Selector

The selector number to display. If this is omitted, all selector values will be displayed.

## !srb <address>

Displays the contents of the specified SCSI request block.

#### PARAMETERS

Address

This is the address of the SCSI request block to examine.

## !sysptes [flags]

This command displays a formatted view of the system page table entries (PTEs).

#### PARAMETERS

Flags

Bit-field of flags indicating which information should be included in the output. Definitions of these bits are as follows:

1: Includes information on the free PTEs.
2: Provides a value and count for each entry.
4: Provides detailed information about each entry.

## !teb <thread-address>

Displays a formatted view of the information contained within a thread environment block. Note that this command does not assume the currently executing thread, unlike most thread- and process-related commands.

#### PARAMETERS

Thread-address

This is the address of the thread that you want to examine. This is not the address of a TEB as derived from the kernel thread block for the thread.

## !thread [address] [flags]

Displays a formatted view of the thread state information for the requested thread. This is the thread information stored in the kernel thread block. If no thread address is provided, the currently executing thread is assumed.

#### PARAMETERS

Address

The address of the thread that is to be examined. A value of –1 (0xffffffff) indicates that the current process should be used; this is necessary to use the Flags field.

Flags

Bit-field of flags indicating which information about the thread is to be displayed. Definitions of these bits are as follows:

2: Displays information about the thread synchronization objects.

4: Displays information about the thread's LPC, addresses, and scheduling information.

Note that due to a bug in the implementation of this command, if '2' is not chosen, '4' will not provide the information described. This may be corrected in a subsequent release of the debugging tools.

## !threadfields

This command displays the names and offsets of the various fields within a kernel thread block. This is useful when attempting to decode thread information.

## !time

Displays information about the system timer variables that control performance counter behavior.

## !timer

Provides a detailed listing of all system timer usage.

## !token <token-address>

Provides a formatted view of a security token object. The fields of the token are listed with the "!tokenfields" command.

### PARAMETERS

Token-address

The address of the token to examine.

## !tokenfields

This command displays the names and offsets (from a token starting address) of the various fields within a token structure. This is useful when attempting to decode a token object.

## !trap <address>

This displays the context saved in the specified trap frame. This is valid only on Intel-based platforms.

### PARAMETERS

Address
: Address of the trap frame that you wish to examine. This can be derived from a stack trace using the built-in "k" command.

## !tss <address>

Displays a formatted view of the saved task state segment (TSS) information for the current processor. The address for the locations of this information can be found by examining the output of the "!pcr" command. This is valid only on Intel-based platforms.

### PARAMETERS

Address
: The address of the saved TSS information.

## !tunnel <address>

Displays the file property tunneling cache information for the given file.

### PARAMETERS

Address
: The address of the file object that you want to examine.

## !trap <address>

Provides the processor context at the specified trap frame address.

#### PARAMETERS

Address
: The address of the trap frame that is to be examined.

## !vad <address>

Provides detail on the virtual address descriptor (VAD) for the given address within the VAD tree.

#### PARAMETERS

Address
: The virtual address of the VAD entry that is to be examined.

## !vcb <vcb-address> [flags]

Displays information about the NTFS volume control block.

#### PARAMETERS

Vcb-address
: The address of the volume control block to examine.

Flags
: Bit-field indicating which information you would like displayed. The valid values are as follows:

1: Include the FCB table for the volume
2: Include the FCB table and FCB entries for all stream files.
4: Include all FCB entries, not just stream files.
8: Display all FCB entries, followed by the VCB. The VCB is redundant output, because there is only one that keeps being repeatedly displayed.

## !version

Displays the version of the kernel extension that is loaded, along with the version of the kernel that it supports.

## !vm

Displays virtual memory statistics maintained by the operating system.

APPENDIX B

# Windows Stop Codes

*This appendix details the bug check codes that you will experience in Windows 2000 blue screens and crash dumps. You should be aware that most of these bug check codes are used internally by the operating system, and understanding the internal bug check codes is hard to do without access to the actual Windows 2000 source code. Microsoft defines the bug check codes in the header file* bugcodes.h. *This header file is installed as part of the Microsoft Windows 2000 Device Driver Kit (DDK). Also, you should be aware that the terms* bug check *and* stop code *are interchangeable in the Windows world.*

*Detail on how to use the debugger to examine a dump is found in Chapter 7 of this book, and a complete description of an NT blue screen is provided in Chapter 3.*

*A bug check is generated when a device calls the routines* KeBugCheck( ) *and* KeBugCheckEx( ). *The routine* KeBugCheck( ) *causes a bug check condition to occur with no parameters. The function* KeBugCheckEx( ), *on the other hand, allows four parameters to be passed as additional information to help diagnose the condition that caused the bug check. These routines are described fully in the DDK documentation.*

# Bug Check Code Listing

The Windows NT bug check codes for versions 4.0 and 5.0 (Windows 2000) are listed below in numerical order. Comments and parameters are noted where they are available and make sense to use. You will note that many bug check codes are unused—they may be relics of previous versions or placeholders for future use. Regardless of their origin or intent, they are included for completeness.

The usage and interpretation describes all of the stop codes as they are used by NT when it ships from Microsoft. You should be aware that third-party device driver writers are free to use the predefined stop codes as they see fit, and such usage may not conform to the descriptions provided here. If you see unexpected parameters from the stop codes, check your stack to ensure that they are not being issued from a third-party device driver.

## APC_INDEX_MISMATCH 0x1

On a checked build of NT, this error will occur when a file system has a mismatched number of *KeEnterCriticalRegion()* and *KeLeaveCriticalRegion()*. This is a problem with the filesystem. If the problem persists, load an unchecked version of the file system.

**PARAMETERS:**

No parameters.

## DEVICE_QUEUE_NOT_BUSY 0x2

This bug check code is not used by current versions of Windows NT.

## INVALID_AFFINITY_SET 0x3

This exception is raised by the exported (and undocumented) routine *KeSetAffinityThread()* when the requested thread affinity is not a subset of the parent process's affinity. This will also occur if the requested affinity is NULL. A stack trace will indicate the caller that issued the *KeSetAffinityThread()* call.

**PARAMETERS:**

No parameters.

## INVALID_PROCESS_ATTACH_ATTEMPT 0x5

When attempting to attach a thread to a process's address space, this bug check will occur if either there is already an address space attached or the thread is executing a deferred procedure call (DPC). This is an internal Windows NT bug check code.

**PARAMETERS:**

1: The process to which we're attempting to attach the thread.
2: The process to which the thread is already attached.
3: A flag indicating whether a kernel APC is in progress.
4: A flag indicating whether the thread is executing a DPC.

## INVALID_PROCESS_DETACH_ATTEMPT 0x6

Occurring only in checked builds, this bug check code indicates that NT is attempting to detach a thread from a process's address space while either there is an APC in progress or the kernel or user APC queues are not empty. This is an internal Windows NT bug check code.

**PARAMETERS:**

No parameters.

## INVALID_SOFTWARE_INTERRUPT 0x7

Not currently used by Windows NT.

## IRQL_NOT_DISPATCH_LEVEL 0x8

Not currently used by Windows NT.

## IRQL_NOT_GREATER_OR_EQUAL 0x9

Unknown at this time what Windows NT uses this bug check code for.

**PARAMETERS:**

Parameters unknown.

## IRQL_NOT_LESS_OR_EQUAL 0xA

This is a very common bug check code that indicates a driver is using an invalid or improper address, usually an errant pointer. The actual code is triggered when a thread accesses pageable memory when the interrupt request level (IRQL) is too high.

With the kernel debugger attached, you should look at the stack trace. This will usually show the offending routine. The address passed in parameter 4 to the bug check will also live within the routine that caused the failure.

### PARAMETERS:

1: Virtual address of the memory referenced.
2: The IRQL at which the access was attempted.
3: Value indicating whether the operation was a read operation or write operation.
   0 = read operation, 1 = write operation
4: Address in the code that referenced the memory.

## NO_EXCEPTION_HANDLING_SUPPORT 0xB

This code is unused by Windows NT at this time.

## MAXIMUM_WAIT_OBJECTS_EXCEEDED 0xC

This bug check is generated when a call to *KeWaitForMultipleObjects()* specifies a wait block array or uses the built-in thread wait block array that exceeds the maximum allowed wait objects (defined in a header file as *MAXIMUM_WAIT_OBJECTS*). A stack trace will show the routine that is causing the error. The solution is to recode your driver to not exceed this limit.

### PARAMETERS:

No parameters.

## MUTEX_LEVEL_NUMBER_VIOLATION 0xD

This code indicates that mutexes have been acquired in the incorrect order. You can use the header file *ddk\inc\exlevels.h* to identify the mutexes that are being acquired in the incorrect order. A stack trace from within the kernel debugger will quickly show the offending routine.

PARAMETERS:

1: The current mutex level of the executing thread.
2: The mutex that you are attempting to acquire.

## NO_USER_MODE_CONTEXT 0xE

This code is unused by Windows NT at this time.

## SPIN_LOCK_ALREADY_OWNED 0xF

This code is unused by Windows NT at this time.

## THREAD_NOT_MUTEX_OWNER 0x11

This code is unused by Windows NT at this time.

## TRAP_CAUSE_UNKNOWN 0x12

This code is unused by the current versions of Windows NT.

## EMPTY_THREAD_REAPER_LIST 0x13

This code is unused by the current versions of Windows NT.

## CREATE_DELETE_LOCK_NOT_LOCKED 0x14

This code is unused by the current versions of Windows NT.

## LAST_CHANCE_CALLED_FROM_KMODE 0x15

This code is unused by the current versions of Windows NT.

## CID_HANDLE_CREATION 0x16

This code is unused by the current versions of Windows NT.

## CID_HANDLE_DELETION 0x17

This code is unused by the current versions of Windows NT.

## REFERENCE_BY_POINTER 0x18

This code is unused by Windows NT at this time.

## BAD_POOL_HEADER 0x19

This bug check code is generated when the operating system sanity checks the header attached to a pool of memory before freeing it. This indicates memory corruption, most likely from an errant pointer in a device driver.

On a free build of Windows NT, this will occur with no parameters from the function *ExFreePool()*. On a checked build, there will be parameters to help diagnose the problem if the code is using tagged memory pools from the function *ExFreePoolWithTag()* (always a good idea when debugging a device driver).

### PARAMETERS:

No parameters on a free build of Windows NT.

—or—

1: Index indicating which field is corrupt in the pool header.

2: Pool entry.

3: Virtual address of the pool entry.

4: 0

## MEMORY_MANAGEMENT 0x1A

This bug check is a "catch-all" code that indicates a problem with the internal consistency of the memory management component of Windows NT. It will occur with or without parameters—parameters that are meaningless without access to the source code for the operating system.

The most likely cause of this bug check is a driver with misbehaving pointers. If you have not installed a new device driver, attempt to boot NT from its last known good state. Failing that, you may have a hardware problem that is corrupting memory.

#### PARAMETERS:

Parameters unknown.

## PFN_SHARE_COUNT 0x1B

This code is unused by the current versions of Windows NT.

## PFN_REFERENCE_COUNT 0x1C

This code is unused by the current versions of Windows NT.

## NO_SPIN_LOCK_AVAILABLE 0x1D

This code is unused by the current versions of Windows NT.

## KMODE_EXCEPTION_NOT_HANDLED 0x1E

This code indicates that an exception occurred in kernel mode that the operating system doesn't know how to deal with. This is a very common bug check condition.

The exception and its address are passed as parameters, and the address of the exception will isolate the driver and function that caused the problem. The address can be checked against the load addresses of the various device drivers within the operating system to determine the driver that caused the problem.

#### PARAMETERS:

1: Actual exception code that wasn't handled.
2: Virtual address of the code that excepted.
3: Parameter 0 of the exception, if any.
4: Parameter 1 of the exception, if any.

## SHARED_RESOURCE_CONV_ERROR 0x1F

This code is not used by the current versions of Windows NT.

## KERNEL_APC_PENDING_DURING_EXIT 0x20

During the termination of a thread, the kernel detected that an APC (asynchronous procedure call) was pending. Passed as one of the parameters to the bug check call is the thread's *APC disable count*. If this parameter is negative, the problem is that an installed filesystem has called *FsRtlEnterFileSystem()* more times than it has called *FsRtlExtiFileSystem()*. A positive value for APC disable count indicates that a filesystem called *FsRtlExitFileSystem()* more often than it called *FsRtlEnterFileSystem()*.

Another thing to check is the current IRQL (also passed as an argument). If the current IRQL is not zero, the problem was probably caused by a device driver's cancel routine returning at an elevated IRQL.

**PARAMETERS:**

1: The virtual address of the APC found pending during exit.
2: The current thread's APC disable count
3: The current IRQL

## QUOTA_UNDERFLOW 0x21

This code is not used by the current versions of Windows NT.

## FILE_SYSTEM 0x22

This error indicates an internal problem within the filesystem. If the problem persists, and you are using the filesystem as delivered from Microsoft, contact its technical support. If you have built the filesystem from the Installable File System Kit (IFS kit) or another source, the problem may be caused by that filesystem driver.

**PARAMETERS:**

1: An indicator of where in the code the problem exists. The high 16 bits include a number that identifies the source file in the filesystem that caused the problem. The low 16 bits of this value indicate a position within the source file.
2: 0
3: 0
4: 0

## FAT_FILE_SYSTEM 0x23

This error indicates an internal problem within the file system. If the problem persists and you are using the filesystem as delivered from Microsoft, contact its technical support. If you have built the filesystem from the IFS kit or another source, the problem may be caused by that filesystem driver.

**PARAMETERS:**

1: An indicator of where in the code the problem exists. The high 16 bits include a number that identifies the source file in the filesystem that caused the problem. The low 16 bits of this value indicate a position within the source file.

2: 0

3: 0

4: 0

## NTFS_FILE_SYSTEM 0x24

This error indicates an internal problem within the NT filesystem. If the problem persists, and you are using the filesystem as delivered from Microsoft, contact its technical support. If you have built the filesystem from the IFS kit or another source, the problem may be caused by that filesystem driver.

**PARAMETERS:**

1: An indicator of where in the code the problem exists. The high 16 bits include a number that identifies the source file in the filesystem that caused the problem. The low 16 bits of this value indicate a position within the source file.

2: 0

3: 0

4: 0

## NPFS_FILE_SYSTEM 0x25

This error indicates an internal problem within the Named Pipe filesystem. If the problem persists and you are using the filesystem as delivered from Microsoft, contact its technical support. If you have built the filesystem from the IFS kit or another source, the problem may be caused by that filesystem driver.

**PARAMETERS:**

1: An indicator of where in the code the problem exists. The high 16 bits include a number that identifies the source file in the filesystem that caused the problem. The low 16 bits of this value indicate a position within the source file.

2: 0

3: 0

4: 0

## CDFS_FILE_SYSTEM 0x26

This error indicates an internal problem within the CD filesystem. If the problem persists, and you are using the filesystem as delivered from Microsoft, contact its technical support. If you have built the filesystem from the IFS kit or another source, the problem may be caused by that filesystem driver.

**PARAMETERS:**

1: An indicator of where in the code the problem exists. The high 16 bits include a number that identifies the source file in the filesystem that caused the problem. The low 16 bits of this value indicate a position within the source file.

2: 0

3: 0

4: 0

## RDR_FILE_SYSTEM 0x27

This error indicates an internal problem within the RDR filesystem. If the problem persists and you are using the filesystem as delivered from Microsoft, contact its technical support. If you have built the filesystem from the IFS kit or another source, the problem may be caused by that filesystem driver.

**PARAMETERS:**

1: An indicator of where in the code the problem exists. The high 16 bits include a number that identifies the source file in the filesystem that caused the problem. The low 16 bits of this value indicate a position within the source file.

2: 0

3: 0

4: 0

## CORRUPT_ACCESS_TOKEN 0x28

This code is unused by the current versions of Windows NT.

## SECURITY_SYSTEM 0x29

This bug check occurs if the security system is asked to perform an unknown, security-related operation on an object. If you encounter this error and can reproduce it, load the checked build of Windows NT and connect the kernel debugger. An assert will fail in place of this bug check and may provide additional information as to the state of the system at the time of the failure.

### PARAMETERS:

No parameters.

## INCONSISTENT_IRP 0x2A

As its name implies, an interrupt request packet (IRP) was found in an inconsistent state. An example of this is an IRP that is marked as pending but was completed.

### PARAMETERS:

1: Virtual address of the IRP that was found to be inconsistent.
2: 0
3: 0
4: 0

## PANIC_STACK_SWITCH 0x2B

This code tells us that the kernel's stack was overrun. This occurs most often when a device driver uses too much stack space, by nesting call stacks too deep or allocating too many stack variables. More rarely, this bug check will occur if there is memory corruption. A stack trace from the kernel debugger will isolate the culpable function.

### PARAMETERS:

No parameters.

## PORT_DRIVER_INTERNAL 0x2C

This code is used by a third-party port driver to indicate an internal error. A stack trace will show the driver that raised the bug check.

**PARAMETERS:**

Parameters unknown.

## SCSI_DISK_DRIVER_INTERNAL 0x2D

This code is used by third-party SCSI disk drivers to indicate an internal error. A stack trace will show the driver that raised the bug check.

**PARAMETERS:**

Parameters unknown.

## DATA_BUS_ERROR 0x2E

This code is caused by a parity error in the main system memory or by accessing a kernel mode address that does not exist.

**PARAMETERS:**

1: Faulting virtual address.
2: Faulting physical address.
3: Processor status register (PSR).
4: Faulting instruction register (FIR).

## INSTRUCTION_BUS_ERROR 0x2F

This bug check code indicates that the operating system detected an error on the instruction bus when running on non–Intel-based platforms. This indicates a hardware problem.

**PARAMETERS:**

No parameters.

## SET_OF_INVALID_CONTEXT 0x30

This code indicates that an error occurred while attempting to manipulate the trap frame on Intel-based platforms. This usually indicates a hardware problem or serious operating system corruption.

**PARAMETERS:**

No parameters.

## PHASE0_INITIALIZATION_FAILED 0x31

This code indicates that the system initialization phase experienced a failure early in the initialization process. Because there are no parameters to this bug check, it is hard to know what failed. More detail can be ascertained by connecting the kernel debugger and examining the stack trace.

**PARAMETERS:**

No parameters.

## PHASE1_INITIALIZATION_FAILED 0x32

This bug check occurs when either the "EX" or "KE" components of the operating system fail to initialize.

**PARAMETERS:**

1: The NT status code that describes why the initialization failed.
2: Indicates location within the source code that the failure occurred.

## UNEXPECTED_INITIALIZATION_CALL 0x33

This bug check occurs when one of the various operating system components is asked to initialize for an unknown initialization phase. This should never occur outside of the development labs. If it does and you can reproduce the problem, get a crash dump to Microsoft.

**PARAMETERS:**

No parameters.

## CACHE_MANAGER 0x34

This error indicates an internal problem within the file cache manager. If the problem persists, contact Microsoft or your computer vendor for technical support.

**PARAMETERS:**

1: An indicator of where in the code the problem exists. The high 16 bits include a number that identifies the source file in the filesystem that caused the problem. The low 16 bits of this value indicate a position within the source file.
2: 0
3: 0
4: 0

## NO_MORE_IRP_STACK_LOCATIONS 0x35

This bug check code occurs when one driver calls another driver using the *IoCallDriver()* facilities and exceeds the amount of stack space allocated in the IRP. If the stack space is exceeded, the driver being called cannot access the parameters for the request. Because the calling driver thinks the packet is valid, memory corruption has probably occurred. The driver that originally issued the *IoCallDriver()* (or issued the IRP directly) is responsible for validating the stack locations prior to issuing the request.

**PARAMETERS:**

1: Virtual address of the IRP.
2: 0
3: 0
4: 0

## DEVICE_REFERENCE_COUNT_NOT_ZERO 0x36

This bug check code indicates that some device driver attempted to delete its device object while another component was still using it. A device driver must not delete one of its device objects while the reference count for the object indicates that it is still being referenced. This is a bug in the calling device driver, because it is the responsibility of the device driver to ensure that the reference counts are zero before attempting the operation. A stack trace will show the offending driver, and the first parameter to the bug check code lists the virtual address of the device object that's being deleted.

**PARAMETERS:**

1: Address of the device object.
2: 0
3: 0
4: 0

## FLOPPY_INTERNAL_ERROR 0x37

An internal error occurred in the floppy disk driver. If you can easily reproduce the problem, you should get a crash dump to the support engineers at Microsoft.

**PARAMETERS:**

Parameters unknown.

## SERIAL_DRIVER_INTERNAL 0x38

An internal error occurred in the serial port driver. If you can reproduce the problem, you should get a crash dump to the support engineers at Microsoft.

**PARAMETERS:**

Parameters unknown.

## SYSTEM_EXIT_OWNED_MUTEX 0x39

This code is not used by the current versions of Windows NT.

## SYSTEM_UNWIND_PREVIOUS_USER 0x3A

This code is not used by the current versions of Windows NT.

## SYSTEM_SERVICE_EXCEPTION 0x3B

This code is not used by the current versions of Windows NT.

## INTERRUPT_UNWIND_ATTEMPTED 0x3C

This code is not used by the current versions of Windows NT.

## INTERRUPT_EXCEPTION_NOT_HANDLED 0x3D

This code appears on non-Intel platforms when the processor receives an interrupt that it does not recognize.

### PARAMETERS:

Parameters unknown.

## MULTIPROCESSOR_CONFIGURATION_NOT_SUPPORTED 0x3E

This bug check indicates that a multiprocessor has mismatched processors. Windows NT running on a multiprocessor system requires that all of the processors be of the same type and level. Either all processors must have floating point support or no processors should. This stop code will also occur if you install Windows NT 4.0 on a multiprocessor 80386 machine.

An example of mismatched processors would be mixing an Intel 80486 CPU with a Intel Pentium CPU within the same system. Another example is mixing a 400-MHz Pentium II with a 200-MHz Pentium II on the same motherboard.

### PARAMETERS:

No parameters.

## NO_MORE_SYSTEM_PTES 0x3F

This code indicates that the operating system has exhausted its supply of page table entries (PTEs). This is almost always caused by a device driver that does not clean up after itself correctly. You can examine the PTE situation in the kernel with the "!sysptes" command in the Windows kernel debugger.

### PARAMETERS:

No parameters.

## TARGET_MDL_TOO_SMALL 0x40

This bug check occurs when a driver attempts to map an MDL into another MDL and the target MDL is not large enough to hold the source pages (with a call to *IoBuildPartialMdl()*). This is almost always a driver bug. A stack trace will uncover the misbehaving function.

**PARAMETERS:**

No parameters.

## MUST_SUCCEED_POOL_EMPTY 0x41

A driver has attempted to allocate memory and indicated that the allocation "must succeed" (indicated with a flag to *ExAllocatePool()*) and that there was no memory available to satisfy the allocation request.

**PARAMETERS:**

1: The size of the request that failed.
2: The number of pages used in the nonpaged pool.
3: The number of requests from nonpaged pool that are greater than PAGE_SIZE.
4: The total number of pages available.

## ATDISK_DRIVER_INTERNAL 0x42

An internal error has occurred within the IDE disk driver. A crash dump should be taken and forwarded to support engineers at Microsoft.

**PARAMETERS:**

Parameters unknown.

## NO_SUCH_PARTITION 0x43

This code is currently unused by Windows NT.

## MULTIPLE_IRP_COMPLETE_REQUESTS 0x44

This bug check code appears when a device driver attempts to complete an IRP that has already been completed (with a call to *IoCompleteRequest()).* This can be caused by a couple of different scenarios. First, two drivers can believe that they are the rightful owners of the IRP and each attempt to complete it. In this case, the stack trace will give you only one of the two drivers—it won't give you the first. Second, a device driver can actually attempt to complete the IRP twice, in which case, a stack trace will be fruitful and the driver will have to be corrected.

**PARAMETERS:**

1: Virtual address of the IRP.
2: 0
3: 0
4: 0

## INSUFFICIENT_SYSTEM_MAP_REGS 0x45

On non-Intel platforms, this bug check occurs when the operating system attempts to allocate virtual memory map registers and that fails. This indicates a hardware problem.

**PARAMETERS:**

No parameters.

## DEREF_UNKNOWN_LOGON_SESSION 0x46

This bug check occurs when the security system is asked to remove a logon session that it did not know existed.

**PARAMETERS:**

No parameters.

## REF_UNKNOWN_LOGON_SESSION 0x47

This code is unused on current versions of Windows NT.

## CANCEL_STATE_IN_COMPLETED_IRP 0x48

This stop code occurs when an I/O Request Packet (an IRP) has a cancel routine specified but is also being cancelled by the I/O subsystem. This indicates that the IRP no longer belongs to a driver but that it can be cancelled. This predominantly happens when a driver mishandles the IRP or when there are two threads (or drivers) accessing the fields of the same IRP.

### PARAMETERS:

1: Pointer to the IRP that the I/O subsystem is attempting to cancel.
2: 0
3: 0
4: 0

## PAGE_FAULT_WITH_INTERRUPTS_OFF 0x49

This bug check code indicates that a driver is using an invalid or improper address, usually an errant pointer. It could also occur if a device driver is using pageable memory within a region on code that executes with interrupts disabled. The actual code is triggered when the virtual memory system attempts to page in memory when interrupts are disabled.

With the kernel debugger attached, you should look at the stack trace. This will usually show the offending routine. The address passed in parameter 4 to the bug check will also live within the routine that caused the failure. This code appears to be unused in current implementations of Windows NT.

### PARAMETERS:

Parameters unknown.

## IRQL_GT_ZERO_AT_SYSTEM_SERVICE 0x4A

This code does not appear to be used by the current versions of Windows NT.

## STREAMS_INTERNAL_ERRROR 0x4B

This code indicates that an internal error occurred within the stream subsystem of the Windows NT operating environment.

**PARAMETERS:**

Parameters unknown.

## FATAL_UNHANDLED_HARD_ERROR 0x4C

This bug check code indicates that there was a catastrophic error during the system boot process. There are numerous potential causes. The cause code that is delivered in parameter 2 offers up the best explanation. Potential values for this parameter follow:

**PARAMETERS:**

1: NT Status of failing operation, if any.
2: The failure parameter. The possible values for this parameter are:

   0x218—This parameter code indicates that a critical registry hive could not be loaded because it is either missing or corrupt.

   0x21A—This parameter tells us that one of the critical system processes (either winlogon or csrss) has ceased execution. The NT status code in the first parameter will provide some insight as to the failing error.

   0x221—This parameter indicates that either a system driver or DLL was determined to be corrupt. The stop screen will show the name of this file.

3: 0
4: 0

## NO_PAGES_AVAILABLE 0x4D

This bug check occurs when the operating system needs memory and there are no pages available for it. Ensure that you have sufficient memory. If you do and this problem persists, you probably have a device driver or other component that is allocating memory and never freeing it (a memory leak).

**PARAMETERS:**

1: The number of dirty pages.
2: The number of physical pages in machine.
3: The extended commit value in pages.
4: The total commit value in pages.

## PFN_LIST_CORRUPT 0x4E

This stop code occurs when corruption is detected in the page frame database (PFN) table. It is almost exclusively caused by a driver that overwrites the wrong memory locations with an errant pointer.

**PARAMETERS:**

1: The number 1.
2: The list head value that was corrupt.
3: The number of pages available in the pool.
4: The number 0.

—or—

1: The number 2.
2: The entry in list being removed.
3: The highest physical page number.
4: The reference count of entry being removed.

## NDIS_INTERNAL_ERROR 0x4F

This bug check code indicates an internal error within an NDIS driver located on your system. A stack trace will show you the offending device driver.

**PARAMETERS:**

Parameters unknown.

## PAGE_FAULT_IN_NONPAGED_AREA 0x50

There are two broad pools of memory in the Windows NT kernel address space. There is the *paged pool,* which is memory that can be allocated and paged in and out of the backing store. There is also the *nonpaged pool,* which is always resident in memory and cannot be paged in and out of the page file.

This bug check code indicates that the memory management system received a page fault when accessing data (or instructions) located in the nonpaged pool. This bug check indicates either severe corruption or a hardware problem.

**PARAMETERS:**

1: Virtual address that Windows NT is trying to fault in.
2: Flag indicating whether the fault was caused by a write instruction: 1 if true, 0 if false.

3: Flag indicating whether the previous mode was kernel mode or a user-mode application.
4: Fault-specific value indicating where in the memory management code the bug check occurred.

## REGISTRY_ERROR 0x51

This stop code tells us that something is wrong with the registry. There is a number of things that could be at issue with the registry.

If the stack trace indicates that the current thread is a system worker thread (which you can tell by *CmpWorker* being on the stack), it is a fairly simple matter to isolate the problem thread. The method that you can use to determine the culprit thread is to execute the following on the kernel debugger attached to the failed machine:

```
dd CmpRegistryMutex+18 L1
!thread <value from above listed command>
```

This should provide you with the thread and the stack that made the registry call that caused the corruption.

This code can also occur if there is a failure in the registry refresh code, which is used only by the security subsystem. This may be simply a problem of the volume containing the registry hive files being full. This is especially likely on primary or backup domain controllers with large numbers of accounts in the SAM.

Finally, this bug check can occur if there is a problem reading the registry hive from the underlying physical volume. This could indicate a hardware problem.

### PARAMETERS:

Parameters are unknown.

## MAILSLOT_FILE_SYSTEM 0x52

This error indicates an internal problem within the filesystem. If the problem persists, and you are using the filesystem as delivered from Microsoft, contact its technical support. If you have built the filesystem from the IFS kit or another source, the problem may be caused by that filesystem driver.

### PARAMETERS:

1: An indicator of where in the code the problem exists. The high 16 bits include a number that identifies the source file in the filesystem that caused the problem. The low 16 bits of this value indicate a position within the source file.

2: 0

3: 0

4: 0

## NO_BOOT_DEVICE 0x53

This bug check code is not issued by the current versions of Windows NT. If Windows NT can initialize to the point that it can detect that there is no boot device, it will issue the bug check code INACCESSIBLE_BOOT_DEVICE (0x7B).

## LM_SERVER_INTERNAL_ERROR 0x54

This bug check code indicates that there was an error internal to the LANMAN subsystem in the Windows NT kernel. A stack trace will indicate the offending routine. A crash dump should be sent to the support team at Microsoft.

#### PARAMETERS:

Parameters unknown.

## DATA_COHERENCY_EXCEPTION 0x55

This bug check code is not used by the current versions of Windows NT.

## INSTRUCTION_COHERENCY_EXCEPTION 0x56

This bug check code is not used by the current versions of Windows NT.

## XNS_INTERNAL_ERROR 0x57

This bug check code is internal to the XNS component of Windows NT. It is undocumented and indicates a problem with a shipping Windows NT software component.

#### PARAMETERS:

Parameters unknown.

## FTDISK_INTERNAL_ERROR 0x58

This bug check occurs when you attempt to boot from a primary partition that was revived from a mirror set. The registry indicates that the mirror in this case is okay, when it really is not. You must reboot from the shadow.

**PARAMETERS:**

No parameters.

## PINBALL_FILE_SYSTEM 0x59

This error indicates an internal problem within the filesystem. If the problem persists and you are using the file system as delivered from Microsoft, contact its technical support. If you have built the filesystem from the IFS kit or another source, the problem may be caused by that filesystem driver.

**PARAMETERS:**

1: An indicator of where in the code the problem exists. The high 16 bits include a number that identifies the source file in the filesystem that caused the problem. The low 16 bits of this value indicate a position within the source file.
2: 0
3: 0
4: 0

## CRITICAL_SERVICE_FAILED 0x5A

If there is a critical failure during the boot process, the operating system attempts to boot off of the "last known good" instance of Windows NT. If the critical failure continues, this bug check is issued. The parameters are apparently meaningless and are hard-coded to the described values.

**PARAMETERS:**

1: 5
2: 9
3: 0
4: 0

## SET_ENV_VAR_FAILED 0x5B

If there is a critical failure during the boot process, the operating system attempts to boot off of the "last known good" instance of Windows NT. If the loader cannot set the environment to point at the last known good instance of Windows NT, this bug check will occur. The parameters are apparently meaningless and hard-coded to the described values.

**PARAMETERS:**

1: 5
2: 10
3: 0
4: 0

## HAL_INITIALIZATION_FAILED 0x5C

This bug check code indicates that there was an error when the hardware abstraction layer (HAL) attempted to initialize either the hardware or its own internal data structures. This usually indicates either a hardware problem or a HAL that is mismatched with the hardware.

**PARAMETERS:**

No parameters.

## HEAP_INITIALIZATION_FAILED 0x5D

This bug check code does not appear to be used by the currently shipping versions of Windows NT.

## OBJECT_INITIALIZATION_FAILED 0x5E

This bug check occurs when the Object Manager component of the Windows NT operating system fails to initialize during the phase 0 initialization.

**PARAMETERS:**

No parameters.

## SECURITY_INITIALIZATION_FAILED 0x5F

This bug check occurs when the Security Manager component of the Windows NT operating system fails to initialize during the phase 0 initialization.

**PARAMETERS:**

No parameters.

## PROCESS_INITIALIZATION_FAILED 0x60

This bug check occurs when the process subsystem within the Windows NT operating system fails to initialize during the phase 0 initialization.

**PARAMETERS:**

No parameters.

## HAL1_INITIALIZATION_FAILED 0x61

This bug check code occurs during the phase 1 initialization, when the HAL attempts to start all of the processors in a multiprocessor system and is unable to do so.

**PARAMETERS:**

No parameters.

## OBJECT1_INITIALIZATION_FAILED 0x62

This bug check code occurs when there is an error in initializing the Object Manager component of Windows NT during the phase 1 initialization of the system.

**PARAMETERS:**

No parameters.

## SECURITY1_INITIALIZATION_FAILED 0x63

This bug check appears when there is an error initializing the Security Manager component of the Windows NT operating system during the phase 1 initialization of the system.

**PARAMETERS:**

No parameters.

## SYMBOLIC_INITIALIZATION_FAILED 0x64

During the phase 0 system initialization, the operating system attempts to create a symbolic link to "\SystemRoot." This bug check code indicates that this operation failed. The first passed parameter provides the NT status code from the attempted link operation.

During the phase 1 system initialization, the operating system attempts to create a directory object and symbolic links for the "\ARCNAME" directory. If any of this fails, this bug check code will be generated. The status code from the failed operation is passed as the first parameter.

**PARAMETERS:**

1: The NT status code of the attempting link operation.
2: Integer representing where within the code the failure occurred.
3: 0
4: 0

## MEMORY1_INITIALIZATION_FAILED 0x65

This bug check code indicates that the Memory Manager component of Windows NT failed to initialize correctly during the phase 1 initialization of Windows NT.

**PARAMETERS:**

No parameters.

## CACHE_INITIALIZATION_FAILED 0x66

During the phase 1 initialization of the operating system, the loader attempts to bring the Cache Manager into operation. This bug check code indicates that this was a failure.

### PARAMETERS:

No parameters.

## CONFIG_INITIALIZATION_FAILED 0x67

This bug check code indicates that the initialization code could not make either the "\REGISTRY\MACHINE\SYSTEM" or the "\REGISTRY\MACHINE\HARDWARE" registry keys available for some reason. Two possible causes are a corrupt registry or low memory.

### PARAMETERS:

No parameters.

## FILE_INITIALIZATION_FAILED 0x68

This bug check code indicates that the filesystem runtime component of the operating system failed to initialize properly.

### PARAMETERS:

No parameters.

## IO1_INITIALIZATION_FAILED 0x69

Initialization of the I/O system or the Plug-N-Play component has failed during the phase 1 initialization of Windows NT when this bug check occurs. This is almost exclusively the result of either misconfiguration of the machine by the user or setup having made some bad decisions when the operating system was installed.

### PARAMETERS:

No parameters.

## LPC_INITIALIZATION_FAILED 0x6A

This bug check code indicates that the LPC dispatch component of Windows NT failed to initialize for some reason.

**PARAMETERS:**

No parameters.

## PROCESS1_INITIALIZATION_FAILED 0x6B

This code occurs when the process subsystem fails to initialize during the phase 1 initialization of Windows NT.

**PARAMETERS:**

1: The status code of the failed initialization operation.
2: 0
3: 0
4: 0

## REFMON_INITIALIZATION_FAILED 0x6C

During the phase 1 initialization of the operating system, the security Reference Monitor failed to initialize properly.

**PARAMETERS:**

No parameters.

## SESSION1_INITIALIZATION_FAILED 0x6D

This stop code indicates that there was a failure during the machine initialization. If you encounter this, you should attempt to boot from an alternate saved configuration. If the machine continues to fail, you may need to reload.

**PARAMETERS:**

1: Indicates the NT status code that caused the initialization failed.
2: 0
3: 0
4: 0

## SESSION2_INITIALIZATION_FAILED 0x6E

This stop code indicates that there was a failure during the machine initialization. If you encounter this, you should attempt to boot from an alternate saved configuration. If the machine continues to fail, you may need to reload.

**PARAMETERS:**

1: Indicates the NT status code that caused the initialization failed.
2: 0
3: 0
4: 0

## SESSION3_INITIALIZATION_FAILED 0x6F

This stop code indicates that there was a failure during the machine initialization. If you encounter this, you should attempt to boot from an alternate saved configuration. If the machine continues to fail, you may need to reload.

**PARAMETERS:**

1: Indicates the NT status code that caused the initialization failed.
2: 0
3: 0
4: 0

## SESSION4_INITIALIZATION_FAILED 0x70

This stop code indicates that there was a failure during the machine initialization. If you encounter this, you should attempt to boot from an alternate saved configuration. If the machine continues to fail, you may need to reload.

**PARAMETERS:**

1: Indicates the NT status code that caused the initialization failed.
2: 0
3: 0
4: 0

## SESSION5_INITIALIZATION_FAILED 0x71

This stop code indicates that there was a failure during the machine initialization. If you encounter this, you should attempt to boot from an alternate saved configuration. If the machine continues to fail, you may need to reload.

**PARAMETERS:**

1: Indicates the NT status code that caused the initialization failed.
2: 0
3: 0
4: 0

## ASSIGN_DRIVE_LETTERS_FAILED 0x72

This stop code indicates that the system was unavailable to assign drive letters to logical drives. This causes the system to fail.

**PARAMETERS:**

Parameters are unknown.

## CONFIG_LIST_FAILED 0x73

This bug check code indicates that one of the core system registry hives is either corrupt or unreadable for some reason. If you continually encounter this bug check code, start your system from an alternate system configuration or restore the registry with the Emergency Repair Disk (ERD).

**PARAMETERS:**

1: 5
2: 2
3: The index of the failing hive in the list of hives.
4: A pointer to a UNICODE string containing the name of the hive file.

## BAD_SYSTEM_CONFIG_INFO 0x74

This bug check indicates either that the SYSTEM hive is corrupt or, more likely, that some critical keys and values are not present. Booting from an alternate configuration may solve the problem, or the registry may need to be restored with the ERD.

**PARAMETERS:**

1: 1
2: A value indicating where in the configuration routine the failure occurred.
3: 0
4: 0

## CANNOT_WRITE_CONFIGURATION 0x75

This stop code occurs when the SYSTEM hive files need to be expanded to hold additional information during the system initialization process but cannot. This indicates either that there is no space on the device or that the registry files are on read/only media.

**PARAMETERS:**

1: 5
2: A value indicating where in the configuration routine the failure occurred.
3: 0
4: 0

## PROCESS_HAS_LOCKED_PAGES 0x76

This bug check occurs whenever a process attempts to exit while it has pages locked for I/O operations. It is caused by a driver that isn't cleaning up properly.

**PARAMETERS:**

1: The address of the offending process.
2: The number of locked pages.
3: The number of private pages.
4: 0

## KERNEL_STACK_INPAGE_ERROR 0x77

This stop code will occur if the kernel experiences an error bringing a page of memory from the disk to main memory. This is often caused by either a hardware failure with the disk or controller or a bad block in the system paging file.

A hardware failure will be the obvious candidate if the first and second arguments to this bug check are zero. If the first argument is not zero, it contains the NT status code of the failing operation. There are a couple of common NT status codes that will point to the problem:

A status code of STATUS_INSUFFICIENT_RESOURCES indicates that you may be running out of nonpaged pool. This could be a device driver that is leaking memory or an insufficient amount of memory in your machine. If the status is STATUS_DEVICE_DATA_ERROR or STATUS_DISK_OPERATION_FAILED, there is a high probability that the problem is a bad block in the paging file.

**PARAMETERS:**

1: 0
2: 0
3: The PTE value of the page you're trying to page in.
4: The address of the stack signature.

—or—

1: The NT status code.
2: The I/O operation status code.
3: The page file number that you're attempting to page from.
4: The offset into the page file for the current operation.

## PHASE0_EXCEPTION 0x78

An error that occurs during the earliest initialization of the kernel will trigger this stop code. A stack trace will not really show anything useful. You should retry the boot with an alternate configuration.

**PARAMETERS:**

No parameters.

## MISMATCHED_HAL 0x79

This stop code happens when the HAL file (*hal.dll*) and the NT kernel (*ntoskrnl.exe*) are mismatched. If you receive this stop code, you most likely have a multiprocessor version of the HAL and a uniprocessor version of the kernel, or vice versa.

**PARAMETERS:**

1: The type of mismatch.

type 1: The release levels mismatch (something is out of date). The remaining parameters in this case are:

2—The major release level of *ntoskrnl.exe*

3—The major release level of *hal.dll*

type 2: The build types mismatch. The remaining parameters in this instance are:

2—The build type of *notskrnl.exe*

3—The build type of *hal.dll*. The valid build types are:

0—free multiprocessor-enabled build

1—checked multiprocessor build

2—free uni build

type 3: MCA computers require a MicroChannel-specific HAL. This type would mean that there's a mismatch with a MicroChannel HAL. The remaining parameters in this case are:

2—The machine type as detected by *ntdetect.com*. A value of 2 indicates a MicroChannel-architecture machine is detected.

3—The machine type that HAL supports. A value of 2 indicates that MicroChannel was detected.

## KERNEL_DATA_INPAGE_ERROR 0x7A

When the kernel cannot page in a page of memory that it needs, it will cause this stop code to occur. The most usual cases of this bug check are bad blocks in the paging file or a disk controller error.

### PARAMETERS:

1: The lock type that was held on the page (the values 1, 2, 3, or a PTE address).
2: The NT status code for the read operation.
3: The current process, or virtual address for lock type 3, or the PTE.
4: The virtual address that could not be faulted in.

## INACCESSIBLE_BOOT_DEVICE 0x7B

During the init of the I/O system, it is possible that the driver for the boot device failed to initialize the device that the system is attempting to boot from. Or it is possible for the file system that is supposed to read that device either to fail its init or to simply not recognize the data on the boot device as a file system structure that it recognizes. In the former case, the arg #1 is the address of a unicode string data struct that is the ARC name of the device from which the boot was being attempted. In the latter case, the arg #1 is the address of the device object that could not be mounted.

If this is the initial setup of the system, this error can occur if the system was installed on an unsupported SCSI or disk controller. Note that some controllers are supported only by drivers that are in the Windows Driver Library (WDL), which requires the user to do a customer install. See the WDL for more information on that.

This error can also be caused by the installation of a new SCSI adapter or disk controller or by repartitioning the disk with the system partition. If this is the case, on i386 systems, the *boot.ini* file must be edited or, on ARC systems, setup must be run. See the Advanced Server System Administrator's User Guide from Microsoft for information on changing *boot.ini*.

If the arg is a point to an ARC name string, the format of the first two (and in this case, only) longwords will be:

USHORT length
USHORT maxlength
PVOID buffer

That is, the first longword will contain something like 00800020, where 20 is the actual length of the unicode string, and the next longword will contain the address of the buffer. This address will be in system space, so the high order bit will be set.

If the arg is a point to a device object, the format of the first work will be:

USHORT type

That is, the first work will contain a 0003, where the type code will always be 0003.

Note that this makes it immediately obvious whether the arg is a pointer to an ARC name string or a device object, because a unicode string can never have an odd number of bytes, and a device object will always have a type code of 3.

#### PARAMETERS:

1: Pointer to the device object or UNICODE string of ARC name.
2: 0
3: 0
4: 0

## BUGCODE_PSS_MESSAGE 0x7C

Although this code is included in *bugcode.h,* it is not really a bug check code. The kernel uses this as a pointer to a message to print during the dump process. It is included here for completeness, but it is not a code that you will ever see.

## INSTALL_MORE_MEMORY 0x7D

You will see this code when there is not enough memory to boot NT. Check your system requirements to ensure that you have an adequate machine to run the version of NT that you are attempting to load.

### PARAMETERS:

1: The number of physical pages found in the system.
2: The lowest physical page address in the system.
3: The highest physical page address in the system.
4: 0

## UNEXPECTED_KERNEL_MODE_TRAP 0x7F

This means a trap occurred in kernel mode that the kernel isn't allowed to have/catch (bound trap) or that is always instant death (double fault). The first number in the bugcheck parentheses is the number of the trap (8 equals double fault, etc). Consult an Intel i386 family manual to learn more about what these traps are.

A "kb" and "!trap" on the appropriate frame (which will be the "ebp" that goes with a procedure named "KiTrap.") will show where the trap was taken.

### PARAMETERS:

1: Trap number
2: 0
3: 0
4: 0

## NMI_HARDWARE_FAILURE 0x80

This bug check occurs with no further information when a catastrophic hardware failure is detected. If you see this message, and it recurs, you should contact your hardware vendor. It is almost always a hardware problem that causes this stop code to appear.

**PARAMETERS:**

No parameters.

## SPIN_LOCK_INIT_FAILURE 0x81

This bug check code occurs when there is an error initializing a spinlock resource. A stack trace should point out the offending code.

**PARAMETERS:**

1: The address of the spinlock that isn't initializing correctly.
2: 0
3: 0
4: 0

## SETUP_FAILURE 0x85

This stop code is not currently used by Windows NT.

## MBR_CHECKSUM_MISMATCH 0x8B

During the boot process, the system verifies the checksum of the disk's master boot record (MBR) against a previous checksum stored by the system loader. If there is a mismatch, this stop code appears. The most frequent cause of this is a boot-sector virus.

**PARAMETERS:**

1: The disk signature from the MBR.
2: The MBR checksum, as calculated by the NT loader.
3: The MBR checksum, as calculated by the system.
4: 0

## BUGCODE_PSS_CRASH_INIT 0x8C

Although this code is included in *bugcode.h,* it is not really a bug check code. The kernel uses this as a pointer to a message to print during the dump process. It is included here for completeness, but it is not a code that you will ever see.

## BUGCODE_PSS_CRASH_PROGRESS 0x8D

Although this code is included in *bugcode.h,* it is not really a bug check code. The kernel uses this as a pointer to a message to print during the dump process. It is included here for completeness, but it is not a code that you will ever see.

## BUGCODE_PSS_CRASH_DONE 0x8E

Although this code is included in *bugcode.h,* it is not really a bug check code. The kernel uses this as a pointer to a message to print during the dump process. It is included here for completeness, but it is not a code that you will ever see.

## PP0_INITIALIZATION_FAILED 0x8F

This bug check occurs if there is a failure in the Plug-N-Play manager during the phase 0 initialization.

### PARAMETERS:

No parameters.

## PP1_INTIALIZATION_FAILED 0x90

This message occurs if phase 1 initialization of the kernel-mode Plug-N-Play manager failed. This is where we do most of our initialization, including setting up the environment (registry, etc.) for drivers to call subsequently during I/O init.

### PARAMETERS:

No parameters.

## WIN32K_INIT_OR_RIT_FAILURE 0x91

This bug check code is not used on the current versions of Windows NT.

## UP_DRIVER_ON_MP_SYSTEM 0x92

If a driver was built as a "uniprocessor-only" driver and you attempt to execute or load this driver on a multiprocessor machine, this stop code will appear. The passed parameter will point out the address of the driver that is incompatible.

**PARAMETERS:**

1: The base address of the misbehaving driver.
2: 0
3: 0
4: 0

## INVALID_KERNEL_HANDLE 0x93

This stop condition occurs if kernel-mode code, such as a driver, attempts to close an invalid handle. This is usually a bug in the caller, which can easily be found from a simple stack trace. Ensure that your code closes only handles that either have been opened or haven't previously been closed.

**PARAMETERS:**

1: The handle that *ZwClose()* was called with.
2: A zero indicates that a protected handle was closed. A "1" indicates that an invalid handle was closed.
3: 0
4: 0

## KERNEL_STACK_LOCKED_AT_EXIT 0x94

This rare bug check code indicates an internal consistency problem in the kernel. It occurs when a kernel stack is not flagged as "swappable" at the time of a thread exit. This most likely indicates an errant pointer and will be very difficult to look for.

**PARAMETERS:**

Parameters are unknown.

## PNP_INTERNAL_ERROR 0x95

This stop code indicates that an error occurred that is internal to the Plug-N-Play subsystem.

#### PARAMETERS:

No parameters.

## INVALID_WORK_QUEUE_ITEM 0x96

This bug check code appears when the kernel routine *KeRemoveQueue()* attempts to dequeue a queue entry whose forward or back pointer fields are not set (are NULL). This is often caused by driver code incorrectly using work queues. For example, if an entry is placed onto a work queue twice, this bug check will occur when the system attempts to remove the second instance of the queue item. This happens because the first removal nullified the forward and back pointer fields. This can occur on any system-managed queue.

#### PARAMETERS:

1: The address of the queue entry whose forward or backward link fields are NULL.
2: The address of the queue being referenced.
3: The base address of the ExWorkerQueue array. This will help determine whether the queue in question is an ExWorker-Queue and, if so, the offset from this parameter will isolate the queue.
4: If this is an ExWorkerQueue, this is the address of the worker routine that would have been called if the work item had been valid. This can be used to isolate the driver that is misusing the work queue.

## BOUND_IMAGE_UNSUPPORTED 0x97

When the operating system attempts to load a bound image with *MmLoadSystemImage()*, this stop code will appear. Ensure that the executable image being loaded was not massaged with the “bind.exe” command. This occurs only on checked builds of the operating system.

**PARAMETERS:**

1: The address of the image descriptor for the image being loaded.
2: The address of the base of the image.
3: A pointer to the UNICODE string of the file's directory.
4: The import size.

## END_OF_NT_EVALUATION_PERIOD 0x98

This stop code appears on evaluation copies of Windows NT. It indicates that the trial period for your system has expired.

**PARAMETERS:**

1: The low order 32 bits of your installation date.
2: The high order 32 bits of your installation date.
3: The duration of the trial period in minutes.

## INVALID_REGION_OR_SEGMENT 0x99

When either *ExInitializeRegion()* or *ExInterlockeExtendRegion()* are called with an invalid set of parameters, this stop code will appear.

**PARAMETERS:**

1: The attempted segment address (which must reside on a quad-word boundary).
2: The attempted segment size (which must be greater than the block size plus the size of a segment header).
3: The attempted block size (which must be a multiple of 8 and smaller than the segment size minus the size of the segment header).
4: 0

## SYSTEM_LICENSE_VIOLATION 0x9A

This stop code indicates that a violation of the software license agreement has occurred. This is almost always caused by an attempt to change the license and product information manually within the registry. You must restore your original registry entries to resolve this stop screen.

**PARAMETERS:**

1: 0—Offline product type changes were attempted. The remaining parameters are:

> 2: if 1, the product should be LanmanNT or ServerNT. If 0, it should be WinNT.
>
> 3: The partial serial number of the product.
>
> 4: The first two characters of product type from product options.

1—Offline changes to the NT evaluation unit time period were attempted. The remaining parameters are:

> 2: The registered evaluation time from the first source.
>
> 3: The partial serial number of the product.
>
> 4: The registered evaluation time from alternate source

2—The setup registry key could not be opened. The remaining parameters are:

> 2: The status code associated with the open failure.
>
> 3: 0
>
> 4: 0

3—The setup type value from the setup registry key is missing, so GUI setup mode could not be detected.

> 2: The status code associated with key lookup failure.
>
> 3: 0
>
> 4: 0

4—The system prefix value from the setup registry key is missing.

> 2: The status code associated with the key lookup failure.
>
> 3: 0
>
> 4: 0

5—Offline changes were made to the number of licensed processors.

> 2: The setup code.
>
> 3: The invalid value found in licensed processors.
>
> 4: The officially licensed number of processors.

## UDFS_FILE_SYSTEM 0x9B

This error indicates an internal problem within the UDFS filesystem. If the problem persists and you are using the filesystem as delivered from Microsoft, contact its technical support. If you have built the filesystem from the IFS kit or other source, the problem may be caused by that filesystem driver.

**PARAMETERS:**

1: An indicator of where in the code the problem exists. The high 16 bits include a number that identifies the source file in the filesystem that caused the problem. The low 16 bits of this value indicate a position within the source file.
2: 0
3: 0
4: 0

## MACHINE_CHECK_EXCEPTION 0x9C

This stop code appears whenever there is a fatal error encountered from one of the computer's CPUs or an error accessing main memory. Consult your hardware vendor or the CPU manufacturer's documentation to understand the parameters.

**PARAMETERS:**

On an Intel Pentium system:

1: The low 32 bits from the P5_MC_TYPE MSR.
2: 0
3: The high 32 bits of the P5_MC_ADDR MSR.
4: The low 32 bits of the P5_MC_ADDR MSR.

On Intel Pentium Pro and later (the P6 core) systems:

1: The bank # of the failing memory.
2: The address field of the Mci_ADDR MSR for the MCA bank containing the error condition.
3: The high 32 bits from the Mci_STATUS MSR for the questionable MCA bank.
4: The low 32 bits from the Mci_STATUS MSR for the MCA bank.

Parameters will be different on newer or different architectures.

## INTERNAL_POWER_ERROR 0xA0

This stop code indicates an internal error in the power management code in NT 5.0 and later systems.

**PARAMETERS:**

Parameters unknown.

## PCI_BUS_DRIVER_INTERNAL 0xA1

This bug check occurs when an internal error is detected in the PCI bus drivers. This should occur only if there is either a problem with the PCI bus or a problem with one of the adapters attached to the PCI bus. This occurs only on NT 5.0 and later systems.

**PARAMETERS:**

Parameters unknown.

## MEMORY_IMAGE_CORRUPT 0xA2

This stop code appears after a system has been awakened from a power-management-induced sleep, and the main memory image appears corrupted. Prior to going into a sleep mode, a checksum (CRC) is run on the main memory image. This is compared with a similar checksum that is calculated after wakeup. If they do not match, this bug check occurs. This appears only on NT 5.0 and later systems.

**PARAMETERS:**

Parameters unknown.

## ACPI_DRIVER_INTERNAL 0xA3

This bug check code indicates that an internal error has occurred in the ACPI subsystem of NT 5.0 and later systems.

**PARAMETERS:**

Parameters unknown.

## CNSS_FILE_SYSTEM_FILTER 0xA4

This error indicates an internal problem within the CNSS filesystem. If the problem persists and you are using the file system as delivered from Microsoft, contact its technical support. If you have built the filesystem from the IFS kit or another source, the problem may be caused by that filesystem driver.

PARAMETERS:

1: An indicator of where in the code the problem exists. The high 16 bits include a number that identifies the source file in the filesystem that caused the problem. The low 16 bits of this value indicate a position within the source file.
2: 0
3: 0
4: 0

## ACPI_BIOS_ERROR 0xA5

This stop code is instantiated when NT 5.0 or later detects that the APCI BIOS is not fully compliant with the ACPI specification.

## WINDOWS_NT_BANNER 0x4000007E

This stop code is not used by the current versions of Windows NT.

## WINDOWS_NT_INFO_STRING_PLURAL 0x4000009D

Although this code is included in *bugcode.h,* it is not really a bug check code. The kernel uses this as a pointer to a message to print during the dump process. It is included here for completeness, but it is not a code that you will ever see.

## WINDOWS_NT_RC_STRING 0x4000009E

Although this code is included in *bugcode.h,* it is not really a bug check code. The kernel uses this as a pointer to a message to print during the dump process. It is included here for completeness, but it is not a code that you will ever see.

## DRIVER_POWER_STATE_FAILURE 0x4000009F

This bug check code is triggered when a condition in the device driver has led to an inconsistent power state. This is a problem with the device driver not conforming correctly to the power management functions in NT 5.0 and later.

### PARAMETERS:

Parameters are unknown.

APPENDIX C

# Windows Status Codes

*One of the most frustrating tasks when debugging kernel code or examining a system dump is resolving status codes back to their original meaning. You will find yourself searching through header files time and again, or maybe you even keep a list of the most common ones that you encounter. To help minimize this frustration, I have provided in this appendix a complete listing of Windows 2000 status codes.*

*The status codes are listed in numerical order, for those working backward from code stepping or stack traces. No meaning or interpretation of these codes is provided. Most of them are named appropriately, and the meaning is very often derived from the context in which the error was encountered.*

## Numerical Listing

| | |
|---|---|
| STATUS_SUCCESS | 0X00000000 |
| STATUS_WAIT_0 | 0X00000000 |
| STATUS_WAIT_1 | 0X00000001 |
| STATUS_WAIT_2 | 0X00000002 |
| STATUS_WAIT_3 | 0X00000003 |
| STATUS_WAIT_63 | 0X0000003F |
| STATUS_ABANDONED | 0X00000080 |
| STATUS_ABANDONED_WAIT_0 | 0X00000080 |
| STATUS_ABANDONED_WAIT_63 | 0X000000BF |
| STATUS_USER_APC | 0X000000C0 |
| STATUS_KERNEL_APC | 0X00000100 |
| STATUS_ALERTED | 0X00000101 |
| STATUS_TIMEOUT | 0X00000102 |
| STATUS_PENDING | 0X00000103 |
| STATUS_REPARSE | 0X00000104 |
| STATUS_MORE_ENTRIES | 0X00000105 |
| STATUS_NOT_ALL_ASSIGNED | 0X00000106 |
| STATUS_SOME_NOT_MAPPED | 0X00000107 |
| STATUS_OPLOCK_BREAK_IN_PROGRESS | 0X00000108 |
| STATUS_VOLUME_MOUNTED | 0X00000109 |
| STATUS_RXACT_COMMITTED | 0X0000010A |

| | |
|---|---|
| STATUS_NOTIFY_CLEANUP | 0X0000010B |
| STATUS_NOTIFY_ENUM_DIR | 0X0000010C |
| STATUS_NO_QUOTAS_FOR_ACCOUNT | 0X0000010D |
| STATUS_PRIMARY_TRANSPORT_CONNECT_FAILED | 0X0000010E |
| STATUS_PAGE_FAULT_TRANSITION | 0X00000110 |
| STATUS_PAGE_FAULT_DEMAND_ZERO | 0X00000111 |
| STATUS_PAGE_FAULT_GUARD_PAGE | 0X00000113 |
| STATUS_PAGE_FAULT_PAGING_FILE | 0X00000114 |
| STATUS_CACHE_PAGE_LOCKED | 0X00000115 |
| STATUS_CRASH_DUMP | 0X00000116 |
| STATUS_BUFFER_ALL_ZEROS | 0X00000117 |
| STATUS_REPARSE_OBJECT | 0X00000118 |
| STATUS_OBJECT_NAME_EXISTS | 0X40000000 |
| STATUS_THREAD_WAS_SUSPENDED | 0X40000001 |
| STATUS_WORKING_SET_LIMIT_RANGE | 0X40000002 |
| STATUS_IMAGE_NOT_AT_BASE | 0X40000003 |
| STATUS_RXACT_STATE_CREATED | 0X40000004 |
| STATUS_SEGMENT_NOTIFICATION | 0X40000005 |
| STATUS_LOCAL_USER_SESSION_KEY | 0X40000006 |
| STATUS_BAD_CURRENT_DIRECTORY | 0X40000007 |
| STATUS_SERIAL_MORE_WRITES | 0X40000008 |
| STATUS_REGISTRY_RECOVERED | 0X40000009 |

| | |
|---|---|
| STATUS_FT_READ_RECOVERY_FROM_BACKUP | 0X4000000A |
| STATUS_FT_WRITE_RECOVERY | 0X4000000B |
| STATUS_SERIAL_COUNTER_TIMEOUT | 0X4000000C |
| STATUS_NULL_LM_PASSWORD | 0X4000000D |
| STATUS_IMAGE_MACHINE_TYPE_MISMATCH | 0X4000000E |
| STATUS_RECEIVE_PARTIAL | 0X4000000F |
| STATUS_RECEIVE_EXPEDITED | 0X40000010 |
| STATUS_RECEIVE_PARTIAL_EXPEDITED | 0X40000011 |
| STATUS_EVENT_DONE | 0X40000012 |
| STATUS_EVENT_PENDING | 0X40000013 |
| STATUS_CHECKING_FILE_SYSTEM | 0X40000014 |
| STATUS_FATAL_APP_EXIT | 0X40000015 |
| STATUS_PREDEFINED_HANDLE | 0X40000016 |
| STATUS_WAS_UNLOCKED | 0X40000017 |
| STATUS_SERVICE_NOTIFICATION | 0X40000018 |
| STATUS_WAS_LOCKED | 0X40000019 |
| STATUS_LOG_HARD_ERROR | 0X4000001A |
| STATUS_ALREADY_WIN32 | 0X4000001B |
| STATUS_WX86_UNSIMULATE | 0X4000001C |
| STATUS_WX86_CONTINUE | 0X4000001D |
| STATUS_WX86_SINGLE_STEP | 0X4000001E |
| STATUS_WX86_BREAKPOINT | 0X4000001F |

| | |
|---|---|
| STATUS_WX86_EXCEPTION_CONTINUE | 0X40000020 |
| STATUS_WX86_EXCEPTION_LASTCHANCE | 0X40000021 |
| STATUS_WX86_EXCEPTION_CHAIN | 0X40000022 |
| STATUS_IMAGE_MACHINE_TYPE_MISMATCH_EXE | 0X40000023 |
| STATUS_NO_YIELD_PERFORMED | 0X40000024 |
| STATUS_TIMER_RESUME_IGNORED | 0X40000025 |
| STATUS_GUARD_PAGE_VIOLATION | 0X80000001 |
| STATUS_DATATYPE_MISALIGNMENT | 0X80000002 |
| STATUS_BREAKPOINT | 0X80000003 |
| STATUS_SINGLE_STEP | 0X80000004 |
| STATUS_BUFFER_OVERFLOW | 0X80000005 |
| STATUS_NO_MORE_FILES | 0X80000006 |
| STATUS_WAKE_SYSTEM_DEBUGGER | 0X80000007 |
| STATUS_HANDLES_CLOSED | 0X8000000A |
| STATUS_NO_INHERITANCE | 0X8000000B |
| STATUS_GUID_SUBSTITUTION_MADE | 0X8000000C |
| STATUS_PARTIAL_COPY | 0X8000000D |
| STATUS_DEVICE_PAPER_EMPTY | 0X8000000E |
| STATUS_DEVICE_POWERED_OFF | 0X8000000F |
| STATUS_DEVICE_OFF_LINE | 0X80000010 |
| STATUS_DEVICE_BUSY | 0X80000011 |
| STATUS_NO_MORE_EAS | 0X80000012 |

| | |
|---|---|
| STATUS_INVALID_EA_NAME | 0X80000013 |
| STATUS_EA_LIST_INCONSISTENT | 0X80000014 |
| STATUS_INVALID_EA_FAG | 0X80000015 |
| STATUS_VERIFY_REQUIRED | 0X80000016 |
| STATUS_EXTRANEOUS_INFORMATION | 0X80000017 |
| STATUS_RXACT_COMMIT_NECESSARY | 0X80000018 |
| STATUS_NO_MORE_ENTRIES | 0X8000001A |
| STATUS_FILEMARK_DETECTED | 0X8000001B |
| STATUS_MEDIA_CHANGED | 0X8000001C |
| STATUS_BUS_RESET | 0X8000001D |
| STATUS_END_OF_MEDIA | 0X8000001E |
| STATUS_BEGINNING_OF_MEDIA | 0X8000001F |
| STATUS_MEDIA_CHECK | 0X80000020 |
| STATUS_SETMARK_DETECTED | 0X80000021 |
| STATUS_NO_DATA_DETECTED | 0X80000022 |
| STATUS_REDIRECTOR_HAS_OPEN_HANDLES | 0X80000023 |
| STATUS_SERVER_HAS_OPEN_HANDLES | 0X80000024 |
| STATUS_ALREADY_DISCONNECTED | 0X80000025 |
| STATUS_LONGJUMP | 0X80000026 |
| STATUS_UNSUCCESSFUL | 0XC0000001 |
| STATUS_NOT_IMPLEMENTED | 0XC0000002 |
| STATUS_INVALID_INFO_CASS | 0XC0000003 |

| | |
|---|---|
| STATUS_INFO_LENGTH_MISMATCH | 0XC0000004 |
| STATUS_ACCESS_VIOLATION | 0XC0000005 |
| STATUS_IN_PAGE_ERROR | 0XC0000006 |
| STATUS_PAGEFILE_QUOTA | 0XC0000007 |
| STATUS_INVALID_HANDLE | 0XC0000008 |
| STATUS_BAD_INITIAL_STACK | 0XC0000009 |
| STATUS_BAD_INITIAL_PC | 0XC000000A |
| STATUS_INVALID_CID | 0XC000000B |
| STATUS_TIMER_NOT_CANCELED | 0XC000000C |
| STATUS_INVALID_PARAMETER | 0XC000000D |
| STATUS_NO_SUCH_DEVICE | 0XC000000E |
| STATUS_NO_SUCH_FILE | 0XC000000F |
| STATUS_INVALID_DEVICE_REQUEST | 0XC0000010 |
| STATUS_END_OF_FILE | 0XC0000011 |
| STATUS_WRONG_VOLUME | 0XC0000012 |
| STATUS_NO_MEDIA_IN_DEVICE | 0XC0000013 |
| STATUS_UNRECOGNIZED_MEDIA | 0XC0000014 |
| STATUS_NONEXISTENT_SECTOR | 0XC0000015 |
| STATUS_MORE_PROCESSING_REQUIRED | 0XC0000016 |
| STATUS_NO_MEMORY | 0XC0000017 |
| STATUS_CONFLICTING_ADDRESSES | 0XC0000018 |
| STATUS_NOT_MAPPED_VIEW | 0XC0000019 |

| | |
|---|---|
| STATUS_UNABLE_TO_FREE_VM | 0XC000001A |
| STATUS_UNABLE_TO_DELETE_SECTION | 0XC000001B |
| STATUS_INVALID_SYSTEM_SERVICE | 0XC000001C |
| STATUS_ILLEGAL_INSTRUCTION | 0XC000001D |
| STATUS_INVALID_LOCK_SEQUENCE | 0XC000001E |
| STATUS_INVALID_VIEW_SIZE | 0XC000001F |
| STATUS_INVALID_FILE_FOR_SECTION | 0XC0000020 |
| STATUS_ALREADY_COMMITTED | 0XC0000021 |
| STATUS_ACCESS_DENIED | 0XC0000022 |
| STATUS_BUFFER_TOO_SMALL | 0XC0000023 |
| STATUS_OBJECT_TYPE_MISMATCH | 0XC0000024 |
| STATUS_NONCONTINUABLE_EXCEPTION | 0XC0000025 |
| STATUS_INVALID_DISPOSITION | 0XC0000026 |
| STATUS_UNWIND | 0XC0000027 |
| STATUS_BAD_STACK | 0XC0000028 |
| STATUS_INVALID_UNWIND_TARGET | 0XC0000029 |
| STATUS_NOT_LOCKED | 0XC000002A |
| STATUS_PARITY_ERROR | 0XC000002B |
| STATUS_UNABLE_TO_DECOMMIT_VM | 0XC000002C |
| STATUS_NOT_COMMITTED | 0XC000002D |
| STATUS_INVALID_PORT_ATTRIBUTES | 0XC000002E |
| STATUS_PORT_MESSAGE_TOO_LONG | 0XC000002F |

| | |
|---|---|
| STATUS_INVALID_PARAMETER_MIX | 0XC0000030 |
| STATUS_INVALID_QUOTA_LOWER | 0XC0000031 |
| STATUS_DISK_CORRUPT_ERROR | 0XC0000032 |
| STATUS_OBJECT_NAME_INVALID | 0XC0000033 |
| STATUS_OBJECT_NAME_NOT_FOUND | 0XC0000034 |
| STATUS_OBJECT_NAME_COLLISION | 0XC0000035 |
| STATUS_PORT_DISCONNECTED | 0XC0000037 |
| STATUS_DEVICE_ALREADY_ATTACHED | 0XC0000038 |
| STATUS_OBJECT_PATH_INVALID | 0XC0000039 |
| STATUS_OBJECT_PATH_NOT_FOUND | 0XC000003A |
| STATUS_OBJECT_PATH_SYNTAX_BAD | 0XC000003B |
| STATUS_DATA_OVERRUN | 0XC000003C |
| STATUS_DATA_LATE_ERROR | 0XC000003D |
| STATUS_DATA_ERROR | 0XC000003E |
| STATUS_CRC_ERROR | 0XC000003F |
| STATUS_SECTION_TOO_BIG | 0XC0000040 |
| STATUS_PORT_CONNECTION_REFUSED | 0XC0000041 |
| STATUS_INVALID_PORT_HANDLE | 0XC0000042 |
| STATUS_SHARING_VIOLATION | 0XC0000043 |
| STATUS_QUOTA_EXCEEDED | 0XC0000044 |
| STATUS_INVALID_PAGE_PROTECTION | 0XC0000045 |
| STATUS_MUTANT_NOT_OWNED | 0XC0000046 |

| | |
|---|---|
| STATUS_SEMAPHORE_LIMIT_EXCEEDED | 0XC0000047 |
| STATUS_PORT_ALREADY_SET | 0XC0000048 |
| STATUS_SECTION_NOT_IMAGE | 0XC0000049 |
| STATUS_SUSPEND_COUNT_EXCEEDED | 0XC000004A |
| STATUS_THREAD_IS_TERMINATING | 0XC000004B |
| STATUS_BAD_WORKING_SET_LIMIT | 0XC000004C |
| STATUS_INCOMPATIBLE_FILE_MAP | 0XC000004D |
| STATUS_SECTION_PROTECTION | 0XC000004E |
| STATUS_EAS_NOT_SUPPORTED | 0XC000004F |
| STATUS_EA_TOO_LARGE | 0XC0000050 |
| STATUS_NONEXISTENT_EA_ENTRY | 0XC0000051 |
| STATUS_NO_EAS_ON_FILE | 0XC0000052 |
| STATUS_EA_CORRUPT_ERROR | 0XC0000053 |
| STATUS_FILE_LOCK_CONFICT | 0XC0000054 |
| STATUS_LOCK_NOT_GRANTED | 0XC0000055 |
| STATUS_DELETE_PENDING | 0XC0000056 |
| STATUS_CTL_FILE_NOT_SUPPORTED | 0XC0000057 |
| STATUS_UNKNOWN_REVISION | 0XC0000058 |
| STATUS_REVISION_MISMATCH | 0XC0000059 |
| STATUS_INVALID_OWNER | 0XC000005A |
| STATUS_INVALID_PRIMARY_GROUP | 0XC000005B |
| STATUS_NO_IMPERSONATION_TOKEN | 0XC000005C |

| | |
|---|---|
| STATUS_CANT_DISABLE_MANDATORY | 0XC000005D |
| STATUS_NO_LOGON_SERVERS | 0XC000005E |
| STATUS_NO_SUCH_LOGON_SESSION | 0XC000005F |
| STATUS_NO_SUCH_PRIVILEGE | 0XC0000060 |
| STATUS_PRIVILEGE_NOT_HELD | 0XC0000061 |
| STATUS_INVALID_ACCOUNT_NAME | 0XC0000062 |
| STATUS_USER_EXISTS | 0XC0000063 |
| STATUS_NO_SUCH_USER | 0XC0000064 |
| STATUS_GROUP_EXISTS | 0XC0000065 |
| STATUS_NO_SUCH_GROUP | 0XC0000066 |
| STATUS_MEMBER_IN_GROUP | 0XC0000067 |
| STATUS_MEMBER_NOT_IN_GROUP | 0XC0000068 |
| STATUS_LAST_ADMIN | 0XC0000069 |
| STATUS_WRONG_PASSWORD | 0XC000006A |
| STATUS_ILL_FORMED_PASSWORD | 0XC000006B |
| STATUS_PASSWORD_RESTRICTION | 0XC000006C |
| STATUS_LOGON_FAILURE | 0XC000006D |
| STATUS_ACCOUNT_RESTRICTION | 0XC000006E |
| STATUS_INVALID_LOGON_HOURS | 0XC000006F |
| STATUS_INVALID_WORKSTATION | 0XC0000070 |
| STATUS_PASSWORD_EXPIRED | 0XC0000071 |
| STATUS_ACCOUNT_DISABLED | 0XC0000072 |

| | |
|---|---|
| STATUS_NONE_MAPPED | 0XC0000073 |
| STATUS_TOO_MANY_LUIDS_REQUESTED | 0XC0000074 |
| STATUS_LUIDS_EXHAUSTED | 0XC0000075 |
| STATUS_INVALID_SUB_AUTHORITY | 0XC0000076 |
| STATUS_INVALID_AC | 0XC0000077 |
| STATUS_INVALID_SID | 0XC0000078 |
| STATUS_INVALID_SECURITY_DESCR | 0XC0000079 |
| STATUS_PROCEDURE_NOT_FOUND | 0XC000007A |
| STATUS_INVALID_IMAGE_FORMAT | 0XC000007B |
| STATUS_NO_TOKEN | 0XC000007C |
| STATUS_BAD_INHERITANCE_AC | 0XC000007D |
| STATUS_RANGE_NOT_LOCKED | 0XC000007E |
| STATUS_DISK_FULL | 0XC000007F |
| STATUS_SERVER_DISABLED | 0XC0000080 |
| STATUS_SERVER_NOT_DISABLED | 0XC0000081 |
| STATUS_TOO_MANY_GUIDS_REQUESTED | 0XC0000082 |
| STATUS_GUIDS_EXHAUSTED | 0XC0000083 |
| STATUS_INVALID_ID_AUTHORITY | 0XC0000084 |
| STATUS_AGENTS_EXHAUSTED | 0XC0000085 |
| STATUS_INVALID_VOLUME_LABEL | 0XC0000086 |
| STATUS_SECTION_NOT_EXTENDED | 0XC0000087 |
| STATUS_NOT_MAPPED_DATA | 0XC0000088 |

| | |
|---|---|
| STATUS_RESOURCE_DATA_NOT_FOUND | 0XC0000089 |
| STATUS_RESOURCE_TYPE_NOT_FOUND | 0XC000008A |
| STATUS_RESOURCE_NAME_NOT_FOUND | 0XC000008B |
| STATUS_ARRAY_BOUNDS_EXCEEDED | 0XC000008C |
| STATUS_FOAT_DENORMAL_OPERAND | 0XC000008D |
| STATUS_FOAT_DIVIDE_BY_ZERO | 0XC000008E |
| STATUS_FOAT_INEXACT_RESULT | 0XC000008F |
| STATUS_FOAT_INVALID_OPERATION | 0XC0000090 |
| STATUS_FOAT_OVERFLOW | 0XC0000091 |
| STATUS_FOAT_UNDERFLOW | 0XC0000093 |
| STATUS_INTEGER_DIVIDE_BY_ZERO | 0XC0000094 |
| STATUS_INTEGER_OVERFLOW | 0XC0000095 |
| STATUS_PRIVILEGED_INSTRUCTION | 0XC0000096 |
| STATUS_TOO_MANY_PAGING_FILES | 0XC0000097 |
| STATUS_FILE_INVALID | 0XC0000098 |
| STATUS_ALLOTTED_SPACE_EXCEEDED | 0XC0000099 |
| STATUS_INSUFFICIENT_RESOURCES | 0XC000009A |
| STATUS_DFS_EXIT_PATH_FOUND | 0XC000009B |
| STATUS_DEVICE_DATA_ERROR | 0XC000009C |
| STATUS_DEVICE_NOT_CONNECTED | 0XC000009D |
| STATUS_DEVICE_POWER_FAILURE | 0XC000009E |
| STATUS_FREE_VM_NOT_AT_BASE | 0XC000009F |

| | |
|---|---|
| STATUS_MEMORY_NOT_ALLOCATED | 0XC00000A0 |
| STATUS_WORKING_SET_QUOTA | 0XC00000A1 |
| STATUS_MEDIA_WRITE_PROTECTED | 0XC00000A2 |
| STATUS_DEVICE_NOT_READY | 0XC00000A3 |
| STATUS_INVALID_GROUP_ATTRIBUTES | 0XC00000A4 |
| STATUS_BAD_IMPERSONATION_LEVEL | 0XC00000A5 |
| STATUS_CANT_OPEN_ANONYMOUS | 0XC00000A6 |
| STATUS_BAD_VALIDATION_CASS | 0XC00000A7 |
| STATUS_BAD_TOKEN_TYPE | 0XC00000A8 |
| STATUS_BAD_MASTER_BOOT_RECORD | 0XC00000A9 |
| STATUS_INSTRUCTION_MISALIGNMENT | 0XC00000AA |
| STATUS_INSTANCE_NOT_AVAILABLE | 0XC00000AB |
| STATUS_PIPE_NOT_AVAILABLE | 0XC00000AC |
| STATUS_INVALID_PIPE_STATE | 0XC00000AD |
| STATUS_PIPE_BUSY | 0XC00000AE |
| STATUS_ILLEGAL_FUNCTION | 0XC00000AF |
| STATUS_PIPE_DISCONNECTED | 0XC00000B0 |
| STATUS_PIPE_CLOSING | 0XC00000B1 |
| STATUS_PIPE_CONNECTED | 0XC00000B2 |
| STATUS_PIPE_LISTENING | 0XC00000B3 |
| STATUS_INVALID_READ_MODE | 0XC00000B4 |
| STATUS_IO_TIMEOUT | 0XC00000B5 |

| | |
|---|---|
| STATUS_FILE_FORCED_CLOSED | 0XC00000B6 |
| STATUS_PROFILING_NOT_STARTED | 0XC00000B7 |
| STATUS_PROFILING_NOT_STOPPED | 0XC00000B8 |
| STATUS_COULD_NOT_INTERPRET | 0XC00000B9 |
| STATUS_FILE_IS_A_DIRECTORY | 0XC00000BA |
| STATUS_NOT_SUPPORTED | 0XC00000BB |
| STATUS_REMOTE_NOT_LISTENING | 0XC00000BC |
| STATUS_DUPLICATE_NAME | 0XC00000BD |
| STATUS_BAD_NETWORK_PATH | 0XC00000BE |
| STATUS_NETWORK_BUSY | 0XC00000BF |
| STATUS_DEVICE_DOES_NOT_EXIST | 0XC00000C0 |
| STATUS_TOO_MANY_COMMANDS | 0XC00000C1 |
| STATUS_ADAPTER_HARDWARE_ERROR | 0XC00000C2 |
| STATUS_INVALID_NETWORK_RESPONSE | 0XC00000C3 |
| STATUS_UNEXPECTED_NETWORK_ERROR | 0XC00000C4 |
| STATUS_BAD_REMOTE_ADAPTER | 0XC00000C5 |
| STATUS_PRINT_QUEUE_FULL | 0XC00000C6 |
| STATUS_NO_SPOOL_SPACE | 0XC00000C7 |
| STATUS_PRINT_CANCELLED | 0XC00000C8 |
| STATUS_NETWORK_NAME_DELETED | 0XC00000C9 |
| STATUS_NETWORK_ACCESS_DENIED | 0XC00000CA |
| STATUS_BAD_DEVICE_TYPE | 0XC00000CB |

| | |
|---|---|
| STATUS_BAD_NETWORK_NAME | 0XC00000CC |
| STATUS_TOO_MANY_NAMES | 0XC00000CD |
| STATUS_TOO_MANY_SESSIONS | 0XC00000CE |
| STATUS_SHARING_PAUSED | 0XC00000CF |
| STATUS_REQUEST_NOT_ACCEPTED | 0XC00000D0 |
| STATUS_REDIRECTOR_PAUSED | 0XC00000D1 |
| STATUS_NET_WRITE_FAULT | 0XC00000D2 |
| STATUS_PROFILING_AT_LIMIT | 0XC00000D3 |
| STATUS_NOT_SAME_DEVICE | 0XC00000D4 |
| STATUS_FILE_RENAMED | 0XC00000D5 |
| STATUS_VIRTUAL_CIRCUIT_CLOSED | 0XC00000D6 |
| STATUS_NO_SECURITY_ON_OBJECT | 0XC00000D7 |
| STATUS_CANT_WAIT | 0XC00000D8 |
| STATUS_PIPE_EMPTY | 0XC00000D9 |
| STATUS_CANT_ACCESS_DOMAIN_INFO | 0XC00000DA |
| STATUS_CANT_TERMINATE_SELF | 0XC00000DB |
| STATUS_INVALID_SERVER_STATE | 0XC00000DC |
| STATUS_INVALID_DOMAIN_STATE | 0XC00000DD |
| STATUS_INVALID_DOMAIN_ROLE | 0XC00000DE |
| STATUS_NO_SUCH_DOMAIN | 0XC00000DF |
| STATUS_DOMAIN_EXISTS | 0XC00000E0 |
| STATUS_DOMAIN_LIMIT_EXCEEDED | 0XC00000E1 |

| | |
|---|---|
| STATUS_OPLOCK_NOT_GRANTED | 0XC00000E2 |
| STATUS_INVALID_OPLOCK_PROTOCOL | 0XC00000E3 |
| STATUS_INTERNAL_DB_CORRUPTION | 0XC00000E4 |
| STATUS_INTERNAL_ERROR | 0XC00000E5 |
| STATUS_GENERIC_NOT_MAPPED | 0XC00000E6 |
| STATUS_BAD_DESCRIPTOR_FORMAT | 0XC00000E7 |
| STATUS_INVALID_USER_BUFFER | 0XC00000E8 |
| STATUS_UNEXPECTED_IO_ERROR | 0XC00000E9 |
| STATUS_UNEXPECTED_MM_CREATE_ERR | 0XC00000EA |
| STATUS_UNEXPECTED_MM_MAP_ERROR | 0XC00000EB |
| STATUS_UNEXPECTED_MM_EXTEND_ERR | 0XC00000EC |
| STATUS_NOT_LOGON_PROCESS | 0XC00000ED |
| STATUS_LOGON_SESSION_EXISTS | 0XC00000EE |
| STATUS_INVALID_PARAMETER_1 | 0XC00000EF |
| STATUS_INVALID_PARAMETER_2 | 0XC00000F0 |
| STATUS_INVALID_PARAMETER_3 | 0XC00000F1 |
| STATUS_INVALID_PARAMETER_4 | 0XC00000F2 |
| STATUS_INVALID_PARAMETER_5 | 0XC00000F3 |
| STATUS_INVALID_PARAMETER_6 | 0XC00000F4 |
| STATUS_INVALID_PARAMETER_7 | 0XC00000F5 |
| STATUS_INVALID_PARAMETER_8 | 0XC00000F6 |
| STATUS_INVALID_PARAMETER_9 | 0XC00000F7 |

| | |
|---|---|
| STATUS_INVALID_PARAMETER_10 | 0XC00000F8 |
| STATUS_INVALID_PARAMETER_11 | 0XC00000F9 |
| STATUS_INVALID_PARAMETER_12 | 0XC00000FA |
| STATUS_REDIRECTOR_NOT_STARTED | 0XC00000FB |
| STATUS_REDIRECTOR_STARTED | 0XC00000FC |
| STATUS_STACK_OVERFLOW | 0XC00000FD |
| STATUS_NO_SUCH_PACKAGE | 0XC00000FE |
| STATUS_BAD_FUNCTION_TABLE | 0XC00000FF |
| STATUS_VARIABLE_NOT_FOUND | 0XC0000100 |
| STATUS_DIRECTORY_NOT_EMPTY | 0XC0000101 |
| STATUS_FILE_CORRUPT_ERROR | 0XC0000102 |
| STATUS_NOT_A_DIRECTORY | 0XC0000103 |
| STATUS_BAD_LOGON_SESSION_STATE | 0XC0000104 |
| STATUS_LOGON_SESSION_COLLISION | 0XC0000105 |
| STATUS_NAME_TOO_LONG | 0XC0000106 |
| STATUS_FILES_OPEN | 0XC0000107 |
| STATUS_CONNECTION_IN_USE | 0XC0000108 |
| STATUS_MESSAGE_NOT_FOUND | 0XC0000109 |
| STATUS_PROCESS_IS_TERMINATING | 0XC000010A |
| STATUS_INVALID_LOGON_TYPE | 0XC000010B |
| STATUS_NO_GUID_TRANSLATION | 0XC000010C |
| STATUS_CANNOT_IMPERSONATE | 0XC000010D |

| | |
|---|---|
| STATUS_IMAGE_ALREADY_LOADED | 0XC000010E |
| STATUS_ABIOS_NOT_PRESENT | 0XC000010F |
| STATUS_ABIOS_LID_NOT_EXIST | 0XC0000110 |
| STATUS_ABIOS_LID_ALREADY_OWNED | 0XC0000111 |
| STATUS_ABIOS_NOT_LID_OWNER | 0XC0000112 |
| STATUS_ABIOS_INVALID_COMMAND | 0XC0000113 |
| STATUS_ABIOS_INVALID_LID | 0XC0000114 |
| STATUS_ABIOS_SELECTOR_NOT_AVAILABLE | 0XC0000115 |
| STATUS_ABIOS_INVALID_SELECTOR | 0XC0000116 |
| STATUS_NO_LDT | 0XC0000117 |
| STATUS_INVALID_LDT_SIZE | 0XC0000118 |
| STATUS_INVALID_LDT_OFFSET | 0XC0000119 |
| STATUS_INVALID_LDT_DESCRIPTOR | 0XC000011A |
| STATUS_INVALID_IMAGE_NE_FORMAT | 0XC000011B |
| STATUS_RXACT_INVALID_STATE | 0XC000011C |
| STATUS_RXACT_COMMIT_FAILURE | 0XC000011D |
| STATUS_MAPPED_FILE_SIZE_ZERO | 0XC000011E |
| STATUS_TOO_MANY_OPENED_FILES | 0XC000011F |
| STATUS_CANCELLED | 0XC0000120 |
| STATUS_CANNOT_DELETE | 0XC0000121 |
| STATUS_INVALID_COMPUTER_NAME | 0XC0000122 |
| STATUS_FILE_DELETED | 0XC0000123 |

| | |
|---|---|
| STATUS_SPECIAL_ACCOUNT | 0XC0000124 |
| STATUS_SPECIAL_GROUP | 0XC0000125 |
| STATUS_SPECIAL_USER | 0XC0000126 |
| STATUS_MEMBERS_PRIMARY_GROUP | 0XC0000127 |
| STATUS_FILE_CLOSED | 0XC0000128 |
| STATUS_TOO_MANY_THREADS | 0XC0000129 |
| STATUS_THREAD_NOT_IN_PROCESS | 0XC000012A |
| STATUS_TOKEN_ALREADY_IN_USE | 0XC000012B |
| STATUS_PAGEFILE_QUOTA_EXCEEDED | 0XC000012C |
| STATUS_COMMITMENT_LIMIT | 0XC000012D |
| STATUS_INVALID_IMAGE_LE_FORMAT | 0XC000012E |
| STATUS_INVALID_IMAGE_NOT_MZ | 0XC000012F |
| STATUS_INVALID_IMAGE_PROTECT | 0XC0000130 |
| STATUS_INVALID_IMAGE_WIN_16 | 0XC0000131 |
| STATUS_LOGON_SERVER_CONFICT | 0XC0000132 |
| STATUS_TIME_DIFFERENCE_AT_DC | 0XC0000133 |
| STATUS_SYNCHRONIZATION_REQUIRED | 0XC0000134 |
| STATUS_DL_NOT_FOUND | 0XC0000135 |
| STATUS_OPEN_FAILED | 0XC0000136 |
| STATUS_IO_PRIVILEGE_FAILED | 0XC0000137 |
| STATUS_ORDINAL_NOT_FOUND | 0XC0000138 |
| STATUS_ENTRYPOINT_NOT_FOUND | 0XC0000139 |

| | |
|---|---|
| STATUS_CONTROL_C_EXIT | 0XC000013A |
| STATUS_LOCAL_DISCONNECT | 0XC000013B |
| STATUS_REMOTE_DISCONNECT | 0XC000013C |
| STATUS_REMOTE_RESOURCES | 0XC000013D |
| STATUS_LINK_FAILED | 0XC000013E |
| STATUS_LINK_TIMEOUT | 0XC000013F |
| STATUS_INVALID_CONNECTION | 0XC0000140 |
| STATUS_INVALID_ADDRESS | 0XC0000141 |
| STATUS_DL_INIT_FAILED | 0XC0000142 |
| STATUS_MISSING_SYSTEMFILE | 0XC0000143 |
| STATUS_UNHANDLED_EXCEPTION | 0XC0000144 |
| STATUS_APP_INIT_FAILURE | 0XC0000145 |
| STATUS_PAGEFILE_CREATE_FAILED | 0XC0000146 |
| STATUS_NO_PAGEFILE | 0XC0000147 |
| STATUS_INVALID_LEVEL | 0XC0000148 |
| STATUS_WRONG_PASSWORD_CORE | 0XC0000149 |
| STATUS_ILLEGAL_FOAT_CONTEXT | 0XC000014A |
| STATUS_PIPE_BROKEN | 0XC000014B |
| STATUS_REGISTRY_CORRUPT | 0XC000014C |
| STATUS_REGISTRY_IO_FAILED | 0XC000014D |
| STATUS_NO_EVENT_PAIR | 0XC000014E |
| STATUS_UNRECOGNIZED_VOLUME | 0XC000014F |

| | |
|---|---|
| STATUS_SERIAL_NO_DEVICE_INITED | 0XC0000150 |
| STATUS_NO_SUCH_ALIAS | 0XC0000151 |
| STATUS_MEMBER_NOT_IN_ALIAS | 0XC0000152 |
| STATUS_MEMBER_IN_ALIAS | 0XC0000153 |
| STATUS_ALIAS_EXISTS | 0XC0000154 |
| STATUS_LOGON_NOT_GRANTED | 0XC0000155 |
| STATUS_TOO_MANY_SECRETS | 0XC0000156 |
| STATUS_SECRET_TOO_LONG | 0XC0000157 |
| STATUS_INTERNAL_DB_ERROR | 0XC0000158 |
| STATUS_FULLSCREEN_MODE | 0XC0000159 |
| STATUS_TOO_MANY_CONTEXT_IDS | 0XC000015A |
| STATUS_LOGON_TYPE_NOT_GRANTED | 0XC000015B |
| STATUS_NOT_REGISTRY_FILE | 0XC000015C |
| STATUS_NT_CROSS_ENCRYPTION_REQUIRED | 0XC000015D |
| STATUS_DOMAIN_CTRLR_CONFIG_ERROR | 0XC000015E |
| STATUS_FT_MISSING_MEMBER | 0XC000015F |
| STATUS_ILL_FORMED_SERVICE_ENTRY | 0XC0000160 |
| STATUS_ILLEGAL_CHARACTER | 0XC0000161 |
| STATUS_UNMAPPABLE_CHARACTER | 0XC0000162 |
| STATUS_UNDEFINED_CHARACTER | 0XC0000163 |
| STATUS_FLOPPY_VOLUME | 0XC0000164 |
| STATUS_FLOPPY_ID_MARK_NOT_FOUND | 0XC0000165 |

| | |
|---|---|
| STATUS_FLOPPY_WRONG_CYLINDER | 0XC0000166 |
| STATUS_FLOPPY_UNKNOWN_ERROR | 0XC0000167 |
| STATUS_FLOPPY_BAD_REGISTERS | 0XC0000168 |
| STATUS_DISK_RECALIBRATE_FAILED | 0XC0000169 |
| STATUS_DISK_OPERATION_FAILED | 0XC000016A |
| STATUS_DISK_RESET_FAILED | 0XC000016B |
| STATUS_SHARED_IRQ_BUSY | 0XC000016C |
| STATUS_FT_ORPHANING | 0XC000016D |
| STATUS_BIOS_FAILED_TO_CONNECT_INTERRUPT | 0XC000016E |
| STATUS_PARTITION_FAILURE | 0XC0000172 |
| STATUS_INVALID_BOCK_LENGTH | 0XC0000173 |
| STATUS_DEVICE_NOT_PARTITIONED | 0XC0000174 |
| STATUS_UNABLE_TO_LOCK_MEDIA | 0XC0000175 |
| STATUS_UNABLE_TO_UNLOAD_MEDIA | 0XC0000176 |
| STATUS_EOM_OVERFLOW | 0XC0000177 |
| STATUS_NO_MEDIA | 0XC0000178 |
| STATUS_NO_SUCH_MEMBER | 0XC000017A |
| STATUS_INVALID_MEMBER | 0XC000017B |
| STATUS_KEY_DELETED | 0XC000017C |
| STATUS_NO_LOG_SPACE | 0XC000017D |
| STATUS_TOO_MANY_SIDS | 0XC000017E |
| STATUS_LM_CROSS_ENCRYPTION_REQUIRED | 0XC000017F |

| | |
|---|---|
| STATUS_KEY_HAS_CHILDREN | 0XC0000180 |
| STATUS_CHILD_MUST_BE_VOLATILE | 0XC0000181 |
| STATUS_DEVICE_CONFIGURATION_ERROR | 0XC0000182 |
| STATUS_DRIVER_INTERNAL_ERROR | 0XC0000183 |
| STATUS_INVALID_DEVICE_STATE | 0XC0000184 |
| STATUS_IO_DEVICE_ERROR | 0XC0000185 |
| STATUS_DEVICE_PROTOCOL_ERROR | 0XC0000186 |
| STATUS_BACKUP_CONTROLLER | 0XC0000187 |
| STATUS_LOG_FILE_FULL | 0XC0000188 |
| STATUS_TOO_LATE | 0XC0000189 |
| STATUS_NO_TRUST_LSA_SECRET | 0XC000018A |
| STATUS_NO_TRUST_SAM_ACCOUNT | 0XC000018B |
| STATUS_TRUSTED_DOMAIN_FAILURE | 0XC000018C |
| STATUS_TRUSTED_RELATIONSHIP_FAILURE | 0XC000018D |
| STATUS_EVENTLOG_FILE_CORRUPT | 0XC000018E |
| STATUS_EVENTLOG_CANT_START | 0XC000018F |
| STATUS_TRUST_FAILURE | 0XC0000190 |
| STATUS_MUTANT_LIMIT_EXCEEDED | 0XC0000191 |
| STATUS_NETLOGON_NOT_STARTED | 0XC0000192 |
| STATUS_ACCOUNT_EXPIRED | 0XC0000193 |
| STATUS_POSSIBLE_DEADLOCK | 0XC0000194 |
| STATUS_NETWORK_CREDENTIAL_CONFICT | 0XC0000195 |

| | |
|---|---|
| STATUS_REMOTE_SESSION_LIMIT | 0XC0000196 |
| STATUS_EVENTLOG_FILE_CHANGED | 0XC0000197 |
| STATUS_NOLOGON_INTERDOMAIN_TRUST_ACCOUNT | 0XC0000198 |
| STATUS_NOLOGON_WORKSTATION_TRUST_ACCOUNT | 0XC0000199 |
| STATUS_NOLOGON_SERVER_TRUST_ACCOUNT | 0XC000019A |
| STATUS_DOMAIN_TRUST_INCONSISTENT | 0XC000019B |
| STATUS_FS_DRIVER_REQUIRED | 0XC000019C |
| STATUS_NO_USER_SESSION_KEY | 0XC0000202 |
| STATUS_USER_SESSION_DELETED | 0XC0000203 |
| STATUS_RESOURCE_LANG_NOT_FOUND | 0XC0000204 |
| STATUS_INSUFF_SERVER_RESOURCES | 0XC0000205 |
| STATUS_INVALID_BUFFER_SIZE | 0XC0000206 |
| STATUS_INVALID_ADDRESS_COMPONENT | 0XC0000207 |
| STATUS_INVALID_ADDRESS_WILDCARD | 0XC0000208 |
| STATUS_TOO_MANY_ADDRESSES | 0XC0000209 |
| STATUS_ADDRESS_ALREADY_EXISTS | 0XC000020A |
| STATUS_ADDRESS_CLOSED | 0XC000020B |
| STATUS_CONNECTION_DISCONNECTED | 0XC000020C |
| STATUS_CONNECTION_RESET | 0XC000020D |
| STATUS_TOO_MANY_NODES | 0XC000020E |
| STATUS_TRANSACTION_ABORTED | 0XC000020F |
| STATUS_TRANSACTION_TIMED_OUT | 0XC0000210 |

| | |
|---|---|
| STATUS_TRANSACTION_NO_RELEASE | 0XC0000211 |
| STATUS_TRANSACTION_NO_MATCH | 0XC0000212 |
| STATUS_TRANSACTION_RESPONDED | 0XC0000213 |
| STATUS_TRANSACTION_INVALID_ID | 0XC0000214 |
| STATUS_TRANSACTION_INVALID_TYPE | 0XC0000215 |
| STATUS_NOT_SERVER_SESSION | 0XC0000216 |
| STATUS_NOT_CLIENT_SESSION | 0XC0000217 |
| STATUS_CANNOT_LOAD_REGISTRY_FILE | 0XC0000218 |
| STATUS_DEBUG_ATTACH_FAILED | 0XC0000219 |
| STATUS_SYSTEM_PROCESS_TERMINATED | 0XC000021A |
| STATUS_DATA_NOT_ACCEPTED | 0XC000021B |
| STATUS_NO_BROWSER_SERVERS_FOUND | 0XC000021C |
| STATUS_VDM_HARD_ERROR | 0XC000021D |
| STATUS_DRIVER_CANCEL_TIMEOUT | 0XC000021E |
| STATUS_REPLY_MESSAGE_MISMATCH | 0XC000021F |
| STATUS_MAPPED_ALIGNMENT | 0XC0000220 |
| STATUS_IMAGE_CHECKSUM_MISMATCH | 0XC0000221 |
| STATUS_LOST_WRITEBEHIND_DATA | 0XC0000222 |
| STATUS_CLIENT_SERVER_PARAMETERS_INVALID | 0XC0000223 |
| STATUS_PASSWORD_MUST_CHANGE | 0XC0000224 |
| STATUS_NOT_FOUND | 0XC0000225 |
| STATUS_NOT_TINY_STREAM | 0XC0000226 |

| | |
|---|---|
| STATUS_RECOVERY_FAILURE | 0XC0000227 |
| STATUS_STACK_OVERFLOW_READ | 0XC0000228 |
| STATUS_FAIL_CHECK | 0XC0000229 |
| STATUS_DUPLICATE_OBJECTID | 0XC000022A |
| STATUS_OBJECTID_EXISTS | 0XC000022B |
| STATUS_CONVERT_TO_LARGE | 0XC000022C |
| STATUS_RETRY | 0XC000022D |
| STATUS_FOUND_OUT_OF_SCOPE | 0XC000022E |
| STATUS_ALLOCATE_BUCKET | 0XC000022F |
| STATUS_PROPSET_NOT_FOUND | 0XC0000230 |
| STATUS_MARSHALL_OVERFLOW | 0XC0000231 |
| STATUS_INVALID_VARIANT | 0XC0000232 |
| STATUS_DOMAIN_CONTROLLER_NOT_FOUND | 0XC0000233 |
| STATUS_ACCOUNT_LOCKED_OUT | 0XC0000234 |
| STATUS_HANDLE_NOT_CLOSABLE | 0XC0000235 |
| STATUS_CONNECTION_REFUSED | 0XC0000236 |
| STATUS_GRACEFUL_DISCONNECT | 0XC0000237 |
| STATUS_ADDRESS_ALREADY_ASSOCIATED | 0XC0000238 |
| STATUS_ADDRESS_NOT_ASSOCIATED | 0XC0000239 |
| STATUS_CONNECTION_INVALID | 0XC000023A |
| STATUS_CONNECTION_ACTIVE | 0XC000023B |
| STATUS_NETWORK_UNREACHABLE | 0XC000023C |

| | |
|---|---|
| STATUS_HOST_UNREACHABLE | 0XC000023D |
| STATUS_PROTOCOL_UNREACHABLE | 0XC000023E |
| STATUS_PORT_UNREACHABLE | 0XC000023F |
| STATUS_REQUEST_ABORTED | 0XC0000240 |
| STATUS_CONNECTION_ABORTED | 0XC0000241 |
| STATUS_BAD_COMPRESSION_BUFFER | 0XC0000242 |
| STATUS_USER_MAPPED_FILE | 0XC0000243 |
| STATUS_AUDIT_FAILED | 0XC0000244 |
| STATUS_TIMER_RESOLUTION_NOT_SET | 0XC0000245 |
| STATUS_CONNECTION_COUNT_LIMIT | 0XC0000246 |
| STATUS_LOGIN_TIME_RESTRICTION | 0XC0000247 |
| STATUS_LOGIN_WKSTA_RESTRICTION | 0XC0000248 |
| STATUS_IMAGE_MP_UP_MISMATCH | 0XC0000249 |
| STATUS_INSUFFICIENT_LOGON_INFO | 0XC0000250 |
| STATUS_BAD_DL_ENTRYPOINT | 0XC0000251 |
| STATUS_BAD_SERVICE_ENTRYPOINT | 0XC0000252 |
| STATUS_LPC_REPLY_LOST | 0XC0000253 |
| STATUS_IP_ADDRESS_CONFLICT1 | 0XC0000254 |
| STATUS_IP_ADDRESS_CONFLICT2 | 0XC0000255 |
| STATUS_REGISTRY_QUOTA_LIMIT | 0XC0000256 |
| STATUS_PATH_NOT_COVERED | 0XC0000257 |
| STATUS_NO_CALLBACK_ACTIVE | 0XC0000258 |

| | |
|---|---|
| STATUS_LICENSE_QUOTA_EXCEEDED | 0XC0000259 |
| STATUS_PWD_TOO_SHORT | 0XC000025A |
| STATUS_PWD_TOO_RECENT | 0XC000025B |
| STATUS_PWD_HISTORY_CONFLICT | 0XC000025C |
| STATUS_PLUGPLAY_NO_DEVICE | 0XC000025E |
| STATUS_UNSUPPORTED_COMPRESSION | 0XC000025F |
| STATUS_INVALID_HW_PROFILE | 0XC0000260 |
| STATUS_INVALID_PLUGPLAY_DEVICE_PATH | 0XC0000261 |
| STATUS_DRIVER_ORDINAL_NOT_FOUND | 0XC0000262 |
| STATUS_DRIVER_ENTRYPOINT_NOT_FOUND | 0XC0000263 |
| STATUS_RESOURCE_NOT_OWNED | 0XC0000264 |
| STATUS_TOO_MANY_LINKS | 0XC0000265 |
| STATUS_QUOTA_LIST_INCONSISTENT | 0XC0000266 |
| STATUS_FILE_IS_OFFLINE | 0XC0000267 |
| STATUS_EVALUATION_EXPIRATION | 0XC0000268 |
| STATUS_ILLEGAL_DL_RELOCATION | 0XC0000269 |
| STATUS_LICENSE_VIOLATION | 0XC000026A |
| STATUS_DL_INIT_FAILED_LOGOFF | 0XC000026B |
| STATUS_DRIVER_UNABLE_TO_LOAD | 0XC000026C |
| STATUS_DFS_UNAVAILABLE | 0XC000026D |
| STATUS_VOLUME_DISMOUNTED | 0XC000026E |
| STATUS_WX86_INTERNAL_ERROR | 0XC000026F |

| | |
|---|---|
| STATUS_WX86_FOAT_STACK_CHECK | 0XC0000270 |
| STATUS_WOW_ASSERTION | 0XC0009898 |
| RPC_NT_INVALID_STRING_BINDING | 0XC0020001 |
| RPC_NT_WRONG_KIND_OF_BINDING | 0XC0020002 |
| RPC_NT_INVALID_BINDING | 0XC0020003 |
| RPC_NT_PROTSEQ_NOT_SUPPORTED | 0XC0020004 |
| RPC_NT_INVALID_RPC_PROTSEQ | 0XC0020005 |
| RPC_NT_INVALID_STRING_UUID | 0XC0020006 |
| RPC_NT_INVALID_ENDPOINT_FORMAT | 0XC0020007 |
| RPC_NT_INVALID_NET_ADDR | 0XC0020008 |
| RPC_NT_NO_ENDPOINT_FOUND | 0XC0020009 |
| RPC_NT_INVALID_TIMEOUT | 0XC002000A |
| RPC_NT_OBJECT_NOT_FOUND | 0XC002000B |
| RPC_NT_ALREADY_REGISTERED | 0XC002000C |
| RPC_NT_TYPE_ALREADY_REGISTERED | 0XC002000D |
| RPC_NT_ALREADY_LISTENING | 0XC002000E |
| RPC_NT_NO_PROTSEQS_REGISTERED | 0XC002000F |
| RPC_NT_NOT_LISTENING | 0XC0020010 |
| RPC_NT_UNKNOWN_MGR_TYPE | 0XC0020011 |
| RPC_NT_UNKNOWN_IF | 0XC0020012 |
| RPC_NT_NO_BINDINGS | 0XC0020013 |
| RPC_NT_NO_PROTSEQS | 0XC0020014 |

| | |
|---|---|
| RPC_NT_OUT_OF_RESOURCES | 0XC0020016 |
| RPC_NT_SERVER_UNAVAILABLE | 0XC0020017 |
| RPC_NT_SERVER_TOO_BUSY | 0XC0020018 |
| RPC_NT_INVALID_NETWORK_OPTIONS | 0XC0020019 |
| RPC_NT_NO_CALL_ACTIVE | 0XC002001A |
| RPC_NT_CALL_FAILED | 0XC002001B |
| RPC_NT_CALL_FAILED_DNE | 0XC002001C |
| RPC_NT_PROTOCOL_ERROR | 0XC002001D |
| RPC_NT_UNSUPPORTED_TRANS_SYN | 0XC002001E |
| RPC_NT_UNSUPPORTED_TYPE | 0XC0020021 |
| RPC_NT_INVALID_TAG | 0XC0020022 |
| RPC_NT_INVALID_BOUND | 0XC0020023 |
| RPC_NT_NO_ENTRY_NAME | 0XC0020024 |
| RPC_NT_INVALID_NAME_SYNTAX | 0XC0020025 |
| RPC_NT_UNSUPPORTED_NAME_SYNTAX | 0XC0020026 |
| RPC_NT_UUID_NO_ADDRESS | 0XC0020028 |
| RPC_NT_DUPLICATE_ENDPOINT | 0XC0020029 |
| RPC_NT_UNKNOWN_AUTHN_TYPE | 0XC002002A |
| RPC_NT_MAX_CALLS_TOO_SMALL | 0XC002002B |
| RPC_NT_STRING_TOO_LONG | 0XC002002C |
| RPC_NT_PROTSEQ_NOT_FOUND | 0XC002002D |
| RPC_NT_PROCNUM_OUT_OF_RANGE | 0XC002002E |
| RPC_NT_BINDING_HAS_NO_AUTH | 0XC002002F |

| | |
|---|---|
| RPC_NT_UNKNOWN_AUTHN_SERVICE | 0XC0020030 |
| RPC_NT_UNKNOWN_AUTHN_LEVEL | 0XC0020031 |
| RPC_NT_INVALID_AUTH_IDENTITY | 0XC0020032 |
| RPC_NT_UNKNOWN_AUTHZ_SERVICE | 0XC0020033 |
| EPT_NT_INVALID_ENTRY | 0XC0020034 |
| EPT_NT_CANT_PERFORM_OP | 0XC0020035 |
| EPT_NT_NOT_REGISTERED | 0XC0020036 |
| RPC_NT_NOTHING_TO_EXPORT | 0XC0020037 |
| RPC_NT_INCOMPLETE_NAME | 0XC0020038 |
| RPC_NT_INVALID_VERS_OPTION | 0XC0020039 |
| RPC_NT_NO_MORE_MEMBERS | 0XC002003A |
| RPC_NT_NOT_ALL_OBJS_UNEXPORTED | 0XC002003B |
| RPC_NT_INTERFACE_NOT_FOUND | 0XC002003C |
| RPC_NT_ENTRY_ALREADY_EXISTS | 0XC002003D |
| RPC_NT_ENTRY_NOT_FOUND | 0XC002003E |
| RPC_NT_NAME_SERVICE_UNAVAILABLE | 0XC002003F |
| RPC_NT_INVALID_NAF_ID | 0XC0020040 |
| RPC_NT_CANNOT_SUPPORT | 0XC0020041 |
| RPC_NT_NO_CONTEXT_AVAILABLE | 0XC0020042 |
| RPC_NT_INTERNAL_ERROR | 0XC0020043 |
| RPC_NT_ZERO_DIVIDE | 0XC0020044 |
| RPC_NT_ADDRESS_ERROR | 0XC0020045 |

| | |
|---|---|
| RPC_NT_FP_DIV_ZERO | 0XC0020046 |
| RPC_NT_FP_UNDERFLOW | 0XC0020047 |
| RPC_NT_FP_OVERFLOW | 0XC0020048 |
| RPC_NT_NO_MORE_ENTRIES | 0XC0030001 |
| RPC_NT_SS_CHAR_TRANS_OPEN_FAIL | 0XC0030002 |
| RPC_NT_SS_CHAR_TRANS_SHORT_FILE | 0XC0030003 |
| RPC_NT_SS_IN_NULL_CONTEXT | 0XC0030004 |
| RPC_NT_SS_CONTEXT_MISMATCH | 0XC0030005 |
| RPC_NT_SS_CONTEXT_DAMAGED | 0XC0030006 |
| RPC_NT_SS_HANDLES_MISMATCH | 0XC0030007 |
| RPC_NT_SS_CANNOT_GET_CALL_HANDLE | 0XC0030008 |
| RPC_NT_NULL_REF_POINTER | 0XC0030009 |
| RPC_NT_ENUM_VALUE_OUT_OF_RANGE | 0XC003000A |
| RPC_NT_BYTE_COUNT_TOO_SMALL | 0XC003000B |
| RPC_NT_BAD_STUB_DATA | 0XC003000C |
| RPC_NT_CALL_IN_PROGRESS | 0XC0020049 |
| RPC_NT_NO_MORE_BINDINGS | 0XC002004A |
| RPC_NT_GROUP_MEMBER_NOT_FOUND | 0XC002004B |
| EPT_NT_CANT_CREATE | 0XC002004C |
| RPC_NT_INVALID_OBJECT | 0XC002004D |
| RPC_NT_NO_INTERFACES | 0XC002004F |
| RPC_NT_CALL_CANCELLED | 0XC0020050 |

| | |
|---|---|
| RPC_NT_BINDING_INCOMPLETE | 0XC0020051 |
| RPC_NT_COMM_FAILURE | 0XC0020052 |
| RPC_NT_UNSUPPORTED_AUTHN_LEVEL | 0XC0020053 |
| RPC_NT_NO_PRINC_NAME | 0XC0020054 |
| RPC_NT_NOT_RPC_ERROR | 0XC0020055 |
| RPC_NT_UUID_LOCAL_ONLY | 0XC0020056 |
| RPC_NT_SEC_PKG_ERROR | 0XC0020057 |
| RPC_NT_NOT_CANCELLED | 0XC0020058 |
| RPC_NT_INVALID_ES_ACTION | 0XC0030059 |
| RPC_NT_WRONG_ES_VERSION | 0XC003005A |
| RPC_NT_WRONG_STUB_VERSION | 0XC003005B |
| RPC_NT_INVALID_PIPE_OBJECT | 0XC003005C |
| RPC_NT_INVALID_PIPE_OPERATION | 0XC003005D |
| RPC_NT_WRONG_PIPE_VERSION | 0XC003005E |

# INDEX

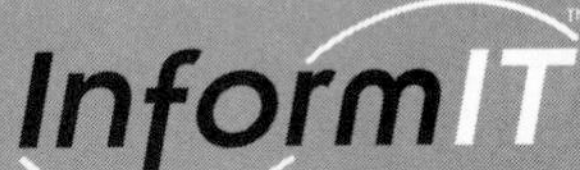


Solutions from experts you know and trust.

Topics

Operating Systems
Web Development
Programming
Networking
Certification
and more...

Expert Access

Free Content

www.informit.com

- Free, in-depth articles and supplements
- Master the skills you need, when you need them
- Choose from industry leading books, ebooks, and training products
- Get answers when you need them - from live experts or InformIT's comprehensive library
- Achieve industry certification and advance your career

Visit InformIT today and get great content from PH PTR

Prentice Hall and InformIT are trademarks of Pearson plc / Copyright © 2000 Pearson

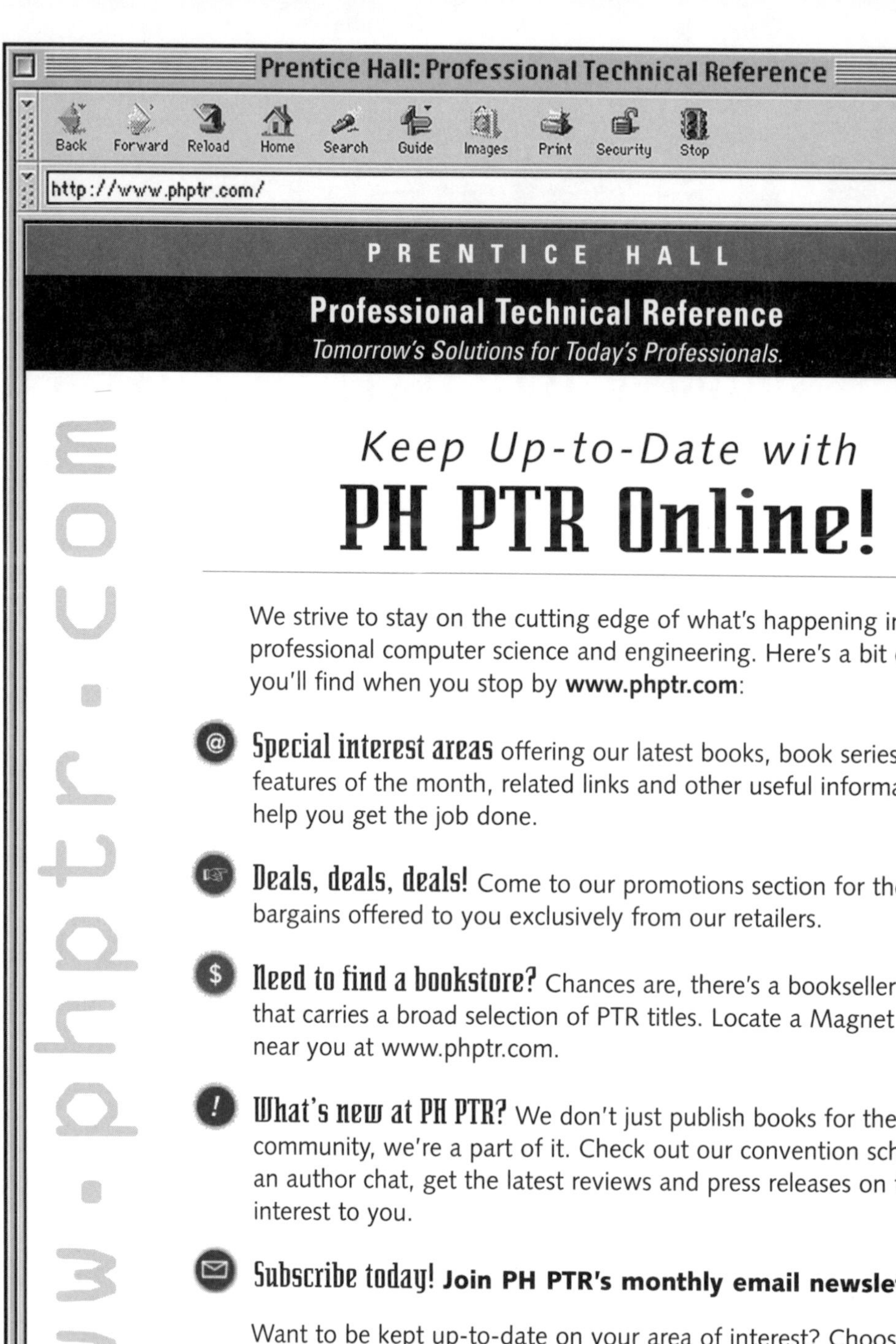
Prentice Hall: Professional Technical Reference
Back Forward Reload Home Search Guide Images Print Security Stop
PH PTR
http://www.phptr.com/
PRENTICE HALL
Professional Technical Reference
Tomorrow's Solutions for Today's Professionals.
www.phptr.com
Keep Up-to-Date with
PH PTR Online!
We strive to stay on the cutting edge of what's happening in professional computer science and engineering. Here's a bit of what you'll find when you stop by www.phptr.com:
Special interest areas offering our latest books, book series, software, features of the month, related links and other useful information to help you get the job done.
Deals, deals, deals! Come to our promotions section for the latest bargains offered to you exclusively from our retailers.
Need to find a bookstore? Chances are, there's a bookseller near you that carries a broad selection of PTR titles. Locate a Magnet bookstore near you at www.phptr.com.
What's new at PH PTR? We don't just publish books for the professional community, we're a part of it. Check out our convention schedule, join an author chat, get the latest reviews and press releases on topics of interest to you.
Subscribe today! Join PH PTR's monthly email newsletter!
Want to be kept up-to-date on your area of interest? Choose a targeted category on our website, and we'll keep you informed of the latest PH PTR products, author events, reviews and conferences in your interest area.
Visit our mailroom to subscribe today! http://www.phptr.com/mail_lists